Language, Gl
the Making of a Tanzanian
Beauty Queen

ENCOUNTERS

Series Editors: Jan Blommaert, *Tilburg University, The Netherlands*, Ben Rampton, *King's College London, UK*, Anna de Fina, *Georgetown University, USA* and Marco Jacquemet, *University of San Francisco, USA*

The Encounters series sets out to explore diversity in language from a theoretical and an applied perspective. So the focus is both on the linguistic encounters, inequalities and struggles that characterise post-modern societies and on the development, within sociocultural linguistics, of theoretical instruments to explain them. The series welcomes work dealing with such topics as heterogeneity, mixing, creolization, bricolage, cross-over phenomena, polylingual and polycultural practices. Another high-priority area of study is the investigation of processes through which linguistic resources are negotiated, appropriated and controlled, and the mechanisms leading to the creation and maintenance of sociocultural differences. The series welcomes ethnographically oriented work in which contexts of communication are investigated rather than assumed, as well as research that shows a clear commitment to close analysis of local meaning making processes and the semiotic organisation of texts.

Full details of all the books in this series and of all our other publications can be found on http://www.multilingual-matters.com, or by writing to Multilingual Matters, St Nicholas House, 31–34 High Street, Bristol BS1 2AW, UK.

Language, Globalization and the Making of a Tanzanian Beauty Queen

Sabrina Billings

MULTILINGUAL MATTERS
Bristol • Buffalo • Toronto

To H.S., for her honesty, generosity, and inspiration

Library of Congress Cataloging in Publication Data
Billings, Sabrina J.
Language, Globalization and the Making of a Tanzanian Beauty Queen/Sabrina Billings.
Encounters: 2
Includes bibliographical references and index.
1. English language–Social aspects–Tanzania. 2. Tanzania–Languages–Social aspects.
3. English language–Tanzania–Rhetoric. 4. Beauty contests–Tanzania. I. Title.
PE3432.T36B55 2013
427'.9678–dc23 2013023705

British Library Cataloguing in Publication Data
A catalogue entry for this book is available from the British Library.

ISBN-13: 978-1-78309-075-4 (hbk)
ISBN-13: 978-1-78309-074-7 (pbk)

Multilingual Matters
UK: St Nicholas House, 31–34 High Street, Bristol BS1 2AW, UK.
USA: UTP, 2250 Military Road, Tonawanda, NY 14150, USA.
Canada: UTP, 5201 Dufferin Street, North York, Ontario M3H 5T8, Canada.

The policy of Multilingual Matters/Channel View Publications is to use papers that are natural, renewable and recyclable products, made from wood grown in sustainable forests. In the manufacturing process of our books, and to further support our policy, preference is given to printers that have FSC and PEFC Chain of Custody certification. The FSC and/or PEFC logos will appear on those books where full certification has been granted to the printer concerned.

Typeset by R. J. Footring Ltd, Derby
Printed and bound in Great Britain by Short Run Press Ltd

Contents

Figures

Acknowledgements

This volume is the result of the institutional, professional and personal help of many. Funding for the fieldwork portions of this work was provided by the National Science Foundation (USA), the University of Chicago and the Fulbright College of Arts and Sciences at the University of Arkansas. The book grew out of my dissertation research and I must thank Salikoko Mufwene and Michael Silverstein for their guidance and support during that iteration of the project, and Jan Blommaert for his continued intellectual mentorship. I am also very grateful to the editors of this series for making this book possible.

I am indebted to many people, especially Kili Kubisiak, Francis Mwaijande, Prisca Mwaijande, Charles Bwenge and Francis Onduso for fruitful conversations and input about matters of Tanzanian language and culture. Special thanks go to Happiness Samson, whose help, patience and insight have been invaluable to this project. And of course, none of the research would have been possible without the collaboration of the many young women whose experiences on and off stage are at the heart of the story I tell here. I must also thank organizers and trainers of the Miss Tanzania pageant and of the many local competitions who allowed me to observe training sessions, to interview participants and to record the events.

On a personal note, I am deeply indebted to my parents, Joan and Barry Billings, for their ongoing support and understanding. To my hatchlings, Gus and June, I give huge thanks for waiting patiently for this book to be completed. Finally, I have difficulty expressing my gratitude for the intellectual and emotional companionship of Jesse Casana, whose contributions to this project are immeasurable.

Note

Every reasonable effort has been made to locate, contact and acknowledge copyright owners. Any errors will be rectified in future editions.

1 Introduction

It could be, of course, that there was something more than
mere physical appearance behind this.
Alexander McCall Smith, *Morality for Beautiful Girls* (2002: 114)

Real Women, Real Lives, Real Language

'Will you be my sponsor?' With the solemnity of a priest, a beauty contestant uttered these words to me as she followed me home after my first visit to watch a pageant rehearsal. She sought money to re-enroll in secondary school, explaining that her small earnings from winning a lower-level pageant went to her family and that she still needed money to pay for delinquent school fees. Though certainly not my first encounter with structural inequality, it was the first time I really considered how these pageants could be about far more than the language ideologies I had initially set out to study. This contestant's request made clear to me several things: that she was struggling with some hard realities; that she saw pageants as a way to better her life; that education seemed to be an answer to her troubles; and that she believed by looking at me that I had more than she did. Furthermore, her use of English with me was significant. Even though earlier she had only heard me speak Swahili as I introduced myself to the group and chatted with the pageant director, her choice of language clued me into a way of reckoning links between language value and personhood that extended beyond the strictly local setting of my study.

This book is as much about lives as it is about pageants. In particular, it is about average Tanzanians, mostly young women, living in cities, getting by but often just barely. Many reside with their families, some live on their own or with friends, and sustenance is almost always a collective effort. These women, though living in what for many people is an isolated corner of the world, consider themselves part of the world, interacting with products, ideas and ways of being in wide global circulation. In many cases, they live rather local lives, in the sense that they may infrequently leave their own neighborhood or city, let alone their own region or country, and may only rarely interact with people from far away. Yet, in pageants, they expertly mix second-hand clothing from the United States with inexpensive items from China or India into fashion-forward outfits; they are as likely to perform dance numbers to local Bongo Flava hip-hop music, or to South African pop diva Brenda Fassie, as to Beyoncé. They speak on stage about subjects such as HIV/AIDS which bridge local, regional and global concerns. Their language use in the competition is likewise reflective of their locality as well as of their place as citizens of the world.

In Tanzania, beauty pageants are wildly popular, with minute details of the contests and their participants appearing frequently in newspapers and other media. And while the media and individuals frequently condemn contestants, especially claiming their *utovu wa nidhamu* ('lack of good behavior') pageants remain a popular spectator sport, and contestants and winners often become, at least ephemerally, national celebrities. Nonetheless, finding qualified and willing contestants sometimes proves difficult. Newspaper advertisements appear during the weeks leading up to the preliminary pageants encouraging young women to submit applications, luring them with the promise of cash and other prizes; however, often this is not enough. Local pageant directors actively recruit girls, by going to their schools, and especially their homes, where parental resistance can be strong. In one case, a pageant director, herself a former Miss Tanzania and now a wife, mother and career woman, said she used her status and accomplishments to present herself to parents as a role model for their daughters. A confident, successful and articulate woman, yet one who embraces motherhood and her role as a wife, she sells pageants as a stepping stone to a prosperous, modern Tanzanian life.

In this way, the director emphasizes another part of the perceived experience of beauty queens – their ability to escape from life-as-usual in Tanzania. Young women who participate do so in part as a way to engage in an aesthetic cosmopolitanism, as well as in hopes of winning prizes, scholarships and money. In addition, many become involved for the opportunity to get out – of their town, of their lifestyle, of poverty or, even, of Tanzania. Newspapers remind their readers of the glamorous lives of former national beauty queens. Reports laud the successes of Miss Tanzania 1967, living in Germany, Miss Tanzania 1996, residing in Italy, and Miss Tanzania 1999, who pursued a degree in the United States. Others have achieved fame and fortune outside of their title as national beauty queen, such as Miss Tanzania 2000, Jacqueline Ntuyabaliwe, who became an East African pop music star performing under the name K-Lyinn. These stories help contestants imagine possibilities in their own lives that might arise out of competing in pageants. While many young women participate in pageants for fun, they also see them as one of their few means of escape, a route to a dream of securing an education and their independence, often perceived as possible only elsewhere.

So, despite the manifold ways in which young urban Tanzanian women tap into and integrate a wide array of locally sourced and international resources for aesthetic, practical and identity-making purposes, they are nonetheless sensitive to their particular place on the global periphery. Many hold ambitions of leaving where they are, for a bigger regional city, for the capital city, Dar es Salaam, for neighboring Kenya, for South Africa, for Dubai, for London or for the United States – anywhere where opportunity is seen as greater than where they are at the moment (which is almost everywhere). They seek independent, stylish and modern lives, away from paternal or conjugal authority, and English is often understood as a critical tool in fashioning their own, mobile, futures. Beauty pageants offer both an opportunity to engage in the aesthetics of globalization and a glimmer of hope for a new, prosperous and independent life.

When I first began studying language use in beauty pageants, years ago as part of my dissertation research, I was impressed by the fact that everyone at these events seemed to be having a lot of fun. Full of music, dance, fashion and humor, Tanzanian beauty pageants are truly a great time for everyone involved. Yet, as I continued researching them and maintained contact with my consultants and friends from my fieldwork, I started to recognize the ways in which pageants also provide a lens into the structuring and gendering of inequality in Tanzania. Language plays an important role, but so do other symbolic resources that are linked with language in terms of their acquisition and interpretation. At once a source of hope, disappointment and cosmopolitan creativity, pageants engage the imagination of many young women who see beauty queens as the kind of woman they strive to be.

To frame this study as concerning real people and life opportunities, I will begin with two vignettes. The first retells the fairy-tale life of the most successful Miss Tanzania in the institution's history, a highly anomalous yet also salient story to the young women in this project for whom her life represents the potential that pageants – and very little else – offer them. The second vignette describes the life of Justina, a typical contestant, for whom the promise of pageantry failed to come through. Together, these stories frame what is possible, as well as what is probable, for the contestants in this study.

Happiness becomes Millen

Looking every bit the international beauty icon, Happiness Magese is tall and stunning, with long limbs and smooth, light-brown skin, shiny straight hair falling far down her back, and graceful, self-assured movement.[1] In 2001, Happiness won the Miss Tanzania crown and has since become a national celebrity. At the time of her competing in the Miss Tanzania competition, she was an English-language university student specializing in law in Dar es Salaam. After winning the title (but not performing well at Miss World) and spending a few years in Tanzania seeking to turn her experience into a modeling career, Happiness earned her breakout job on the cover of *Kenyan Cosmopolitan* magazine. Soon thereafter she moved to South Africa, where she signed with a prominent modeling agency, changed her first name to 'Millen' and became a near-household name there. After gaining significant success on the African continent and in Europe doing

Figure 1.1 Millen (Happiness) Magese, Miss Tanzania 2001, on the cover of a pan-African fashion magazine. Note the variant spelling of 'Milen'

print and runway work, she moved to New York in 2009 and signed with Ford Modeling Agency. She currently walks the runways of Paris, Milan and New York, and is, as is often noted, the only black face of Ralph Lauren. This career trajectory is extremely unlikely for the young women in this study. Millen is the only Miss Tanzania winner[2] to have done well as an international model, despite the fact that most young women see the events as a platform for just that. While several winners have secured other kinds of success within Tanzania, none has achieved the kind of mobile, global, cosmopolitan life that Millen has. As a product of her upbringing, her education and her career, she speaks a pan-African version of the standard English, at once full of exotic charm but also fully fluent. Her language thus serves both as an index of her success and as a tool for having achieved it. Even her name change signals a move from a local identity to a translocal one; while 'Happiness' is certainly an English *word*, it is not, outside of some African contexts, typically an English *name*. Changing her name to Millen marked, as well as ushered in, her new identity as a truly cosmopolitan, borderless, international beauty icon (Figure 1.1).

Justina

When I first met her, Justina lived with her mother and younger brother in a two-room wattle-and-daub house with a concrete floor in the northern city of Arusha. Adjacent was the one-room house of her older brother Charles, who had a new baby. While neither dwelling had running water, Charles's had electricity and pirated cable television, on which Justina eagerly watched local and international music videos when time and un-predictable power delivery permitted. The families shared three goats and several chickens, which they kept in a corner of their courtyard, a cheerful space with potted plants dotting the edges of the swept dirt. Justina's parents – divorced for many years – were ethnically Maasai, but, unlike her parents and older brother, she did not speak the language.

From the beginning, Justina struggled to raise enough money to stay in secondary school. She repeatedly had to drop out, because her mother, who earned a small living through her sewing and mending, did not have enough money for school fees. Sometimes, she could resume her schooling thanks to a windfall from Charles, who worked in the dangerous and largely un-controlled tanzanite mines of the region. Charles would vanish for weeks at a time to work, then return to Arusha's black market to sell whatever rough stones he had found, a process which yielded an unpredictable and barely sustaining income for his family. Finally, in the middle of her secondary education, Justina dropped out permanently. Now her younger brother was also secondary-school age, and the family thought it was important for him to have at least some higher education.

Justina worked during this time, helping her sister-in-law buying and reselling second-hand clothing. After several months, she enrolled in a local computer course thanks to another contribution from Charles. Upon completion of the course, Justina tried to obtain a job as a receptionist in several of the local hotels and tourism companies catering to the international safari clientele, a line of work in which she was very interested. However, potential employers repeatedly turned her away due to her poor English skills. It was at this point, at the age of 18, that Justina enrolled in a local beauty pageant. She liked the idea of performing in the contemporary dance routines, as well as wearing a fancy evening gown and high-heeled shoes for the first time. Even more captivating to her, scholarships were available to a local tourism school, and cash was also among the prizes.

While Justina finished in the top three in the city-level pageant, she failed to gain a place in the regional pageant (again, her language and communication skills may have, in part, been at issue here, though so were her brown-stained teeth, a result of fluorosis from high fluoride levels in water, common in the region). Disappointed, she used her small pageant earnings, as well as help from a family friend, to enroll in a travel and tourism school in downtown Arusha. Here, she took half-day classes for four months, on the subjects of airline ticketing, accounting and English. Justina graduated from the program with honors, and her school arranged an internship for her with a mid-range tourist hotel in central Dar es Salaam. When she arrived, however, the hotel manager put her to work as a cleaning woman rather than as a receptionist, again because of her inadequate English. Justina stayed at the hotel for two months, until she contracted malaria and had to return to her family in Arusha for recovery;[3] since she was too ill to work, she could not afford her housing in the capital. Pending another big find by her brother, she planned to attend an English school across the border in Nairobi, where she believed language teachers would be more qualified.

Together, the life stories of Millen and Justina serve as an instructive starting point for this book. Millen's career trajectory is the fantasy for many young Tanzanian women who participate in pageants and who have followed Millen's movements in newspapers since her name was still 'Happiness'. Justina's life, on the other hand, is typical of the struggles of many young urban women in Tanzania to survive, be independent and find some enjoyment and meaning in life. Her participation in pageants was at once a pleasurable engagement with contemporary fashion and beauty as well as an ambitious attempt at escape. Both women participate – through pageants, clothing, media and travel – in a globalized world, yet they do so in extremely different ways, which belie stark inequalities in Tanzania. The pageants that gave Justina hope for escape and Millen a bona fide career as an international fashion model offer a glimpse into the forces that shape urban Tanzanian lives, as both a part of and on the fringes of our inter-connected world.

Pageants as Global and Local

While contests of feminine beauty of one kind or another have been around for hundreds, if not thousands, of years, with precursors for example in ancient Greece (Pomeroy, 1975) and medieval England (Banner, 1983), the modern beauty pageant has its most direct lineage in the past century or so in the United States. It was in 1921 that beauty pageants really took off, with the introduction of the Miss America competition in Atlantic City, New Jersey (Ballerino Cohen et al., 1996b). Soon after the original Miss America[4] contest, similar beauty pageants started to appear outside of the United States, and in the years following World War II they became a truly global phenomenon. England, where Queens of May contests already had a long history, was the quickest to catch on (Synnott, 1989). However, it did not take long for France, Turkey and other nations, including newly independent African countries such as Tanzania, to begin hosting their own national beauty pageants, where it is likely the spirit of nationalism fostered their spread (Ballerino Cohen et al., 1996b). Indeed, pageants worldwide began to embrace the contests as showcases for patriotism, citizenship and scholarship, and it is these ideals which remain largely the image that national beauty pageant enterprises tend to circulate today (Ballerino Cohen et al., 1996b; Deford, 1971).

Regardless, however, of the meanings promulgated by the pageant industry, citizens, participants and critics make their own sense of these spectacles. Today in the United States, for example, pageants are often loved as kitsch entertainment, disregarded as frivolous pop culture or embraced, typically by those involved, as scholarship opportunities and career stepping-stones (Banet-Weiser, 1999). American feminists have focused for decades on pageants as degrading and alienating, while post-feminists such as Camille Paglia and Naomi Wolf have stressed the agency of women who participate in such events (see overview in Banet-Weiser, 1999).

Yet these understandings do not find much traction in other parts of the globe, where the existence of pageants often signals emergent personae and positionalities vis-à-vis others, perceived as more 'traditional'. It has been argued that 'beauty contests are places where cultural meanings are produced, consumed, *and* rejected, where local, global, ethnic and national, national and international cultures and structures of power are engaged in their most trivial but vital aspects' (Ballerino Cohen *et al.*, 1996b: 8). While often self-consciously modeling themselves on Western, particularly American beauty pageants, the contests vary greatly: in the ways in which beauty is manifested; in discourses about femininity, authenticity and culture; and how local hierarchies of value and goodness are determined, displayed and disputed on pageant stages. These meanings are made visible not only through language but also through elements of feminine beauty, fashion, grooming and more.

While pageants are always necessarily made local, they are also often, simultaneously, *felt* as a cultural borrowing from the West. In many cases, pageants serve as an emblem of modernity, progress and cosmopolitanism (Besnier, 2002; Borland, 1996; Dewey, 2008; Johnson, 1996; Schulz, 2000). Through bodily adornment, shaping and carriage, contestants self-consciously mark themselves as knowledgeable of Western norms in fashion and styling. And it is not just the contestants themselves who bear such indexicalities. Pageants frequently take place in a city's most up-to-date performance facility, and the entire spectacle of lights, dance, music and talk together allows audiences to participate in the performance of a modern, translocal, cosmopolitan sensibility. For others, however, a deep sense that pageants are indeed foreign produces debate, tension and controversy over the extent to which they are a harbinger of irrevocable changes in local norms and values (see Chapter 3).

Language and Globalization

Homogenization, hybridity or multivocality?

The spread of pageants worldwide (Ballerino Cohen *et al.*, 1996a) is a clear example of the complex set of phenomena that is commonly understood as globalization. Coupland (2010: 1) discusses the now widely accepted claim that, 'whatever globalization is, it isn't an altogether new phenomenon'. The movements of people, products, money and ideas that help characterize globalizing phenomena have, through imperial and colonial encounters, been shaping people's lives throughout history (e.g. Kellner, 1989). Yet Coupland concludes that 'while globalization is certainly not without precedent, its scale and scope *are* new' (2010: 2; cf. Appadurai, 1996). Globalization involves a 'time–space compression', a speeding up of the transactions and interactions that have been going on for a very long time (Harvey, 1989: 240). The physical, economic, cultural and political interconnectedness facilitated by new technologies and, in some cases, loosened geographic and financial boundaries, allow for a much faster pace of change, and these changes are felt as new to people. Nonetheless, the qualitative nature of these changes is open to debate. Is globalization a source of good, bringing technological advances, positive social change and longer lives to people worldwide (e.g. Stiglitz, 2002)? Or is it largely a source of bad, exacerbating global inequalities through exploitative practices in trade and production (e.g. Hobsbawm, 2007)? Or must we consider the tensions between 'flow' and 'closure' (Meyer & Geschiere, 1999)?

With regard to language and globalization, two prominent and opposing strands have emerged, each built on the belief that linguistic diversity is desirable, yet differing in what *counts* as linguistic diversity. One strand concerns the notions of language death and endangerment; according to this perspective, it is the spread of English and, to a much lesser extent, other global languages that has resulted in the documented wiping out of linguistic diversity (e.g. Nettle & Romaine, 2000). Many scholars of language shift (e.g. Mühlhäusler, 1996; Nettle & Romaine, 2000; Skutnabb-Kangas, 2000) insist that it is the forces of globalization and mass media, themselves linked largely with former colonial languages, especially English, which are to a great degree responsible for the disappearance of minority languages worldwide. This view, however, is rooted in fundamentally flawed theories of the relationship between language and society, and the nature of language itself, as revealed in particular by the rhetoric and terminology used by their proponents, such as *killer language*, *linguicide* and *linguistic genocide* (for critiques, see Mufwene, 2004; Silverstein, 1998; Stroud, 2001). Such metaphors, and the theories they reflect, strip speakers of agency, give languages themselves disembodied qualities of good and evil, and fail to recognize the ways in which even 'foreign' linguistic material gets remade and made local as it moves from place to place. As Woolard (1989: 365) has reminded us, 'the metaphors we use affect the theories we build'.

The other strand of literature considers, rather than the homogenizing forces of globalization, the ways in which globalization has circulated linguistic and other materials to be made locally available and relevant. In this body of work, researchers consider how users of English make the language their own by localizing linguistic and cultural materials into hybrid forms. Pennycook (2007) examines global hip-hop and the ways in which English, and in particular African-American vernacular, speech practices are melded with various South Asian linguistic resources to produce local, popular musical forms, that at once reference hip-hop's roots and at the same time reflect and stand for a reordering of the linguistic and cultural practices embedded in hip-hop. Indeed, countless studies have shown convincingly that language users in Africa (e.g. Higgins, 2009; McLaughlin, 2009; Spitulnik, 1999) and across the globe (cf. Jacquemet, 2005) employ English and other erstwhile 'imperial' or 'dominant' linguistic materials for interactional and symbolic effects. Rather than simply flattening linguistic diversity, globalizing processes offer an opportunity for new, locally meaningful forms to flourish.

In her work *English as a Local Language*, Higgins (2009) enlists the work of Bakhtin (1981) to develop a framework for understanding hybrid language practices in urban Tanzanian as well as kindred practices worldwide. In particular, it is Bakhtin's notion of *multivocality* that is especially useful, as it frames the sociolinguistic phenomena Higgins (2009) analyzes at both the interactional and societal levels. On the interactional level, multivocality refers to the layered and contested meanings that occur in all speech (Bakhtin, 1981; cf. Silverstein & Urban, 1996) but can be especially present when one employs markedly hybrid linguistic forms, due to the array of meanings and contexts upon which such speech draws. On the societal level, Higgins takes multivocality to refer to the interplay of, in Bakhtin's terms, *centripetal* and *centrifugal* forces, or forces that serve, respectively, to pull practices towards a normative center, or to push them out from one. Since, according to Bakhtin, centripetal and centrifugal forces are always present in all speech, employing the notion of societal multivocality, Higgins argues, helps us to avoid polarizing understandings of English as either solely a menace to linguistic diversity or as a purely creative force in the lives of postcolonial subjects.

Higgins' (2009) use of the notion of multivocality to understand hybrid linguistic practices is effective in several ways. First, this approach recasts such linguistic practices as, rather than anomalous, commonplace in postcolonial and multilingual settings. Second, it frames such varieties as successful in communicative and symbolic functions, rather than as failures in the mismatch with standard forms. In this way, multivocality is also a framework that seems to apply well to other hard-to-categorize varieties, registers and genres, such as crossing (e.g. Rampton, 1995), styling (e.g. Bucholtz & Trechter, 2001; Coupland, 2007) and passing (e.g. Bucholtz, 1995; Goffman, 1959; Renfrow, 2004), in which centrifugal rather than centripetal forces are more prominently at work in shaping particular codes for particular functions and spaces. Third, Higgins makes clear that English need not be seen as a 'killer' language, but rather as an interactional and symbolic tool that speakers have reworked with other, 'indigenous' as well as non-local resources. Finally, her study shows us that what English is, is as diverse as the people who speak it, and can be understood only in particular contexts of use.

The work of Higgins (2009), Pennycook (2007) and others that focuses on linguistic hybridity and multivocality addresses what is recognized by cultural anthropologists more broadly: as commodities, ideas, people and language move through space and time, their significance and substance get reworked into new categories of meaning. An American cast-off shirt donated to help the needy becomes a fashion-forward statement of cosmopolitan identity in urban Zambia (Hansen, 2000). The ideal of romantic love as exemplified in Hollywood films becomes, when embraced by urban Nairobi women, a stance against patriarchy and in support of personal and financial independence (Spronk, 2009). These processes, while ever-increasing in pace and scale in the era of globalization, are not new in character. Even in cases of more overt coercion, culture is never adopted wholesale when introduced into a new context:

> Conquered and colonized societies, to take the obvious example, were never simply made over in the European image, despite the persistent tendency of Eurocentric scholars to speak as if they were. Rather, citizens struggled, in diverse ways and with differing degrees of success, to deploy, deform, and defuse imperial institutions. (Comaroff & Comaroff, 1993: xi–xii)

In beauty pageants in the postcolonial setting of Tanzania, we see the localization of a global genre, in linguistic and other terms. While pushing contestants towards a Western normativity in body, style and language, pageants in Tanzania simultaneously make local sense. Local norms, practices and ideologies, as well as local resources, give shape to contestants' self-construction as beauty queens and provide frameworks for evaluation. Though some discussion casts the events and their contestants as 'foreign', for many, beauty queens represent an emerging ideal of urban Tanzanian womanhood. At the same time, the self-conscious integration of recognizable bits of symbolic material as indeed foreign is essential in signaling the user (here the contestant) as suitably cosmopolitan and modern. On this score, I adopt the semiotic perspective of Agha (2007), who envisions how linguistic and non-linguistic symbolic materials are often linked together as comparable and belonging together, a topic to which I will return in subsequent chapters. In terms of language, English is a cornerstone of pageant success, yet what that English sounds like, and what speaking it means in these events, is informed by a complex of local ideologies, practices and institutions.

Truncated linguistic competencies

From an analytic point of view, the notions of multivocality and linguistic hybridity push language researchers to question what exactly they mean by 'language'. Language users increasingly, and perhaps now even more often than not, use bits from diverse languages and varieties in ways that would, under the rubric of static 'languages', be considered non-fluent, fragmented or even gibberish (Jacquemet, 2005). Yet, often, they do so with élan, conveying complex meanings on both the denotational and the symbolic planes. In other words, real language competence – or knowing how to use language – has little to do with mastery over a named language but instead with what 'counts' as competence in particular environments (Blommaert et al., 2005). Blommaert et al. (2005) introduce the notion of 'truncated multilingualism' to refer to the repertoires available to speakers in globalized environments with access to a mélange of linguistic materials.

For decades, scholars (e.g. Hymes, 1996; Silverstein, 1998) have drawn our attention to the significant problem in sociolinguistics and related fields of focusing on languages as static clusters of grammar, phonology and words, indicated by names such as French, English, Turkish and so forth, rather than on their real-life instantiations. In such formulations – the norm in many language-concerned disciplines – 'crucial *differences within the language complex* became invisible or were just blotted out' (Blommaert, 2005: 391, emphasis in original), because too much attention is paid to language monoliths, which, empirically speaking, are nonexistent. Instead, the socially significant linguistic parameters of difference among speakers are typically not those which can be identified by language names, but are, rather, 'particular varieties – repertoires, registers, styles, genres, and modes of usage' (Blommaert, 2005: 391). Others have made similar arguments: 'the true subject is not "language" alone, but repertoire – the mixes of means and modalities people actually practice and experience' (Hymes, 1996: 207; see also Silverstein, 1998).

Critically, the issue of avoiding language monoliths as the object of study also concerns the indexicalities of language. Not only must we steer clear of a view of language as static, predetermined clusters of grammar, phonology and words, but we must also avoid ones that take their indexicalities as static and predetermined.[5] Speakers use their 'means and modalities' in regimented as well as unique ways – or in Silverstein's (1976) words, 'presupposing' and 'creative' ways – to index emergent, yet socially identifiable, identities (Agha, 2007; Bucholtz & Hall, 2004; Silverstein, 2003a). On the ground, there is no such thing as a unified English, for example, nor is there a singular social meaning embodied by English. People mix, meld, borrow and bend linguistic materials into locally meaningful bundles, in ways that often defy easy naming (Blommaert *et al.*, 2005). These bundles – at once socially coherent and interactionally flexible – shape people's lived environments and index meaningful social positions much more diverse and complex than static formulations allow.

For example, in Ben Rampton's landmark work on inter-ethnic youth communication in urban England, he describes 'language crossing' as occurring when 'speakers … briefly adopted codes which they didn't have full and easy access to' (Rampton, 1995: 298). The youth in his study, some of Anglo descent using Panjabi, others of Pakistani origin using Jamaican Creole, could not in any way be considered fluent in the 'crossing' code, yet they were able to mobilize 'foreign' linguistic material in creative and socially meaningful ways (see also Cutler, 1999). These speakers show in fact great competence in using an array of language materials to contest racial boundaries and discourses.

In another example, Jacquemet, in his study of urban Albanians, presents the notion of 'transidiomatic practices' to describe 'the communicative practices of transnational groups that interact using different languages and communicative codes simultaneously present in a range of communicative channels, both local and distant' (Jacquemet, 2005: 264–265). Jacquemet illustrates how linguistic fragments from American pop music, Italian telenovelas and an online advertising campaign intersect to popularize the Albanianized transidiomatic floater *don uorri* – 'don't worry' – as an indexical icon of its speakers as multilingual and attuned to international pop cultural references. It also serves as a blithe self-mocking of the masculine stereotype of a southern European mafia don. The adept layering of linguistic with sociocultural knowledge, acquired through electronic media as well as face-to-face contact among transnational people, make clear that competence in real-life situations has little to do with bounded, named linguistic systems (see also Dyers, 2009).

In each of these cases, local linguistic practices involving an apparent hodgepodge of linguistic elements prove meaningful in specific settings. In beauty pageants, the ways in which English materials are mobilized are often highly fragmented and non-standard, but also powerfully indexical of status, education and the like. More often than not, these varieties serve contestants well in conveying to audiences and judges information about themselves they wish to be known. Yet when taken out of a strictly local context, their indexicalities get reordered and their meanings shift in hierarchical and regimented ways. It is to this topic that I now turn.

Inequality and a Sociolinguistics of Mobility

Scales, orders of indexicality and polycentricity

While globalization's capacity to spread cultural materials, as well as bodies, far and wide creates opportunities for local linguistic innovation, such innovation can at the same time function as an icon and engine of inequality. Researchers have convincingly illustrated that globalization is not just a source of opportunity, linguistic or otherwise. Rather, one of its fundamental characteristics is its capacity to exacerbate inequalities within and across states (e.g. Hobsbawm, 2007) and across a range of dimensions, including gender (e.g. Freeman, 2000; Mills, 2003), ethnicity and race (e.g. Hattery *et al.*, 2008) and age (e.g. Baars *et al.*, 2006). The opportunities offered by globalizing processes for increased wealth, mobility and access to a dizzying diversity of world products are in large part experienced by the minority of the world's population, located primarily in global centers, while such opportunities are to a great degree made possible by the labor of those located primarily in global peripheries (Hobsbawm, 2007).

From a sociolinguistic point of view, local linguistic practices undergo shifts in their indexicalities after they move. In other words, while they effect positive communicative meanings when used in specific, local environments, once they are relocated, their value often plummets. The kinds of non-standard English-language street signs appearing as symbolic capital across the globe (e.g. Blommaert, 2010; Higgins, 2009; see also Chapter 2) reappear regularly in travelers' photoblogs (e.g. engrish.com) to illustrate the innocent, provincial use of English by people who are now reframed as semi-illiterate. The semiotically complex transidiomatic practices employed by urban Albanians (Jacquemet, 2005) surely become referentially perplexing indices of speakers' lives on the global fringes when transplanted to urban Italy itself, the centering space in many respects of their social world. And when the urban, multi-ethnic youth of Rampton's (1995) study bring their crossing and other hybrid practices out of their neighborhood and into normative institutions such as schools, their language use is likely no longer to be valued as boundary-breaking and identity-building but, instead, is taken as non-standard, sub-par and even subversive (e.g. Jaspers, 2005). In each of these cases, the local value of a particular variety is only one side of the coin; the other side is that the 'globalized' forms spoken most naturally by the people in the examples above serve as positive symbolic and interactional resources only in limited spaces. While serving to enrich local experience, and on occasion moving out of the local to secure some kind of translocal visibility and utility (Heller, 2010b; Pennycook, 2007), these varieties typically do not help speakers much in their quest to change the material reality of their lives, but instead afford their users rather slim opportunities for social or geographic mobility. Invaluable for face-to-face meaning-making, their value quickly plummets outside of a strictly local setting: global, yes; exportable, no.

In his *Sociolinguistics of Globalization*, Blommaert tells us that 'the traditional concept of "language" is dislodged and destabilized by globalization' (Blommaert, 2010: 2), the latter being a set of processes that, 'even if not new in substance ... are new in intensity, scope, and scale' (Blommaert, 2010: 1; see also Hobsbawm, 2007; Wallerstein, 2004). In the past, sociolinguists – such as Labov (1966, 1972), and the generations of scholars following in his footsteps – have considered language practices as grounded in a specific horizontal space, such as the village, the city or the country, with social stratification being part of a 'snapshot' of this stationary location. Today, the increased pace, distance and frequency with which people, words, objects and ideas move, and the repercussions on lives of such movement, together challenge the compartmentalization of peoples, cultures and languages that has been characteristic of studies of language and culture for many decades. Blommaert argues for a 'sociolinguistics of mobility' which focuses 'not on language-in-place but language-in-motion, with various spatio-temporal frames interacting with one another' (Blommaert, 2010: 5). Key to his sociolinguistics of mobility are three conceptual building blocks: scale, orders of indexicality and polycentricity.

For Blommaert (2010), a sociolinguistic 'scale' is a metaphor that allows us to envision the ways in which practices, norms and standards for language exist in strata, informed by social, political and cultural factors. The notion of scale is particularly useful, thus, for framing sociolinguistic phenomena in terms of inequality, as '[a]ccess to and control over scales is unevenly distributed' (Blommaert, 2010: 5). In this view, the notion of scales evokes vertical, hierarchical dimensions that are always at play in interaction, and which can be foregrounded or backgrounded even over the course of a single interaction. One's ease in moving up and down scale levels is a signal of, and indeed a factor in creating, one's social mobility.

This brings us to the second building block, that of orders of indexicality. As linguistic resources move through scales, say, from the local to the global, their functions and meanings shift. Such shifts 'involve a reordering of normativity' (Blommaert, 2010: 22), and these shifts are, to a degree, regimented and predictable, and point to the '(non-)exchangeability of particular linguistic or semiotic resources across places, situations and groups' (Blommaert, 2010: 38–39). The French spoken by a professor at the University of Kinshasa may index her locally as an educated elite, though in Paris it, along with other salient features of her origin, may mark her to many as an unwanted immigrant of low status.

Finally, and connected to the first two concepts, is polycentricity. The notion of polycentricity in a sociolinguistics of mobility recognizes that people orient towards different centers and institutions simultaneously, with 'multiple – though never unlimited – batteries of norms to which one can orient and according to which one can behave' (Blommaert, 2010: 40). A student may provide a tongue-and-cheek answer to the teacher, which simultaneously orients to the expectations of student–teacher pair–part exchange while also orienting towards the student's desire to position herself positively vis-à-vis her cohort. Yet while people's behaviors, use of language and interpretations are simultaneously informed by different centers, some centers have authority over others, in a structured, ordered way. The joking student will find that her orientation to her cohort works only within that immediate age and class set, while the expectations of the teacher likely are more broadly rewarded.

In pageants in general, the interplay of scales, orders of indexicality and polycentricity is often striking. Tensions between locally and more widely recognized regimes of meaning exist at every level of competition, with simultaneous, overlapping and sometimes contradictory orientations towards differing systems of normativity and value. For example, in Tanzanian pageants, contestants must please local audiences with a degree of modesty in their dress, at the same time that they are aware of international expectations in segments such as the swimsuit competition, and want to position themselves to judges and organizers as a suitable Miss World delegate.

Yet the struggle between local and non-local – that is, generalizable – value and meaning is not a struggle between equals but rather reflects power differentials across individuals, places and institutions. Wilk (1998: no page) points out about pageants that 'The continuing lesson is that the local is subordinated to the national, and the national to the global'. Simultaneous scales of orientation and judgment influence pageant happenings but, ultimately, it is the highest possible scale level where the judgment is most authoritative, where the contestant's valuation offers the potential for escape and opportunity that she seeks. For a Tanzanian beauty queen, her ability to mobilize the appropriate linguistic variety is critical at each level, though what counts as appropriate takes a different shape at each turn.

In sum, Blommaert's (2010) sociolinguistics of mobility is useful in this project as it acknowledges that globalizing forces introduce and reorder the tools of and norms for linguistic and other semiotic behaviors within pageants. At the same time, this approach makes clear that in pageants, as elsewhere, multiple orientations – to the family, to the community, to school, to the nation-state, to the global stage – influence behaviors and evaluations simultaneously. Finally, a sociolinguistics of mobility puts power relations at the heart of these processes, acknowledging the structured authority and value of certain scales, orders of indexicality and centers over others, and seems to be as relevant for linguistic as for non-linguistic meaning-making.

The state-as-switchboard scalar level

A salient characteristic of globalization seems to be the capacity of money, cultural products and ideas to move around globally without passing through state gatekeepers (Kearney, 1995), and hence some scholars have predicted the state's imminent demise (e.g. Appadurai, 1996; Castells, 1996). Yet, while transnational flows are undeniably a defining characteristic of our era, a consensus has arisen among many scholars that the state indeed maintains relevance (cf. Hobsbawm, 2007; Wallerstein, 2004), even if what exactly its functions are may be variable and in flux. Many scholars argue for the vital role that the state has in distributing resources differentially, serving as the gatekeeper for international investment, and controlling migration, emigration and immigration.

Blommaert (2005: 396) has called the state 'a switchboard' that is critical in a globalized era, in structuring access to and the distribution of economic, social, cultural and symbolic capital, including language. The state has important effects on people's language use and on the construction of valuation schemes, which, while informed by global practices and preferences, are in large part interpreted through state-level actors (cf. Hobsbawn, 2007; Wallerstein, 2004). In other words, the state orients people towards international models of language, education and governance, at the same time that it controls local access to infrastructure as well as to symbolic, legal and value-making resources (Blommaert, 2005: 396). Asylum cases offer a clear example of the significance of this scalar level's role in global processes, in which states adopt a 'modernist reaction to postmodern realities' (Blommaert, 2010: 172), including a steadfast clinging to a monoglot ideology (cf. Silverstein, 1996) in the face of linguistic hybridity. The monoglot ideology results in decisions which render asylum seekers illegitimate and even language-less, jeopardizing their chances to stay in the host country and even threatening repatriation to a country that is not their own (e.g. Corcoran, 2004; Maryns, 2006).

The centrality of the state in organizing the ideologies and practices we see in pageants and in urban Tanzania more generally is prominent in several ways. The Tanzanian state has historically been influential, if not fully successful, in its attempts to shape national culture, elements of which are both performed and contested on the pageant stage (Chapter 3). Concerned about the negative influence of both foreign and ethnic practices on a nascent national identity, the Tanzanian government has attempted to regulate certain practices and products deemed incongruent with that ideal. Tanzanian beauty pageants, as Western-origin spectacles, come under the state's watchful eye and, while deeply controversial, occur as state-monitored and supported events that, at least by some estimation, reflect and uphold a version of official Tanzanian national culture. In particular, some policing of language and the female body surface in concrete form in pageant regulations (Chapters 3 and 4). More subtly, the linguistic practices employed by contestants in these events, while influenced by international norms, are structured in part by regional and socioeconomic hierarchies, themselves influenced by state-level processes (Chapters 4 and 5). Critically, the state is central to these discussions, as Tanzanians often understand social, political and cultural change, and personal and national success on the global stage, to be the provenance of the government. Many put their faith in the ability of state institutions to mold behaviors, values and opportunities in the name of building a better Tanzania, as I will discuss further in Chapters 2 and 6.

Language as a resource

In Tanzanian beauty pageants, one's ability to mobilize linguistic and other symbolic resources has the capacity to make or break one's hopes and dreams. In particular, language becomes perhaps the most essential resource for success and is characterized by steep inequalities of access. Here, I consider briefly an understanding of language *as a resource*, as opposed to other paradigms that emphasize language primarily as a closed system.

Many scholars (e.g. Blommaert, 2010; Bucholtz & Hall, 2004; Heller, 2010a, 2010b) argue that language should be seen primarily in its capacity to serve as a 'resource', actively used for achieving all kinds of semiotic, interactional and even monetized work, all located within social hierarchies of value. Bucholtz (2004, 2006, 2009) takes as her concern the central role of slang and youth language as a resource in interactionally constructing speaker identities, difference and lived environments (see also Eckert, 1989; Mendoza-Denton, 2008). For her, a language-as-resource paradigm is critical in an era in which differences of race and ethnicity are, more than ever, widely visible through media and face-to-face interactions. Along with gender, they are highly malleable categories, adopted by 'outsiders' in novel ways (see e.g. Rampton, 1995), and with a range of potential and highly fluid meanings. Linguistic and other semiotic materials are not inextricably linked to particular identities but instead can shift meanings in use, with even an identical bit of language taken to index polarized racial categories (see also Ochs, 1992, for a similar discussion of language and gender). Racial, ethnic and gendered identities are emergent through interaction, and the range of such identities is wide, even within a single high school.

For Blommaert (2005, 2010), a language-as-resource perspective is central when considering language use in this era, characterized more by super-diversity than by static speech communities. The high mobility of people and their ways of speaking highlights the stratified ways in which such varieties – and their speakers – are differently valued in different spaces. A central concern for Blommaert is the ways in which language facilitates or constrains social mobility and access to opportunity and institutions, especially for speakers with linguistic resources from the global periphery, as in the case of asylum seekers in Western countries (see also Blommaert, 2009; Corcoran, 2004; Maryns, 2006). In many such circumstances, the linguistic materials at hand defy easy categorization, from both the point of view of normative institutions as well as that of traditional linguistics. While often considered highly multilingual in a home environment, these speakers come to be seen as having no language at all, utterly voiceless, when seen from the perspective of schools, state agencies and even main-stream neighbors. Viewing language as a resource is critical in this line of thinking, in that it considers what language can actually do for people in particular environments.

Heller (2010a, 2010b) focuses on the ways in which language functions as a specific kind of resource: a commodity, available for exchange for goods or money in particular markets. Language-as-commodity, she argues, has taken front and center in a globalized economy, in which standard varieties of dominant languages are often sought for offshore call centers (e.g. Cameron, 2001; Cowie, 2007), while non-standard, hybrid and minority varieties become commodified in niche marketing campaigns (Kelly-Holmes, 2005; see also Higgins, 2009) as well as in hip-hop and other music that has come to have value in the global marketplace (e.g. Sarkar & Winer, 2006; see also Perullo & Fenn, 2000; Pennycook, 2007). For Heller, a language-as-resource paradigm:

> can draw on Bakhtinian notions of heteroglossia, on Foucauldian ideas of discourse, and on Bourdieuan ideas of markets to reimagine languages as communicative resources, socially constructed in uneven, unequal, distributed social spaces. These circulate – also unevenly and unequally – through social networks and communicative archipelagos,

in ways which make them more or less accessible to speakers, as the latter have greater or lesser interest in mobilizing them in their own communicative action. (Heller, 2010b: 361)

The context of beauty pageants puts language-as-resource in high relief. Contestants manipulate linguistic (and other) tools to perform specific personae and achieve particular goals on stage as part of the evaluative process. The shape of these resources, though, is variable, as is access to the resources that count as good at particular scale levels. Furthermore, as these young women resume their regular routines, as students, as drop-outs, as career-seeking young women, their access to, quest for and command over various linguistic resources stands out as an orienting factor in their lives.

Globalization, Cosmopolitanism and (Gendered) Citizens of the World

But inequality is not the only lens through which to consider globalization, and the notion of cosmopolitanism gives us another perspective which emphasizes the identity-making and pleasurable effects of global flows on people's lives. For Besnier, cosmopolitanism refers to:

a particular disposition (in the sense of Bourdieu's habitus) towards difference associated with super-national flows. In its most common usage, cosmopolitanism assumes access to particular symbolic capital that transcends and puts into perspective the local context. The cosmopolitan Western urbanite, for example, 'controls' symbols of other locales, including languages, exotic foods and tastes, and non-local ways of apprehending the everyday. (Besnier, 2007: 69)

From this point of view, a critical aspect of cosmopolitanism is the consumption and display of a particular cadre of globally sourced goods and practices that are taken locally as signifiers of a particular kind of select global membership. Usually, then, cosmopolitanism is thought to be a characteristic of elites, who have the money, education and free time to acquire – through travel, books, shopping, theater-going, private classes, etc. – such signifiers (Hannerz, 1996). Indeed, very often the cosmopolite is associated with white male privilege (Ram, 2008; Stivens, 2008).

Yet others contend that, especially in this globalized era, cosmopolitanism can be enacted by nearly anyone. Werbner envisions cosmopolitanism as being 'about reaching out across cultural differences through dialogue, aesthetic enjoyment, and respect; of living together with difference'

(Werbner, 2008b: 2). Since, she argues, cosmopolitanism is always rooted in a particular time and place, it is locally emergent and, hence, as is true any time there are cultural 'borrowings' at hand, is embodied in unexpected ways. Hannerz (1996) tells us that some cosmopolites attempt to 'master' entire cultures, while others pick and choose the parts that appeal to them, and either strategy offers the potential for marking oneself as a cosmopolitan. Thus, the fact one need not have access to 'entire cultures' means that, through access to the bits of culture flowing through global scapes, enacting cosmopolitanism is possible even for people without much in the way of means or mobility (see e.g. Robbins, 1998; Wardle, 2000).

Providing two case studies from his fieldwork in the South Pacific archipelago of Tonga, Besnier (2007) illustrates how cosmopolitanism can be imagined by people who have little access to material resources. First, Besnier takes us to Tongan flea markets, or *fea*, shabby, makeshift stalls where sellers and buyers gather to exchange international second-hand goods – clothing, household products, grooming items – usually remitted by relatives living abroad (see also Besnier, 2004). While all segments of Tongan society shop at *fea* because they offer international products not available in local shops, many shoppers like these improvised markets because they feel welcome in them and, critically, because they are sometimes able to afford the products on offer (see Hansen, 2000, for similar discussions of Zambian second-hand clothing markets). But the *fea* experience is as much about browsing as it is about buying, offering a sensory engagement with products from abroad. It is also a social occasion, where people talk about the much-felt tensions between local codes of sartorial feminine decency and highly valued Western fashion sense.

For the second case study, Besnier (2007) overviews his research on Tongan transgender beauty pageants (Besnier, 2002). In these events, members of the local transgender community compete in a prominent national event to wear the crown of Miss Galaxy. During the event, 'girls' don exotic outfits envisaged as the national costumes of distant lands, places with which the contestants likely have no connection but simply find captivating. Contestants also shape their bodies to conform, to the extent possible, with Western ideals of femininity. While marginalized and often poor members of society, the transgender pageant participants display their appreciation and knowledge of cultural difference through the aesthetics of their clothes and bodies.

In both of these Tongan cases, a critical component of participants' cosmopolitan imaginings is their use of English. In the flea markets, shoppers and sellers use more English in their small talk than they do in any other context. The use of English on stage at Miss Galaxy is also central to the performance of cosmopolitanism, and in fact the entire event is oriented around English language use. Language – often truncated, hybrid varieties whose value is wholly local – is thus essential to the cosmopolitan imaginings of Tongans, which in many cases they experience as a very real part of their lives.

In addition to the positive, largely aesthetic, cosmopolitanism described above, cosmopolitanism also has a political dimension. Thus, Hannerz notes that:

> cosmopolitanism has two faces, a cosmopolitanism with a happy face, enjoying new cuisines, new musics, new literatures. Political cosmopolitanism, is often a cosmopolitanism with a worried face, trying to come to grips with very large problems. (Hannerz, 2004: 71)

'Cosmopolitics' (Hannerz, 2005), then, can suggest an engagement with human rights and environmental issues that at once may occur far from the cosmopolitan's front door but which are nonetheless thought to be important social causes because they point to our shared humanity and world.

Pageants in Tanzania bear both the happy and the worried faces of cosmopolitanism, in myriad ways. Contestants as well as audiences embrace Western music, fashion and physical aesthetics in fashioning themselves as keyed into the wider world (Chapter 4). As I discuss in Chapter 6, pageants at least perfunctorily celebrate not just Western cultural difference, but also other kinds of diversity, seen in the selection of a Miss Tanzania of South Asian origin. At the same time, pageants orient around a cosmopolitan humanitarianism, seen especially during the question-and-answer session (Chapter 3). While given a nationalist spin, questions typically concern issues wracking many parts of the world, such as homelessness, child abuse and, especially, HIV/AIDS. Contestants who answer such questions with the appropriate dose of informed caring earn favor with audiences and judges. Simultaneously, for audience members, attending such an event, with an eye to stylish women and stylish humanitarian campaigns, enhances their own self-understanding as members of the local cosmopolitan community.

Yet just *wanting* to be cosmopolitan does not necessarily make one so. Hence, cosmopolitanism also involves a question of competence, which, 'with regard to alien cultures itself entails a sense of mastery, as an aspect of the self. One's understandings have expanded, a little more of the world is somehow under control' (Hannerz, 1996: 240). And competence – linguistic or otherwise – is necessarily in the eye of the beholder. As Besnier (2004) makes painfully clear, competence in a locally good-enough cosmopolitan

English can make or break a contestant's bid for Miss Galaxy. Hence, we embark again upon the notion of inequality; while *anyone* can adopt a cosmopolitan sensibility, some people, in any given context, are *more* cosmopolitan than others, at least in part due to unequal access to signs of cosmopolitan-ness. Furthermore, some varieties of cosmopolitanism are more mobile across scales and spaces than others; they still succeed in indexing cosmopolitanism when used away from home. Other, more vernacular cosmopolitanisms (Bhabha, 1996; Werbner, 2008a; cf. the 'vernacular globalization' of Appadurai, 1996) become, ironically, indexical of cosmopolitanism's opposite – parochialism – when on the move.

In this study, we will see vernacular cosmopolitanisms that are felt as real and significant to those using them. Contestants wear not only high heels and evening gowns, but also versions of Maasai ethnic dress and Indian saris (Chapter 6). They expound their views of famine, disease and strife, conveying an awareness of and sensitivity to the global downtrodden. Yet a successfully cosmopolitan contestant becomes laughably provincial – through her dress, hairstyle and, indeed, language – as she moves up the pageant hierarchy and towards the Miss Tanzania pageant (Chapter 4). And even Miss Tanzania, once she reaches the pageant pinnacle of Miss World, may feel woefully uncosmopolitan when competing against women from Madrid, Rio and Delhi (Chapter 7). The quest for the crown becomes, again, one structured by hierarchical, though polycentric, scales, and language use plays out as a primary focus of attention.

Finally for this project, the notion of cosmopolitanism helps frame gendered responses to aesthetic, educational, linguistic, vocational and aspirational facets of globalization that get distilled in and around beauty pageants (Besnier, 2007). Contestants' onstage performance, through self-adornment, linguistic showmanship and political messaging, makes clear their gendered orientation towards a global cosmopolitanism befitting an international beauty queen or runway model – the ultimate dream for many. Offstage, their particular strategies for securing an education, a career and social and geographic mobility are also gendered, as well as age-graded and urban, in response to a more widely felt lack of opportunity in Tanzania. In that, for these young women, such strategies are often more centrifugal than centripetal in nature, their responses can be understood as manifestations of a cosmopolitan sensibility in the age of globalization. This last point reminds us of the fallacy of gendering globalization and cosmopolitanism as masculine, a reminder critical when considering the seemingly local and, hence, implicitly 'feminine', lives and activities of what Freeman (2001: 1008) has called '"small-scale" individuals', people such as the Tanzanian beauty contestants in this study.

Fieldwork

Fieldwork for this research was conducted during four extended stays in Tanzania, including two long periods in Arusha and Dar es Salaam, and shorter stays in Morogoro and Mwanza, between 2001 and 2007 (Figure 1.2). In addition, I collected online interviews and newspaper coverage that inform this work, through to 2012.

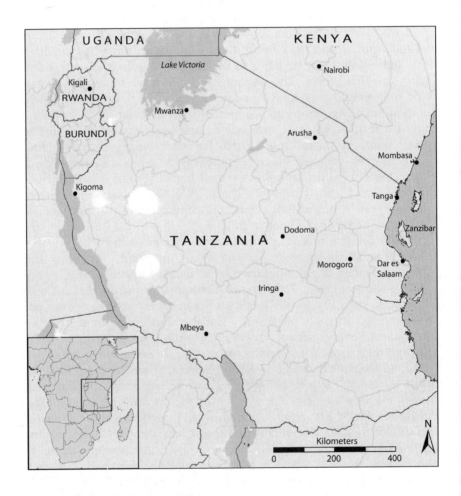

Figure 1.2 Map of Tanzania
Credit: Jesse Casana, map data courtesy of ESRI, Inc

Research design

My original research design was aimed at gathering data which would reveal ideologies about language use in urban Tanzania, and my approach was to integrate multiple kinds of evidence, from the most explicit meta-pragmatic commentaries elicited in interviews to implicit evidence gleaned, for example, from patterns of code choice. Constituting the heart of the data were eight beauty pageants which I attended and recorded, as well as three more pageant recordings which I obtained. In addition, I interviewed 27 contestants and five pageant organizers. The intention of these interviews was to gather background information, to elicit metasemiotic descriptions about expectations for contestants and others during the events, and to collect samples of offstage spoken Swahili and English, as well as to make contacts for later home visits. Prior to several competitions, I also attended rehearsals, which usually occurred daily during the preceding week or two. By watching practices, I was able to get a sense of the emergent nature of the final, live 'text', a 'natural history' of a week or two's worth of the pageants' coming-into-being through intensive correction, creative inspiration and modification (cf. Silverstein & Urban, 1996).

Following the pageants, I conducted several focus groups, during which I showed pageant video excerpts in order to seek clarification of specific pageant moments as well as to understand local value judgments about language, beauty, dress and comportment. My data also include hundreds of newspaper articles taken from extensive reportage of these and other topical events, contextualizing this study within broader discourses in Tanzania about gender, sexuality, language and education. More informally, I established friendly relationships with several contestants and organizers, visiting their homes, meeting their families and sharing meals with them. We engaged in typical gendered activities, such as browsing clothing markets, watching children, going to the salon (*salooni* locally) and talking about celebrities and popular music.

The juxtaposition of various kinds of data was fruitful, in part by revealing contradictions. In some cases, these contradictions emphasized the naturalized aspect of some ideologies, while in other cases they pointed to competing ideologies, held by a single person or by a variety of people. For example, discourses about the equality of English and Swahili abound offstage in interviews, yet pageant data showed that, in fact, the two languages were not equal, but that, rather, winners were far more likely to speak English than Swahili. Likewise, in interviews, participants emphasized that local ethnic languages were out of place in pageants because of mutual incomprehensibility, yet, on the one hand, English was used even though many people do not understand it well, and, on the other hand, local ethnic languages do indeed make an appearance in certain pageant contexts.

The present volume expands the original research (Billings, 2006, 2009, 2011a, 2011b), to include a greater emphasis on gender as well as non-linguistic features constituting local understandings of Tanzanian beauty queens and modern Tanzanian femininity. In many cases, the original fieldwork data has proved useful for these purposes. In addition, online interviews and many additional newspaper articles have been drawn on, especially with regard to gender, ethnicity, language and education, both within pageants and in urban Tanzanian society more generally.

Researching Tanzanian beauty pageants

It is perhaps not surprising that some Tanzanians with whom I came in contact might have come away with assumptions about me that did not match my own view of my role there, or that my research interests were sometimes mapped onto me as somehow representative of my own identity. These are observations that have been frequently noted by those who have conducted fieldwork, and such misunderstandings present the potential for an array of ramifications for the research itself (e.g. Setel, 1999). I was a young, single, white American woman, working my way through cities and across the country, usually alone, to study, of all things, beauty pageants. These various aspects of my being contributed to a range of interpretations about who I was and what I was up to. Because I was American and white, contestants and others assumed on numerous occasions that I was a judge or a coach, brought in to impart my knowledge of how things are done in the West. Others took my skin color and national origin as indexical of my being in a financial position to be a pageant or contestant sponsor. Because I was relatively young, female and interested in beauty pageants, some community members thought that I was a *malaya* ('prostitute') – a view that extended to those I was studying. The fact that I was constantly on the move, sometimes at night, certainly contributed to that perception. Others viewed my interest as evidence that I had myself taken part in such events back home (see Banet-Weiser, 1999, for similar reactions). The fact that I was always asking a lot of questions and sometimes writing things down led some, in particular certain pageant organizers, to see me suspiciously, nervous that I was planning to exploit them or the contestants.

While, over time, I believe that most people with whom I had any regular contact saw me in a way that more or less matched my own sense of self and purpose, some interpretations created ramifications for the ways in which I collected and analyzed data. For example, I had originally planned to interview contestants prior to events, but when I realized their uncertainty about my role, I found them far more forthcoming once the events were over. Likewise, I found organizers more willing to talk about the pageants after the fact, less nervous that a sensational news story would overshadow the pageant proceedings. On the other hand, my presence at rehearsals seemed largely unnoticed, perhaps because I was observing rather than interviewing, and because I agreed not to record them. Certainly, repeat contact led to greater trust, and these issues diminished over the course of my fieldwork. Still, handling requests from contestants to sponsor their pageant participation or their education was an ongoing challenge, as was navigating uncharitable interpretations of my character by fellow audience members when pageants rolled past the midnight hour. Making visible my pad of paper and pencil – perhaps odd accessories for a raucous nighttime show – seemed to assuage people's assumptions, as did bringing along a friend when possible.

At the intersection of work and play: Transcriptions, translations and focus groups

Transcripts and rough translations of pageant proceedings were made primarily in Tanzania with the help of a pageant contestant who worked with me as an assistant. We usually met at a local hotel bar, where we could sit outside in the courtyard and enjoy Fantas and chips while pouring over video-recordings. Depending on the availability of electricity and the status of my batteries, we would view the original recordings on the small screen of my video-camera, or else on my laptop. After no more than a few days working like this, I realized the great potential for drawing in others' opinions – the technology in and of itself was of great interest, as were, perhaps secondarily, the controversial and entertaining pageants. Frequently, friends, as well as employees and customers of the hotel, would join us, generously sharing their opinions and analyses of the pageant proceedings.

My initial research plan involved more formalized focus groups, in which participants would be asked to view or listen to segments of the events and then answer questions about the suitability and quality of language use. Early during the period of time dedicated to transcriptions, I attempted a couple of these and found the results disappointing. The participants were reticent to speak and seemed to be telling me what they thought I wanted to hear. In the meantime, however, the impromptu 'focus groups' had taken off, occurring most days in conjunction with transcription and translation sessions with my assistant. I quickly recognized the rich potential of these encounters and began planning questions based on my knowledge that we would be visited each day by other participants, eager to share their analyses, opinions and judgments on the ever-captivating topics of language and beauty.

The Book

Just as I understand language to be interwoven with other features in real life, so does my analysis integrate, to a great degree, discussions of linguistic and non-linguistic data. That said, Chapters 2, 4 and 5 concern more directly matters of language and communication, while the emphasis in Chapters 3, 6 and 7 is to a larger extent on non-linguistic symbolic behaviors. Here I will briefly overview the contents of each chapter.

Offering critical background to the entire book, Chapter 2 provides a discussion of the sociolinguistic landscape of Tanzania with regard to Swahili and English, the co-official languages of the country. Beginning with an overview of the theoretical notion of language ideologies, the chapter addresses how ideologies have been in play in shaping language use, as well as categories of personhood, in modern Tanzania. I review how language in education has long been a topic of debate and how the key tenets of the debate are informed by ideological associations of Swahili and English. I then move to a discussion of hybrid linguistic varieties and urban Tanzanian identities, before offering conclusions about the interplay of multivocality with the existence of life-shaping hierarchies of linguistic value.

Chapter 3 moves on to Tanzanian beauty pageants themselves. Here, I analyze the ways in which pageants reflect, perform and contest under-standings of Tanzanian national identity and the role of the feminine in constructing that identity. First, I overview historic attempts to formulate a unified national identity, which have often focused on efforts to control femininity and ethnicity, especially in urban spaces. Next, I bring forth data from pageants in which contestants and other participants enlist signs and discourses representative of the nation in framing themselves and the event as bona fide. Finally, I address the issue of the problematic place of women in the city who, through their education, clothing and activities, represent either the promise or the downfall of a modern Tanzanian.

Chapters 4 and 5 concern in particular the issue of linguistic inequality, as informed by spatial as well as class-based hierarchies which cast English as superior to Swahili. In both chapters, we see contestants' attempts to index themselves, largely through language, as educated elites, yet we also see variation in terms of what actually counts as good English. Dar es Salaam sits at the pageant pinnacle, and tastes and practices more common there give form to interpretations of goodness and value for the national beauty queen. What is more, an understanding of contestants as schoolgirls serves as a model for their behavior as well as a basis for critiques against them. Ultimately, hierarchies of value extend beyond language and education and subsume the entire feminine being, whose characteristics that would qualify her for Miss Tanzania are acquirable not just through schooling but even more perhaps through an upper-class, transnational upbringing.

In Chapter 6, I turn to ethnicity and race in pageants in the context of the ideological construction of Tanzania as color-blind. Like most public and urban events in Tanzania, beauty pageants are widely understood as zones in which racial and ethnic differences should be irrelevant. Yet the space of performance opens up room for grappling with Tanzanian ethnicity, the strategy of double-voicing allowing performers to create distance between themselves and the ethnic personae of their routines. Furthermore, the fact that, in a recent year, a Miss Tanzania of South Asian origin was selected brought to the fore concerns over inequality, gender and race in forging Tanzania's identity and its future.

Finally, in the concluding Chapter 7, I discuss the trope of *kutafuta maisha*, 'looking for life', as a way of framing the quest for mobility and opportunity in Tanzania, among contestants and other urban Tanzanians in pursuit of a better life. Building on this trope, I take a look at discourses surrounding Miss Tanzania's perennial failure at the Miss World competition in terms of hierarchies of value, indexical re-orderings and polycentricities. Finally, I revisit the life of Justina, the pageant contestant from the beginning of the present chapter, to illustrate how some of the key ideas of the book have played out in the life of a particular young Tanzanian woman.

Notes

(1) I use pseudonyms for most contestants' names in this book. However, when discussing contestants who have achieved some fame or notoriety, as in the case of Happiness Magese, I use their real names.

(2) In 2007, Tanzania began participating in another international pageant circuit, that of Miss Universe. That year, Miss Universe Tanzania went on to finish relatively high – sixth place – at the Miss Universe competition. She has since secured a reasonably successful international career in fashion modeling. However, this project reports on Tanzania's participation in the Miss World circuit, which has historically been the dominant pageant organization in the country.

(3) Arusha is much higher in elevation and has a more moderate climate than Dar es Salaam, which is on the coast. Hence, malaria is less common in Arusha, and it is said that Arushans as well as other northern residents have less immunity and malaria-avoidance know-how than people from the coast.

(4) The name Miss America was coined in 1921 but not used officially until many years later (Banet-Weiser, 1999).

(5) For example, although profoundly influential, Labov's work (e.g. 1966, 1972) has not escaped serious criticism. Critics (e.g. Dorian, 1982; Romaine, 1982) have pointed to several fundamental problems with a Labovian approach. For instance, the class categories he employed were taken as independent variables, as a given rather than discoverable through ethnographic fieldwork. Furthermore, class seemed to be independent of, rather than co-produced by, the linguistic forms used by members of the speech community. Likewise, critics of traditional approaches to codeswitching have illustrated the flexibility of social meanings that may be indexed by variable use of 'mixed' varieties (Meeuwis & Blommaert, 1998; Urciuoli, 1998; Zentella, 1997).

2 Language Ideologies, Linguistic Registers and the Sociolinguistic Landscape of Swahili and English in Tanzania

'Kiswa-English' in Parliament will therefore be unacceptable. Once this rule is enacted, it will certainly be a good beginning and a message well sent to all and sundry that there is a lot of prestige for one to start and end one's speech or normal talk in Kiswahili....
Open letter to the Speaker of the Parliament
(wa Kuhenga, 2012), *Daily News Online*

Primary level teachers need to speak proper English. No doubt the government will help them....
Tanzanian Minister for Education and Vocational Training,
reported in Kimati (2010), *Daily News Online*

English language is one of the aspects excluding Tanzanians from job markets ... experts have called upon the government to introduce English interview skills into the primary and secondary schools curriculum, to equip students with knowledge and skills necessary when seeking jobs on national and international job markets.
Robi (2012), *Daily News Online*

During my tenure at the EAC [East African Community], I was so upset with Tanzanian graduates who feared their Kenyan counterparts just because of the English language....
Former East African Community (EAC) Secretary-General,
reported in Mwakyusa (2011), *Tanzania Daily News*

China, Japan, and many other nations have been able to make their language scientific but ours cannot be used in modern technology. So the best is to invest a lot in learning English.
Senior lecturer in the Department of Economics at the University
of Dar es Salaam, reported in Kalokola (2011), *The Citizen*

The power of language – its capacity to build nations and create citizens, to forge relationships or create fissures across groups of people, to deliver an education, to bring people closer to God – has long been a concern in Africa. Fardon and Furniss (1994) argue that, in Africa, language is often either characterized by a dearth (lacking grammatical, conceptual, ortho-graphic or other necessary components) or a glut (too many languages, too many people, too much ethnolinguistic difference). This dearth-or-glut understanding has frequently been thought to render particular African languages or repertoires ineffective for particular purposes (Fabian, 1986). Indeed, in Tanzania, as elsewhere in Africa, language is often constructed as a problem, for individuals, communities, institutions and the nation-state. But meanwhile, Africans successfully go about their daily business manipulating complex linguistic toolboxes to meet their communicative needs.

In a newspaper story, a Tanzanian reporter outlined an exchange that had recently occurred during a sitting of Parliament (Tarimo, 2011). In the session, MP Mohamed Missanga blamed students' low scores on the previous year's national exams on low competence in English:

> It is not only students because even teachers are not very competent in written and spoken English. These and other factors contributed to last year's poor performance. (Tarimo, 2011)

MP Missinga urged the government to consider how it might remedy the situation, by improving English fluency, exam performance and quality of education in Tanzania. To this critique, the Educational and Vocational Training Deputy Minister, Philip Malugo, denied any connection between poor English and low scores on the exams, stating that 55% of students passed the English portion and nearly 60% passed the Swahili portion. Thus:

> On the basis of this comparison, it is unreasonable to conclude that the Form Four students failed because they didn't know English. (Tarimo, 2011)

In other words, students performed poorly all round, so how could English be to blame? Like the Deputy Minister, another MP, Freeman Mbowe, did not doubt the value of English as the medium of instruction in secondary school, but he did recognize possibilities for improving the quality of the teaching of English that students receive in school. He proposed that the government allow more qualified English teachers from neighboring Uganda and Kenya, where citizens are believed to have a higher level of competence in standard English, to come to Tanzania to teach in secondary schools (Tarimo, 2011).

This exchange, which received some traction in the local press, is just one instantiation of a decades-old concern about the medium of instruction in Tanzanian secondary school, and many threads in the report underscore ideological formulations about language. These include: (1) the unwavering allegiance to English as the medium of instruction, in spite of some evidence that might implicate it in poor student outcomes; (2) the understanding of English as best acquired through education; (3) the implicit assumption that it is clear which variety of English is at issue; (4) the apparent, though also largely implicit, disagreement over the role of Swahili in constructing an education; (5) a faith in the government's ability to effect change in language use; (6) the locating of better speakers of English outside of the country; (7) the very fact that the language medium of classroom instruction is a debatable issue and a reportable piece of news.[1] Many of these ideologies are likewise reflected in this chapter's epigraphic newspaper quotes, all of which express commonly held, if sometimes divergent, views about language, society and opportunity in Tanzania.

In this chapter, I discuss the sociolinguistic place of Swahili[2] and English in Tanzania, especially in terms of the language ideologies that structure linguistic difference in socially meaningful ways. Swahili, while traditionally a language of the coast, is today the national language and is spoken by most Tanzanians, as a second or third language if not as a first (Mazrui & Mazrui, 1995; Whiteley, 1969). Most urbanites go about much of their daily affairs in one of many registers of Swahili. It is also the official language of primary schools and Parliament and is used widely across other institutions and settings. Despite being an indigenous language associated with self-reliance as well as independence from colonial control, Swahili today carries far less prestige than English, the language of the former colonial power, Great Britain (Blommaert, 1999a; Mulokozi, 1991). English, though it is co-official with Swahili, is nonetheless considered the language of 'higher' functions and elite business; of particular importance to this chapter, it is also the medium of instruction in secondary school and beyond. At the same time, what English actually looks like, both inside and outside of school walls, is complex; it is often 'mixed' with Swahili and, indeed, not every 'English' is equally elite. Tanzania is also home to immense linguistic and ethnic diversity, with over 120 local ethnic languages documented (Gordon, 2005).[3] Yet these ethnolinguistic differences, through decades of policies, discourses and practices aimed at creating a unified Tanzanian nation-state, have been largely erased from urban, public contexts, including schools (Blommaert, 1999a; Wedin, 2005). I will elaborate upon the topic of language and ethnicity in Chapter 6, keeping my focus here on Swahili and English.

I begin by presenting some of the key issues in current formulations of language ideologies as they relate to my investigation, including a discussion of the notion of register. I then turn to an overview of critical points in East African sociolinguistic history, especially when discussion and debate over

Swahili and English language use and utility has occurred. In many cases, these moments have configured language as a powerful tool, at the same time that it has been seen as somehow too much, too little, or in some other way not quite right and in need of top-down remedies. Next, I move on to the particular case of language and education debates in Tanzania, in which I elaborate on many of the issues brought up in the parliamentary debate discussed above. Finally, I overview some of the documented urban register phenomena in Tanzania in terms of how these registers are understood as representative of identifiable social personae and hence subject to ideological formulations. Both of these last topics will lay a foundation for the discussions of contestants' language use and evaluation presented in Chapters 4 and 5.

Language Ideologies

Language ideologies and life consequences

At the heart of this chapter is a study of language ideologies. Irvine (1989: 255) understands language ideologies as 'the cultural system of ideas about social and linguistic relationships, together with their loading of moral and political interests'. In other words, there is a powerful link between linguistic forms and the ways in which people (organized in an array of formations such as communities, classes, villages, states, etc.) perceive those forms. Furthermore, as an analytic tool, language ideologies offer a means of understanding the regularized connections between linguistic and non-linguistic forms and, in so doing, they are extremely useful for shedding light on how language structure and use deeply matter for the political and social realities of speakers (Eisenlohr, 2006).

Case studies have effectively used the concept of language ideologies as a means of making sense of an assortment of sociolinguistic phenomena that directly affect people's lives. Several notable projects (e.g. Hill, 1998; Hoffman, 2006; Silverstein, 1985) have relied on language ideologies to lend coherence and depth of understanding to language shift and change in communities in a variety of places and periods. Other analyses (e.g. Briggs, 1996; Haviland, 2003; Hirsch, 1998) have highlighted the roles played by language ideologies in an array of institutional quarters of social life. Still other studies (e.g. Eisenlohr, 2006; Inoue, 2006) examine the historical and historicizing processes that serve to create relevant social identities and distinctions.

As these cases make clear, ideologies about language are regularly projected onto non-linguistic actions and thus they can, and often do, have important effects on individuals' lived worlds. People's understandings of language use frame concerns about life chances, opportunity and success, and they have often been used as 'justification for widely varying political arrangements' (Gal, 1998: 329). In this study, ideologies about language form and use, and, by extension, about those who use them, will be shown to shape institutional policy and practice, group formations and identity, and individual and gendered communicative strategies and life trajectories.

Multiplicity, contention and distortion

Scholars (Gal, 1998; Woolard & Schieffelin, 1994) have noted that rather than existing in a one-to-one relationship with a given speech community, ideologies are always multiple and varied, often as reflexes of the many meaningful social distinctions recognized by the community itself (Kroskrity, 2000). That language ideologies are multiple leads to another point: that there is often conflict around these ideologies (Blommaert, 1999b; Gal, 1998), and projects have documented subversive discourses and counter-ideologies in an array of scales and arrangements (e.g. Collins, 1998; Spitulnik, 1998). Nonetheless, Kroskrity (1998) argues that, in spite of competing views, there are always dominant ideologies, in terms of both being broadly shared and being linked with the power- and authority-bearing bodies. This observation recalls Urciuoli's (1998) distinction between the inner and outer spheres of interaction; while these two spheres are analytically distinct, the inner sphere is always colored by the outer sphere, but not vice versa. Members of the New York City Puerto Rican communities which she studied remarked that although hybrid Spanish–English varieties sound normal to their own ears, they at the same time recognize that these ways of speaking (and by extension their speakers) are negatively valued by members of the outer sphere and especially by representatives of centering institutions like schools. In Blommaert's (2010) sociolinguistics of mobility, overviewed in Chapter 1, we see a similar ability of people to orient, linguistically and otherwise, to multiple scales (the neighborhood, the school) at the same time that they are aware of the differential worth of the varieties within their repertoire and within a wider schema of value; Chapters 4, 5 and 7 will revisit this idea.

Many scholars (Eisenlohr, 2006; Kroskrity, 2000, Schieffelin et al., 1998) have pointed out that what is meant by 'ideology' in the sense that it is commonly used in linguistic anthropology stands in opposition to the way in which it has been used by other, especially Foucauldian, theorists, according to whom the term implies some kind of perspectival distortion. The former emphasize that, from the semiotic perspective, the notion of ideology is 'neutral' (Eisenlohr, 2006: 17), in that it implies no scientifically provable point of view against which divergent perspectives are measured. These and others have pointed to the 'multiplicity and contention' among language ideologies (Gal, 1998) as evidence that there is no single, ultimate vantage point that determines what is and is not distorted.

Yet while, indeed, the existence of dissimilar valorizations of language structure and use signals to the analyst the existence of ideological understandings, Agha (2007) argues that we should not avoid the inclusion of distortion in formulations of language ideology:

> Whenever competing models of a cultural phenomenon co-exist in a society, *each* of these models distorts the phenomenon from the point of view of *every* other model. Empirically, to claim that a cultural model is ideological is not to distinguish 'distortion'-laden from 'distortion'-free models (such as, say, scientific models) but to comment on the *mutually distorting character of competing positional models.* (Agha, 2007: 396, emphasis in original)

The analytic usefulness of considering distortion thus lies in the fact that speakers themselves understand differing valuation schemes as distortions from a norm. Agha states that:

> particular socially positioned models contrast with each other as alternative systems of normativity. *Each* is ideological from the perspective of *every* other in so far as it gets the (normative) facts incorrect. (Agha, 2007: 157)

The important point here is that speakers themselves view others' ideologies as distorted. Thus, the layered and polycentric nature of ideological valorizations coexists with the fact that speakers often normalize their own practices and valuation schemes at the expense of others.

Registers, ideologies and the standard

As discussed in Chapter 1, language monoliths have no empirical existence. As ideological constructs, they nonetheless are subject to linkages with conceptions of identity, personhood and value and, indeed, have even laid the ideological foundation for the construction of nation-states and for the justification for colonial and imperial projects (Anderson, 1983; Chimhundu, 1992; Errington, 2007; Gal & Irvine, 1995; Makoni & Pennycook, 2007; Woolard & Schieffelin, 1994). Yet, in actual communication, it is specific registers – even if sometimes referred to by speakers as named languages – that typically garner interlocutors' attention, shaping interaction and serving as justification for judgments about their speakers. People understand enregistered, that is, recognized, varieties (Agha, 2007) as indexical of certain qualities and personae, and hence registers are often subject to ideological formulations (Hill, 1998; Kroskrity, 1998).

Silverstein has described registers as 'alternate ways of "saying 'the same' thing"' (Silverstein, 2003a: 212), all the while emphasizing that, in fact, they are never the same. Since each register bears different indexical values, their meaning, of which indexicality is a part, can never be identical. What is more, registers are differentially distributed across a given community, and one's social capital is linked with (both stemming from and emanating out of) one's control over certain registers and their ideological backing (Agha, 2007; Martin, 1992). While a first order of indexicality is presupposed by the context of use, higher orders of indexicality ideologically mark the speaker of the register as a certain kind of person, with certain value-laden qualities (Silverstein, 2003a).

Furthermore, as 'open cultural systems' (Agha, 2007: 158), registers are particularly ideological in nature, in that, as bundled clusters of linguistic or other semiotic materials deemed to belong together, they may be taken up by other users. At this point, the symbolic value of the register gets reworked, and often devalued, by the original speakers. Standard register provides a good example of this phenomenon:

> Standard register in well-developed standard-language communities is, as we know, hegemonic in the sense that ideologically it constitutes the 'neutral' top-and-center of all variability that is thus around-and-below it. This hegemony of standard register differentially sweeps up people of different groups and categories into an anxiety before standard. Hence we can understand the Labovian 'hypercorrection' phenomenon.... (Silverstein, 2003a: 219)

The notion of hypercorrection thus is an ideological interpretation of situated register use; speakers who wish to index themselves as 'top-and-center' people, but who do not fully control the 'top-and-center' standard register, are seen *by standard register speakers* as having committed hyper-correction. Sometimes a register can rise 'above' the standard, as is the case for 'oinoglossia' or 'wine talk', which has 'higher-than-(mere)-Standard indexical value' (Silverstein, 2003a: 226).

While often the standard is ideologically constructed as neutral (Agha, 2007; Silverstein, 2003a), from the point of view of the analyst, the standard often has a very narrow space of use:

In a common ideological view, Standard English is just 'the language,' the baseline against which all other facts of register differentiation are measured. Yet from the standpoint of usage Standard English is just one register among many, highly appropriate to certain public/official settings, but employed by its speakers in alternation with other varieties … which are linked with distinct spheres of social life. (Agha, 2007: 146)

In this chapter and throughout this study, I will demonstrate that metapragmatic discourses about 'English' and 'Swahili' and their apparent virtues abound. Yet, rather than static monoliths, the referents of these terms vary and, indeed, signify particular varieties of language. At times, people talk explicitly about specific named registers but, even then, the substance of the register – its register shibboleths (Silverstein, 2003a) – may shift according to the users and evaluators; what is 'standard' or 'neutral' for one group is in some way marked for another. Ultimately, and as will be outlined in more detail in subsequent chapters, it is these *discourses about language* that shape the ways of speaking themselves, giving form to local understandings of meaningful variety and difference. And since these understandings are not just differential but also hierarchical, they help structure social inequality through the ways in which they construct distinction and value.

Language, Ideologies and the Construction of the Tanzanian Nation-State

It has often been said that Tanzania presents a model of language planning in a highly multilingual society (e.g. Abdulaziz, 1971; Harries, 1968, 1969; Mazrui & Mazrui, 1995; O'Barr, 1976; Whiteley, 1968, 1969). Indeed, in part through language policy and planning, Swahili has become so widely distributed in Tanzania that, in contrast to many African nations, the country operates publicly, to a great degree, in this one indigenous language. This state of affairs has been deemed a triumph because it means that, in official realms, Tanzania has neither the legacy of relying predominantly on a colonial language, nor the logistical and political challenges of operating in multiple indigenous languages.[4] Tanzania's linguistic unity is credited as being responsible for the relative peace and stability enjoyed by the country, especially in comparison with other postcolonial African nations. While this conclusion is certainly based on problematic assumptions about the 'normal', monolingual linguistic profile of a nation (Blommaert, 1996, 1999a), it remains a fact that Swahili – ideologically unified but analytically an overlapping cluster of registers and varieties – is by far the most commonly used language in Tanzania and to this day remains a symbol of the nation's peace and unity. While Swahili had been well established on the East African coast for centuries (Mazrui & Mazrui, 1995; Nurse & Spear, 1985; Whiteley, 1969), it was not until the end of the 18th century that it began to be used inland to any significant degree. Beginning around that time, Swahili-speaking, Arab-led trading caravans began to enter the interior, due to the ever-increasing demand for ivory and slaves (Whiteley, 1969).[5] In addition to carrying out more frequent and extended expeditions, many traders began to set up permanent homes and small slave-trading centers in the interior, leading to ethnically and linguistically mixed communities, and to an even greater need for a lingua franca than required by periodic trading alone (Massamba, 1989).

By the time European missionary activity began in the early 19th century, Swahili was already established as lingua franca over extensive Arab trade routes throughout much of what is today Tanzania (Whiteley, 1969). The first missions were located primarily along these existing trade routes,[6] and we know from missionaries' memoirs that local interpreters of Swahili were easy to come by (Whiteley, 1969). Throughout the missionary period, and especially during its peak between 1860 and 1880, Swahili publications – first language studies, then readers and religious texts – abounded (Whiteley, 1969). Despite the growing study and use of Swahili, however, many missions were reluctant to employ that language with Africans, because they believed their flock would receive the evangelical message better and more truly via their own local ethnic languages rather than Swahili (Wright, 1965).[7]

The colonial period continued, for the most part, to bolster Swahili's dominant position. Soon after establishing control of what is now mainland Tanzania in the 1880s,[8] the German colonial administration realized the need for making clear policies with regard to language within government institutions, and especially in schools, where Africans would be groomed to be low-level officials (Wright, 1965). The use of German was quickly ruled out, largely because the administration was hesitant to relinquish the symbolic control nested in that language (Wright, 1965). Likewise, the official use of local ethnic languages was not an option because of the perceived administrative nightmare of communicating, publishing and teaching in multiple languages (Whiteley, 1969). And while Swahili had been used in many capacities since the inception of the colony, the administration was suspicious about its connections to Islam, especially in the wake of the Maji Maji uprising against colonial rule in 1905 (Wright, 1965).

Later that year, the German linguist Carl Meinhof was enlisted to solve the language problem by de-Islamisizing the language, and his proposal included writing it in Roman script and stripping it of many Arabic-origin lexemes (Mazrui & Mazrui, 1995). All told, Meinhof's endeavors for lexical purification failed, but his recommendation to begin writing the language in Roman script were well received and enabled the German colonial regime to feel more comfortable in embracing Swahili as its administrative language. Following this change, the colony's efforts to use Swahili redoubled (Mazrui & Mazrui, 1995).

When the British assumed control of Tanganyika after World War I, they upheld to a great extent the linguistic status quo established by the German administration, by maintaining Swahili in primary schools, lower segments of the administration and in the military (Wright, 1965). But the British differed ideologically from the Germans in at least two ways: first, they had greater tolerance for minority languages, a position which in turn may have slowed the spread of Swahili throughout the country (Mazrui & Mazrui, 1995); and second, the colonial government believed in the importance of English in the upper levels of education and administration (Mazrui & Mazrui, 1995). This positional superiority of English led to a shift in Africans' associations with both English and Swahili:

> Whereas in German times the acquisition of Swahili represented a first stage towards participating in Government through membership of the junior Civil Service, no further stage in this participation [during the British period] could be achieved through the language. The next stage involved the acquisition of English, and for this reason Swahili was seen increasingly by Tanganyikans as a 'second-class' language. (Whiteley, 1969: 61)

At the same time, however, the British regime was committed to the generalized use of Swahili in non-elite capacities, seeing the need for 'developing' a standard language that would be lexically and grammatically equipped to handle its many administrative functions. In 1930, the colony formed the Inter-Territorial Language Committee with the primary goal of standardizing Swahili and promoting its continued use in primary education and the civil service throughout British East Africa (Whiteley, 1969).[9] While the Committee – lacking a single African member until 1946 – was successful both in establishing a standard, based on the Unguja (Zanzibari) dialect, and in proliferating this standard through publications (Whiteley, 1969), 'it did not elevate the status of Kiswahili as a language capable of rendering high status knowledge' (Roy-Campbell, 2001: 57).[10] English remained the elite language and the vehicle for success, while Swahili stood as the language of the under-educated masses. As I will discuss below, the emphasis placed on language 'development', as well as the essentializing equations of 'English as a language of X' and 'Swahili as a language of Y', whereby English is constructed as superior to Swahili, still hold a central place in discourses about language use and language policy in Tanzania today.

Beginning in the mid-1940s, Tanganyikans involved in the efforts for independence employed Swahili, vehicularly and symbolically, as the language of the emergent nation (Blommaert, 1999a). Despite its absence from elite realms of communication, Swahili was nonetheless considered a 'non-tribal, egalitarian and democratic medium', one which could both appropriately convey the message of freedom and serve as a political symbol for that freedom (Blommaert, 1999a: 88). The fact that it was already widely used as a vernacular in Dar es Salaam, the headquarters of the independence movement, solidified the choice of Swahili in such efforts (Whiteley, 1969). Following independence from Great Britain in 1961, the government, led by President Julius Nyerere and the TANU (Tanganyika African National Union) party,[11] enacted several symbolic and policy moves in the promotion of Swahili. Notable was the decision to make Swahili the national language and the language of Parliament, followed by Nyerere's own historic use of the language in his Republic Day speech to that body in 1962 (Blommaert, 1999a).

Blommaert (1999a) describes a subsequent shift in the way Swahili was conceptualized in the wake of the union between Tanganyika and the islands of Zanzibar and Pemba in 1964. These islands, both exclusively Islamic and Swahili-speaking, as well as committed to socialism, brought to the newly formed country of Tanzania a radicalism previously absent. In this context, English came to represent Swahili's opposite, that is, 'a symbol of neocolonialism, oppression, and imperialism' (Blommaert, 1999a: 91). This dichotomous relationship between English and Swahili was further enforced by the Arusha Declaration of 1967, in which President Nyerere clearly put forth the socialist direction the country was to take, concep-tualized under the phrase *Ujamaa na Kujitegemea* ('African socialism and self-reliance') (Blommaert, 1999a: 91). The Declaration was also successful in continuing the spread of Swahili through, among other things, *Ujamaa* villages, or planned cooperative farming communities based on socialist ideals. By 1973, two million people, coming from diverse ethnic and lin-guistic backgrounds, lived in such villages, in which Swahili was the lingua franca (Abdulaziz-Mkilifi, 1973).

Despite the fervor for Swahilization seen in the early years of *Ujamaa*, President Nyerere, in 1974, announced that Tanzanians were best served by Swahili–English bilingualism as a matter of practicality (Blommaert, 1999a). From that time, and especially in the wake of the liberalization of the Tanzanian economy in the early 1990s, the connections between Swahili and socialism, on the one hand, and English and oppression, on the other, gradually weakened, leading to a complete dissolution of that binary ideological opposition between the two languages (Blommaert, 1999a). Today, while Swahili certainly dominates the linguistic landscape in Tanzania in terms of public communication, and one would have to look long and hard to find a Tanzanian incapable of speaking it, English 'is now more than ever a prestige language' (Blommaert, 1999a: 95). English remains the language of higher education and of other elite functions, and the desire to know it, as an indicator of success and as a key to a better life, is tremendous and near universal.

English as the Medium of Instruction: The Ongoing Debate

During the transition to independence and the *Ujamaa* years of the late 1960s and 1970s, education was central to the discourses of independence and *maendeleo* ('progress'). *Elimu ya Kujitegemea* ('Education for Self-Reliance') was a socialist program, put forth in 1967 on the heels of the Tanzanian socialist manifesto, the Arusha Declaration (see above), which emphasized literacy and primary schooling for all. Primary school in this new vision was to provide a self-contained education for all Tanzanians, the majority of whom would live their lives as farmers, a lauded vocation within the *Ujamaa* framework. The curriculum of primary school was to focus on basic reading, mathematics and agrarian, as well as political, knowledge (Blommaert, 1999a).

Critically, primary school was the vehicle for promoting the acquisition of Swahili for all, and during this era the Tanzanian government made the language the medium of instruction in primary school. While English remained the medium of instruction in secondary school, the government supported its eventual replacement with Swahili there (Mulokozi, 1991). Because English was considered at that time to be too intimately connected to colonialism and capitalism, its use in the school system, as well as elsewhere in the administration, was thought to be at odds with the socialist doctrine outlined in the Arusha Declaration (Blommaert, 1999a). At the same time, the over 100 other languages spoken by Tanzania's citizens were virtually ignored (Blommaert, 1999a), a remarkable feat made possible by the semiotic process of 'erasure' (Irvine & Gal, 2000), in which differences which interfere with a unified ideology are systematically overlooked.

But before Swahili could be used in secondary school, it was thought to need 'development' in terms of technical vocabulary as well as materials. Scores of linguists and other experts were engaged to make this happen (Mulokozi, 1991). Nonetheless, and for largely political and ideological rather than practical reasons (Blommaert, 1999a; Mulokozi, 1991), the changeover never occurred, and still today, apart from the use of Swahili in civics class, English remains the medium of instruction in secondary school and beyond.

The place of English as the medium of secondary school instruction has been the subject of a debate that surfaces regularly in multiple contexts: in public fora such as newspaper letters to the editor and editorials (Qorro, 2006); in governmental contexts such as parliamentary debates, as described at the beginning of this chapter; and in local as well as international scholars' writings about language, education and inequality (Qorro, 2006; see also e.g. Brock-Utne, 2007a, 2007b). Neke characterizes the pro-English side of the debate in terms of a series of ideological equations. For English-medium supporters, English equals, among other things, education and 'the highway to success' (Neke, 2003: 123, 132). In contrast, Swahili equals 'backwardness' as well as 'failures and ignorance' (Neke, 2003: 137, 139). It is a position that is often upheld by policy-makers as well as the general public (Neke, 2003), and these equations surface in very public ways, for example on the Tanzania national website's education page:

The main feature of Tanzania's education system is the bilingual policy, which requires children to learn both Kiswahili and English. English is essential, as it is the language which links Tanzania and the rest of the world through technology, commerce and also administration. The learning of the Kiswahili [sic] enables Tanzania's students to keep in touch with their cultural values and heritage. (www.tanzania.go.tz/educationf.html)

While presenting the language policy as 'bilingual' and hence balanced and equal, the passage echoes the language-ideological equations above. Here, 'English is essential' and is intimately tied with all forms of modern knowledge, as well as with global interconnectivity (i.e. English equals education, English equals a highway). In contrast, Swahili's main importance is to connect students with tradition and the past (i.e. Swahili equals backwardness).

Many proponents of the status quo of English-medium education argue that still, after decades of 'development', Swahili is not up to the task of being used in elite contexts. According to one government official quoted by Roy-Campbell, 'we have not tackled the question of technical language. You encounter a lot of non-technical words, street words, in some Kiswahili texts. This detracts from the seriousness of the subject' (Roy-Campbell, 2001: 117). This statement constructs Swahili as still in need of 'development', not ready for promotion to more elite settings. Such an understanding of the language helps fuel the ideological construction of Swahili as less valuable than English, and hence inappropriate for use in post-primary educational settings. In this view, while Swahili's importance for certain key instrumental and symbolic functions is maintained, it is below English in overall value.

The other side of the debate, often voiced by scholars, advocating Swahili at all levels of schooling, typically concerns the quality of education that students receive (Blommaert, 1999a; Neke, 2003). From this point of view, the current policy is 'a pedagogical absurdity' (Mulokozi, 1991: 9). After seven (primary) years of Swahili-medium instruction, with English taught only as a class, secondary school students are abruptly forced to learn in a language that neither they nor, in many cases, their teachers understand well (Mtesigwa, 2001; Roy-Campbell & Qorro, 1997; Vavrus, 2003; Yahya-Othman, 1990). This is a phenomenon that has been observed in other sub-Saharan educational contexts (e.g. Brock-Utne, 2000, 2002; Serpell, 1993) and will be discussed in some depth in Chapter 5. Martha Qorro (quoted in Neke, 2003: 210–211), a scholar and outspoken advocate for the complete Swahilization of the educational system, compares the Tanzanian situation to that of Europe two centuries ago, when it was finally recognized that 'using Latin as the medium of instruction in education made the majority of its citizens fail to get an education'. The current language policy in Tanzania, it is argued, curtails overall learning potential and holds back the Tanzanian citizenry from a robust and empowering education (Brock-Utne, 2007a, 2007b; Qorro, 2006; Vuzo, 2005).[12] Furthermore, it does not result in learning English and it even curtails the development of students' advanced Swahili skills (Qorro, 2006). In the news story at the beginning of this chapter, the fact that students scored almost equally poorly in both languages on national exams is due, from this perspective, to the fact that while students take portions of the exam *in Swahili*, they were exposed to the subject matter *in English*, and, hence, their acquisition of the material is inadequate.

As Neke (2003) and Roy-Campbell (2001) point out, while many average Tanzanians (including students) agree with the pro-English side of the debate, in the following excerpt from a letter to the editor in the *Guardian*, a prominent English-language newspaper in Tanzania, a secondary student voices an argument against English-medium instruction and in favor of Swahili-medium schools:

... I am a form five student and I feel it's a very row [sic] deal we get from the government by being taught in English, a language we don't comprehend comprehensively.

Majority of students – and I mean throughout the whole country don't understand anything they are taught. Only claming [sic] saves a few who can manage if that is education at all. A few of us very few indeed who are in public schools and knows or rather understands English it's through our own efforts. Even some of our teachers don't understand the language.

What the authorities concerned are not realizing is that they are wasting whole generation in education that will not give them much....
                          Dissatisfied student, Moshi (*Guardian*, 23 July 2003)

In addition to summarizing in a more personal voice many of the arguments that have been offered in favor of all-Swahili education, the student also unintentionally gives weight to the position by the occasional display of the limits of his or her own knowledge of standard English (see Chapters 4 and 5).

Interestingly, neither side of the debate in its current form typically calls directly on issues of nationalism in their arguments, despite the firm ties of the Swahili language with the Tanzanian nation-state. Today, most Tanzanians know Swahili (even if not the standard), regardless of their educational background, and its place as the national language – a medium of communication shared by all Tanzanians regardless of background – is now largely taken for granted. However, the link between medium of instruction and nationalism has surfaced in recent years with regard to the proliferation of private education, where Swahili is sometimes not the medium of instruction even in primary schools. The people who attend these schools, whether elite black Tanzanians, expatriates or local South Asians, are thought to live in a different Tanzania altogether, removed from the struggles and values of average citizens (see Chapter 6). In this privileged realm, Swahili may not be desired or necessary, even for face-to-face daily interactions. In a graduation speech at a private primary school in northern Tanzania, a government official lambasted such institutions for 'eroding the Tanzanian culture', as described in a local newspaper:

The Monduli District Commissioner [DC] Mr. John Kasunga was the chief guest in the ceremony.... Mr. Kasunga underscored the importance of Swahili as both the country's main medium of communication and national symbol adding that it should not be downplayed.

He expressed concern that some privately-owned English Medium Primary Schools were eroding the Tanzanian culture from children's minds by feeding them exotic traditions especially foreign language at the expense of Swahili.

As the result, according to the DC, there are many pupils and students who either cannot speak in Kiswahili or they converse poorly in the National language despite being born and brought up in Tanzanian [sic].

(Minja, 2011)

For this civil servant, Swahili-medium instruction at the primary-school level is necessary to ensure that all Tanzanians speak Swahili. His argument is distinct from those of the independence era because, rather than arguing in favor of Swahili as the national language, he takes its status as such for granted. However, his comments echo *Elimu ya Kujitegemea* in an understanding of a Swahili-language primary education and the ability to speak Swahili as being fundamental to Tanzanian culture and identity. His comments, while couched in nationalist rhetoric, stem from a recognition of social inequalities in Tanzania, whereby only a very small slice of the population has access to wealth, mobility and opportunity. It is this tiny portion of the country that has the greatest access to elite English – through private institutions such as the one at which the commissioner was speaking.

Both sides of the debate agree that Swahili is a national symbol and important for day-to-day communication, and both sides also agree that English is a valuable tool in today's globalized world. Instead, the issue for most is a fundamentally different understanding of the role of language in education. For the pro-English side, English itself is the goal of education, the thing that, more than anything else, marks one as educated and secures one a job, a future and membership in elite circles. Knowing English has to do with accessing local and translocal networks of power and privilege in pursuit of a better life. For the pro-Swahili side, an education has to do with acquisition of knowledge and cognitive skills, which is best secured through a language in which one is already fluent – Swahili. In the latter point of view, one may and should still learn English as a subject in school, but it should not be the medium of instruction for subjects like mathematics, biology and social studies (Qorro, 2006).

In this book, and mirroring some of the arguments made by many of the scholars above, I argue that by locating higher knowledge in a virtually unknowable code, the use of English as the medium of instruction in secondary schools perpetuates a fundamentally unequal relationship between English and Swahili, and hence between the people capable of speaking them (see Chapters 4 and 5). Rather than, as pro-English-medium voices argue, increasing Tanzanians' opportunities for success and global connectivity, the policy further peripheralizes them and exacerbates inequalities on multiple scales. In their own cities and country, it is the miniscule elite, those who may have had the opportunity to attend English-only schools from an early age, who have the greatest chance of securing one of the very limited white-collar jobs, for which English is deemed a requirement. From a regional, East African point of view, many Tanzanians recognize that often good jobs in Tanzania are lost to people from neighboring countries, where knowledge of English is more widespread. One professional voiced the concern as follows: 'Go to the foreign banks. Go to Citibank, to Stanbic and all these places. Plenty of Ugandans. Plenty of Kenyans. Where are the Tanzanians?' (Neke, 2003: 132). The position of the MP quoted at the beginning of the chapter, who argued in favor of allowing Kenyans and Ugandans to take over as secondary school teachers, points to the real threat to jobs and access to opportunity that this favoring of English creates. Finally, from a global perspective, withholding an empowering education in a familiar language from Tanzanians who are eager to learn and succeed certainly has repercussions for taking part in a competitive international ideascape.

In later chapters, I will explore the idea that while, indeed, for most Tanzanians, English, regardless of medium of instruction, is an invaluable part of an education, what is unclear is *which* English is at issue. Chapters 4 and 5 discuss in detail the variable nature of what constitutes educated English, and how these varieties are mobilized, mimicked and sometimes mocked in beauty pageants. Below, I discuss the varieties of Swahili and English that have been analyzed by scholars as indexical of local personae.

Language and Urban Tanzanian Identities

The language hybridity and multivocality overviewed in Chapter 1 as characteristic of the global economy are also part and parcel of the linguistic repertoires of many urban Tanzanians today. As an elite, standard language formally introduced in East Africa through colonialism, English today maintains that position in part through its role as the medium of instruction in post-primary education. Yet schooling is not the only way in which Tanzanians have access to English language material. Even if standard English is the provenance of a higher education, other kinds of English circulate broadly in urban East Africa, through music, television and the internet, and such language material has come to be integrated into a variety of codes accessible to a wide segment of the population. Furthermore, most Tanzanians attend primary school, where they do acquire some English, even if not fluently or in standard form. Hence Tanzanians from many backgrounds use English and Swahili in ways that defy ready categorization and which serve to index their social status, group identities and, at times, cosmopolitan positionalities.

Traditionally, sociolinguistic research has understood such hybrid varieties in terms of codeswitching – the purposeful mixing of two or more distinct codes. Some scholars have described the pragmatic effects of Swahili–English codeswitching, such as topic change (Beardsley & Eastman, 1971), marking of topic or focus (Blommaert, 1999a) or emphasis and expression of emotion (Kishe, 1995). Others have pointed to the social functions made possible by Swahili–English codeswitching, including asserting authority, establishing solidarity and creating distance vis-à-vis one's interlocutors (Kishe, 1995: 260–261). These and other functions have very commonly been noted cross-linguistically as resulting from speakers' juxtaposition of language varieties.

While indeed in Tanzania, as elsewhere, the combining of material perceived as being from different languages serves as a tool for speakers to produce pragmatic and other effects, codeswitching as an analytic framework is typically insufficient from a social scientific perspective. Meeuwis and Blommaert (1998) offer several criticisms of traditional approaches to code-switching, as prominently articulated by Myers-Scotton (1993a, 1993b). First, the authors argue against the faulty assumption that codeswitchers are *necessarily* bilingual in two 'languages', such that they could participate in monolingual conversations in either of the 'languages' (see e.g. Rampton, 1995). Second, they take issue with the premise in codeswitching frameworks that such speech is abnormal, 'marked' and necessarily in need of explanation (see e.g. McLaughlin, 2009; Swigart, 1994). In addition, the 'monolectal' view of codeswitching proposed by Meeuwis and Blommaert (1998) is connected to the notion of register, taking into account the local categories according to which users of these varieties conceive of their own, hybrid ways of speaking (see e.g. Mendoza-Denton, 2008). It becomes clear that static, stalwart indexicalities associated with separate languages do not begin to make sense of many people's normal language use. Instead, the creative and sometimes unexpected things people do with the diversity of linguistic materials around them are better captured by the notion of 'languaging' (Jørgensen, 2008; Jørgensen et al., 2011), a concept which avoids a rigid understanding of language boundaries and indexicalities.

Furthermore, such mixed varieties are in urban Tanzania the norm. These varieties, rather than being created by combining idealized English and Swahili, are often distinct hybrid varieties unto themselves, which, while sometimes employed in a way that capitalizes on the contrast between the two languages, also serve as recognized codes to create and index relevant group distinctions. And while schooling is a primary source for the acquisition of English language material, English has more than one face, and English language materials circulate in a multitude of realms outside the classroom.

In *English as a Local Language*, Higgins (2009), through a series of case studies, discusses the ways in which Tanzanians have localized English language materials into a wide variety of hybrid linguistic practices, each indexical and, in part, constitutive, of particular urban identities. In one case study, Higgins presents an analysis of journalists' newsroom speech. Through a mix of standard English and standard Swahili linguistic materials, as well as monolingual use of each of these varieties, journalists adeptly employ these codes for interactional as well as symbolic functions. On the interactional level, they use these tools to create humor, manage relationships with colleagues and structure discourse. At the same time, their speech constructs in-group relations as well as indexes themselves as members of the elite, having received the education to hold command of both schooled varieties. This variety recalls Blommaert's (1992, 1999a) 'campus Swahili', which is involves standard Swahili smattered with idiosyncratic standard English lexical insertions, most of which have undergone very little semantic shift. Campus Swahili is spoken by the Tanzanian educated elite – *wasomi* – and especially by University of Dar es Salaam faculty, as an informal, in-group code. In formal or outer-sphere communications, *wasomi* use other variants – a more pure Swahili, English or a local ethnic language. Bwenge (2002) likewise describes an elite Swahili–English mixed code used by Tanzanian parliamentarians that serves similar functions.

Turning to a distinctly different context, Higgins (2009) explores the world of East African hip-hop, also characterized by hybrid linguistic forms (see also Perullo & Fenn, 2003). This time, however, the linguistic matter is largely non-standard, and not just Swahili and English, but local languages as well. For these performers, plugged into the international, and especially American, world of hip-hop, use of phrases such as 'get busy' and 'gwan' critically involve re-entextualization (Silverstein & Urban, 1996), according to which a particular bit of language, once imported into a new context, takes on a different meaning. Yet the original meaning does not necessarily disappear completely, and so re-entextualization gives rise to multivocality, offering great opportunity for *double entendre*, humor and even covert messaging – see Stambach's (2000a) discussion of Remy Ongala's 'things with socks'. As an example of multiple levels of re-entextualization, multivocality and verbal humor, Higgins (2009) describes the case of the Kenyan group Gidi Gidi Maji Maji's song 'Unbwogable', a title derived from the

English morphemes *un* and *able* sandwiching the Dholuo word *bwogo* ('to be shaken'). 'Unbwogable', thus meaning un-scare-able, was a song of self-aggrandizement, fitting neatly into both African-American hip-hop as well as into Luo discourses of masculinity. When adopted later in the political campaign of a presidential candidate, Mwai Kibaki, himself a Luo, the song became an anthem for a strong candidate as well as a new Kenya, one in which the fluid mixing of peoples, language and beliefs was to be a corner-stone (see Nyairo & Ogude, 2005).

This engagement by non-elite youth with non-standard and pop cultural elements of English recalls what Blommaert has described as *Kihuni*, a variety spoken by marginalized Dar es Salaam youth (*wahuni* – 'bandits'), consist-ing of 'baffling instances of linguistic mixing, borrowing and relexification in Swahili, English and other languages, and sound play' (Blommaert, 2005: 406). The English borrowings include *pusha* ('drug dealer', from 'pusher'), *dewaka* ('man-of-all-trades', from 'day worker') and *kukrash* ('to disagree', from 'crash' plus the Swahili infinitive marker *ku-*) (Blommaert, 2005: 407). Rather than being connected with education, much of the English use in *Kihuni* comes from its speakers' familiarity, through music, television and inexpensive entertainment newspapers, with African-American hip-hop culture.

In the realm of advertising, Higgins (2009) examines multivocality in billboard and other street-level advertising. In some cases, the language used is similar to the language employed by the newspaper journalists she describes; while sometimes 'mixed', it requires monolingual competence in standard English and/or Swahili. In other cases, signage employs 'localized English', characterized by the use of monolingual English material in non-standard ways. It is a genre similar to one which Blommaert (1999a, 2005; see Chapter 1) has called 'Public English'; while full of 'errors', it is successful in serving as an index of a certain level of education, class and global belonging. In contrast to these indexicalities, Higgins (2009) presents examples of advertisements that employ deeply hybrid, youthful registers characterized by street Swahili and English slang, functioning to draw in a particular segment of the population with humor by reflecting how they actually communicate. In particular, cell phone advertisements creatively employ playful language with slogans such as 'Chombeza time' ('chat time'), with street Swahili *chombeza* meaning 'chat' but also to 'sweet-talk' with someone of the opposite sex. On the interactional level, Higgins shows that the double voicing of some of these hybrid forms may lose that effect over time as they become fully indigenized; on the societal level, the multi-vocality shown here illustrates the widening value of such street forms, through a recognition of the spending power of their speakers.

Finally, in contrast with these highly local varieties, Blommaert (2013) describes Tanzanians' language use on Facebook, which often involves the 'supervernacularized' English register characteristic of electronic exchanges across the globe. 'Heterographic' conventions are readily employed by plugged-in urban Tanzanians, resulting in posts such as 'mornin guyz, ... on ma way 2 college!' (p. 22). Yet even this supervernacularized English is frequently combined with Swahili to form an even more 'dislodged and blended' register (p. 22), and sometimes users incorporate the orthographic conventions of the supervernacular while using monolingual Swahili, as Blommaert describes:

> Thus, '2' can stand for the Swahili syllable 'tu' in, for instance 'wa2' ('watu', 'people'), or to replace the first person plural marker 'tu' as in '2ngoje' ('tungoje', 'let's wait'). The symbol 'w' stands for 'we' as in 'ww' ('wewe', 'you'), and 'c' can replace 'si' in e.g. 'cc' ('sisi', 'we') and 'cendi' ('siendi', 'I'm not going'). (Blommaert, 2013: 23)

Here, the languaging done by Tanzanian Facebook users reflects a familiarity with globally recognized conventions of the digital supervernacular as well as with the conventions of written Swahili. The resulting register is at once cosmopolitan and highly local, emergent yet central in forging a community of online Tanzanians at home and abroad.

In all of these cases, the presence of English material does indexical and identity-building work, but the origins and value of each kind of English are distinct. In the case of the varieties spoken by journalists and professors, the 'standardness' they exhibit is acquired through higher education, and even though English is not used in a pure form, it nonetheless marks the speakers as a particular kind of elite. In the case of the youth varieties, the English is idiomatic, derived mostly from American popular culture, indexing another side of English and its place in global entertainment and youth culture. In advertising, English language material can be manipulated to appeal to various segments of the population by achieving a range of indexical effects. In electronic communication, the international conventions of the supervernacular have become so commonplace and diffuse in urban Tanzania that little knowledge of spoken English is actually needed to employ them, though the more English is included, the more sophisticated the languaging can become, as in the description directly above.

In sum, what is clear is that 'English' in Tanzania is not a singular entity, either in terms of its form or in terms of the ways in which it can signal and construct local urban subjectivities.

Conclusion

Higgins (2009) understands the hybrid varieties she describes as examples of postcolonial performativity (Pennycook, 2001), according to which colonial discourses related to English (and other colonial languages), as well as the language itself, have been reworked and revalued. Indeed, as 'creative responses to the domination of English' (Lee & Norton, 2009: 286), such varieties have emerged worldwide and reflect an ownership of, as well as sometimes an irreverence or even ambivalence towards, English. Critically, Lee and Norton (2009), following Canagarajah's (1999) work on English in Sri Lankan classrooms, emphasize the politics of location in the global order – centers and peripheries – in constructing practices and ideologies involving English. Here, Tanzania's location on the global periphery as well as its history as an English colony help to structure the varieties of available English, the indexicalities with which such varieties are loaded, and the multivocality embedded in them.

In this study, I also emphasize that social and spatial hierarchies *within* Tanzania inform the ways in which English is accessed, (re)claimed and remade. The dynamics of global centers and peripheries certainly play a part here, but as a reflex of a more generalizable dynamic of scales, orders of indexicality and polycentricity (Blommaert, 2010; overviewed in Chapter 1). Even as ideologies about English and Swahili are situated within historical and globalized frameworks, contemporary local hierarchies strongly influence the ways in which linguistic varieties are acquired, employed and evaluated in Tanzania. Furthermore, the state, in its capacity to shape policy, discourses and access to resources, is an important player in structuring language ideologies as well as actual on-the-ground repertoires of Tanzanians today.

Rather than reproducing the 'dearth' and 'glut' dichotomy discussed at the beginning of the chapter, I have intended to present a picture of language use in urban Tanzania as characterized by complexities of form, function and ideological formulations, all with the potential to affect lives. It is a linguistic and ideological landscape shaped as much by historical and global dynamics as by current state-level control over resources and policies, local socioeconomic realities and individual circumstances and preferences. It is one in which speakers creatively engage with linguistic materials at the same time that they seek, especially through education, particular varieties as commodities capable of improving their lives. As is often the case, dominant ideologies seem to privilege some people – some language users – over others, by configuring some varieties and their speakers as more worthy than others, and by informing policies that continue to structure such inequality. In following chapters, especially 4 and 5, I examine pageants themselves to discuss the ways in which local hierarchies of value influence pageant outcomes, themselves indicative of contestants' life trajectories outside of pageants.

Notes

(1) Other ideological constructions regarding education are embedded here as well, such as the belief in testing as a measurement of student learning, but these will not be the focus in this work.

(2) Some scholarship uses the term Kiswahili rather than Swahili. This usage stems from the fact that in the Swahili language, ki- is the prefix for the noun class which includes languages and, thus, Kiswahili means 'the Swahili language' and likewise Kiarabu means 'the Arabic language', Kiingereza' means 'the English language', and so on. In this work, I employ the less marked term Swahili.

(3) Following the norm among many Tanzanian language scholars (e.g. Msanjila, 1999), the term 'local ethnic language' (LEL) will be used in this work to refer to any indigenous language in Tanzania other than Swahili, which, while indeed indigenous to East Africa, has been self-consciously constructed in Tanzania as non-ethnic. Alternatives to local ethnic language have also been suggested, including Mekacha's (1993) 'ethnic community language' (ECL). In official Tanzanian discourse in Swahili, these languages are called *lugha za jamii* ('community languages') or, more recently, *lugha za asili* ('languages of origin').

(4) South Africa is rare among African nations in designating within its constitution 11 official languages. Yet even this much-lauded effort to support linguistic equality and rights is fraught with ideological, administrative and political problems (Makoni, 2003; Mesthrie, 2006; Williams & Bekker, 2008).

(5) Fabian (1986) prefers a 'processual approach' to the question of what has been called Swahili 'diffusion up-country' by others (Whiteley, 1969: 42). Fabian's focus is on 'concentrating less on when, where, and by what means Swahili "arrives" in Katanga [in present-day Democratic Republic of the Congo], than on why and in what form it "emerges" in this area' (Fabian, 1986: 9). His argument for this approach is grounded in the idea that the notion of 'diffusion' is based on a simple spatial metaphor which, analytically speaking, strips the processes of linguistic change of critical historical and political aspects.

(6) Lawuo (1984) emphasizes, however, that motivations and actions of local populations cannot be ignored in terms of the settlement patterns of missionaries. In particular, he gives evidence of the adeptness of Chagga chiefs in luring missionaries to their villages in order to learn more about and gain some control over the emerging coffee trade.

(7) This view fell under what was called at that time the 'Livingstonian principle', by which 'in the final analysis each African community could be consolidated into its Christianity by the efforts of its own indigenous members and by using the conceptual tools of its own indigenous cultures' (Mazrui & Mazrui, 1995: 54). Indigenous languages were considered foremost among these 'conceptual tools'.

(8) During the German colonial period (1885–1919), the area that is now mainland Tanzania, along with Rwanda and Burundi, was called 'German East Africa' (*Deutsch Ostafrika*). After World War I, the British gave the area of mainland Tanzania

the official name 'Tanganyika Territory'. In 1961, the newly independent nation adopted the same name (minus 'Territory'). It was only in 1964, when the Indian Ocean island of Zanzibar and mainland Tanganyika joined together, that the name 'Tanzania' (or, more properly, the United Republic of Tanzania) came into being. The name stems from a combination of **Tan**ganyika and **Zan**zibar (Ofcansky & Yeager, 1997).

(9) The motivation for forming a committee to promote Swahili also came in part from a 1922 visit to East Africa by the Phelps Stokes Commission – an American foundation committed to an investigation into the state of education in Africa (Ofcansky & Yeager, 1997) – which perceived that English was being forced on Africans. The commission recommended that, instead, local languages, especially Swahili, should be used in educational and administrative capacities throughout the Tanganyikan territory (Roy-Campbell, 2001).

(10) In 1964 the committee was nationalized as the Institute of Kiswahili Research, and 10 years later it became a research body of the University of Dar es Salaam, where it remains today (Roy-Campbell, 2001).

(11) Ironically, this pro-Swahili independence party chose an English name for itself. In contrast, the party's successor, CCM (Chama cha Mapinduzi, 'Party of the Revolution'), went with a Swahili name.

(12) Some scholars of education (e.g. Stambach, 1994; Vavrus, 2003) have also discussed the extremely didactic pedagogy that is standard practice in Tanzanian classrooms. For another perspective on the matter of learning and teaching in Africa, see Moore (2006). The topics of education and pedagogy will be discussed further in Chapter 5.

3 'From the Geneva of Africa': Beauty Pageants, National Culture and Tanzanian Femininity

A nation who refuses to learn from foreign culture is nothing but a nation of idiots and lunatics ... [but] to learn from other countries does not mean we should abandon our own.
Julius Nyerere, President's 1962 Inaugural Address (Nyerere, 1967b: 186–187)

Mara nyingi watu wanafikiri kwamba mchezo kama huu ni mchezo wa kihuni, sio mchezo wa kihuni ni mchezo mzuri ... nina hakika kwamba vijana tunaowapeleka si wahuni
[Often people think that a competition like this is a competition of sleazy girls; it's not a competition of sleazy girls, it's a good competition ... I'm sure that these young people are not sleazy.]
Special guest, regional beauty pageant

Pageant Politics: Women's Bodies as Sites of Contestation Over the Nation

While embracing a Western model of pageantry and its concomitant norms and practices, beauty contests worldwide are firmly rooted in the national imaginary. Billig (1995) argues that people buy into a sense of belonging to a unified nation through 'banal nationalism', the repetitive, quotidian and largely taken-for-granted symbols and practices encountered every day in sporting events, money exchanges and turns of phrase, such as *the* prime minister or *the* weather, which express a natural division between us and them. Commonplace signs of nationhood are woven into almost every aspect of beauty pageants. While sometimes self-consciously staged, such signs more likely occur in unremarkable or impromptu ways, and they serve to give legitimacy to the choice of a singular, typically non-representative, woman, as symbolic and even iconic of the entire nation. This facet of pageants recalls a wealth of studies that have considered the ways in which performances and spectacles 'perform the nation' – tying together diverse people and erasing perceived difference – through the use of recognized but often taken-for-granted symbolic practices (e.g. Askew, 2002; Banet-Weiser, 1999; Breed, 2008; Raymos-Zaya, 2003; Reed, 2009). Such performances encourage participants and observers alike to imagine themselves as part of a unified whole.

At the same time, the appropriation of a decidedly Western tradition in beauty pageants challenges understandings of the nation in an especially potent way – through representations of the female form. Pageants have repeatedly stirred tensions, sometimes erupting into violence, in communities around the globe, and often the struggles concern perceived threats to national identity. At the Miss World Pageant of 1996, held in Bangalore, India, widespread riots erupted and Indian protesters threatened mass suicide. For these rioters, holding the pageant in Bangalore was cultural imperialism and globalization at its worst, an affront to a perceived millennia-old Indian identity, embodied by a decidedly home-grown femininity (Banet-Weiser, 1999; Parameswaran, 2004). In 2002, when Miss World took place in Abuja, Nigeria, riots broke out in the conservative Muslim city of Kaduna, where over 200 people were killed. Following a newspaper article claiming that the Prophet Mohammed 'probably would have chosen a wife from among them [the contestants]', fundamentalist Muslims burned much of Kaduna, chanting 'down with beauty' and 'Miss World is sin' (CNN Online, 2002). The protests, while in the name of Islam, unfolded within a nationalist frame; they occurred because the pageant was taking place *in Nigeria*, even if in the religiously 'neutral' city of Abuja, some 200 kilometers away. Race and ethnicity, in conjunction with gender, have likewise motivated conflict over what constitutes a suitable symbol of the nation (see Chapter 6). In 1996, protests surfaced through much of Italy over the selection of a black Caribbean woman as Miss Italia (Banet-Weiser, 1999). And in 1986, Lisa Mahfood, the daughter of Lebanese immigrants, had bottles and oranges as well as racial epithets hurled at her while taking her coronation walk down the platform as Miss Jamaica, by an audience which was shocked and outraged at the selection of a woman seen as white to represent their country (Barnes, 1994).

Such tensions are not, however, constituted exclusively by differences between groups, but are also felt within individuals, for whom there is often an ambivalence and even anxiety about what it is to orient towards the global *and* the local, the national *and* the transnational or cosmopolitan (e.g. Crawford *et al.*, 2008; Dewey, 2008). For example, Crawford *et al.* (2008) describe the attitudes of urban Nepali women to the local rise of beauty pageants. On the one hand, they recognize pageants as an opportunity to empower women in a patriarchal society, to showcase Nepal in global competitions and to reach out to less fortunate segments of society to participate in the 'progress' of the nation. On the other hand, these same women express a strong dislike for the commercialized aspects of the competitions and they worry about the damaging effects the promulgation of pageants might have on young Nepali women's body image.

In Tanzania, beauty pageants, as exclusively urban events, enact a vernacular cosmopolitanism through signs and symbols of elite, fashionable and often globally sourced elements of style, fashion, taste and politics. Renowned performers from Tanzania and abroad take the stage in between competitive segments; audiences don cutting-edge hairstyles and outfits, and prefer drinking South African red wine or Kenyan Tusker beer to the local pilsner that often sponsors the event. The masters of ceremonies (MCs) often speak in stylish and sometimes non-local English. And in their provocative clothing and movements, aimed to resemble international runway models, contestants themselves key into an international, cosmopolitan sensibility.

But Tanzanian beauty pageants also seek a representative of the nation. She must be, by some locally relevant standards, worthy of bearing the title of 'Miss Tanzania', 'Miss Arusha' or 'Miss Mwanza'. Although discussion abounds in newspapers and on city streets about the foreign origin of the qualities of beauty rewarded in Tanzanian pageants – light skin, long straight hair, and tall and trim bodies, it is more often beauty contestants' behavior that garners attention. Pageants are seen to corrupt young Tanzanian women, and this corruption is made most visible on stage by the clothing contestants wear. Such concern over feminine virtue within pageantry is not unique to Tanzania, and Banet-Weiser (1999) overviews the historical tension in the Miss America pageant between its reliance on exposing the female body and its emphasis on establishing the respectability of its participants. Indeed, the equation of woman = nation as embodied by 'the chaste and modest woman', representative of the moral qualities of the nation itself, has frequently been noted in state-sponsored feminine symbols such as in France's Marianne and Germany's Germania (Mosse, 1985: 90; see discussion in Banet-Weiser, 1999), as well as in the United States' Statue of Liberty.[1]

Yet, unlike the symbols of Germania and Marianne, a beauty queen is flesh and blood, capable of making decisions on and off stage that may contradict the ideals she is to stand for, and a new beauty queen is selected every year, ushering in the potential each time for threats to understandings of a national femininity. Furthermore, rather than a symbol that distills and elevates unproblematic values held by the entire populace, no one in Tanzania conceives of beauty queens as straightforwardly representative of the nation, even if they themselves accept her role; voices dismissing the legitimacy of such events and their delegates are too many and too loud to ignore completely. For example, an anecdote well known to many Tanzanians is that, in 1998, the winner of Miss Tanzania was expelled from secondary school for participating in the pageant until a government minister intervened and coerced the school into reinstating her. Finally, and unlike, say, the Statue of Liberty, the sexuality of beauty contestants is prominently on display, and the question of the respectability of contestants and their viability as national representatives is paramount to many.

This chapter seeks to explore how nationalist imaginings are manifested and contested in Tanzanian beauty pageants, primarily through female bodies and voices. From one perspective, these events are the product of global processes, as contestants, organizers and participants self-consciously orient to international tastes, values and norms. Yet, from another perspective, pageants simultaneously engage with the symbolic portfolio of the nation. The 'banal' ways in which what it means to be Tanzanian are performed, critiqued and questioned in and around beauty pageants shed light on the long-term struggles around Tanzanian national culture. These struggles have often played out over the female form and have concerned women's embrace of products and practices considered 'foreign', with the ultimate effect that urban Tanzanian women must navigate a very narrow space of respectability within their own cities as they seek modern and independent lives for themselves.

Beauty Pageants in History and Phenomenology

Going international

Despite the rapid proliferation of beauty contests in the first half of the 20th century as nationalist endeavors (see Chapter 1), it was not until 1951 that national beauty queens were brought together to vie for a title under a single competitive umbrella. In that year, the first international beauty contest was held in London, England, under the name of 'Festival Bikini Contest'. Quickly dubbed 'Miss World' by the British media, this pageant was designed as a one-time event, part of a larger, government-sponsored, 'Festival of Britain', aimed at showcasing the nation's strength and viability in the aftermath of World War II and at assuaging various political tensions with some of its colonies (Lovegrove, 2002). The next year, the American swimwear company Catalina followed suit with the Miss Universe contest, which also brought together beauty contestants from many different nations (Ballerino Cohen et al., 1996b). In the same year, the organizers of the British Miss World pageant decided to make their contest an annual event because of its success and popularity in 1951. With both the American Miss Universe and the British Miss World pageants established, the 1950s saw a brisk growth of beauty pageants globally, as nations throughout the world began to host their own contests in order to participate in the international events. By 1954, 16 countries, mostly European, as well as Turkey, Egypt, Ceylon (present-day Sri Lanka) and the United States, were represented at Miss World, and by 1960 there were 39 delegates, several of whom were from South American and African countries and colonies; Misses Korea and Japan also competed.[2]

While diverse countries from across the globe were sending representatives to Miss World and Miss Universe, black contestants were distinctly missing for the first years of these international pageants. Kenya, Rhodesia (modern Zambia and Zimbabwe) and South Africa sent white contestants during the 1950s and even later. In 1957, the newly independent West African nation of Ghana sent the first black contestant, Monica Amekoafia, to Miss World, a highly symbolic statement of national independence, pride and authenticity. In subsequent years, other independent African nations, including Liberia, Gambia and Nigeria, dispatched black representatives. By 1967, there was significant participation by African nations, including Tanzania, Uganda, Ghana and Nigeria, all represented by black women (Figure 3.1). Today, international beauty pageants have strong representation by numerous sub-Saharan African nations, all of which are now usually – though not always – represented by black women. Yet the issue of race and ethnicity in finding a national representative is still contested ground (Banet-Weiser, 1999; Barnes, 1994), a topic upon which I will elaborate upon in Chapter 6, as well as briefly below.

While other international pageants have proliferated in recent years, Miss World and Miss Universe remain the two most visible. Miss World is a larger competition than Miss Universe; in 2011, there were 113 contestants competing at Miss World, versus 89 at Miss Universe. Miss World also has a stronger orientation to developing nations and the global south; African countries such as Kenya, Uganda, Zimbabwe and Liberia, as well as Eastern European ones like Lithuania, Latvia and Belarus, are among about two dozen countries that participate exclusively in Miss World. One of the primary reasons for this global division in participation is the franchise fee, which, while varying from country to country, tends to be significantly higher for Miss Universe than for Miss World. The United States and India are among several nations participating in both the Miss World and Miss Universe competitions.[3] The Miss World contest is the more relevant to this study because, at the time of the bulk of the research, Tanzania sent

Figure 3.1 Contestants at Miss World 1967: (from left) Misses Tanzania (Theresa Shayo), Uganda, Ghana and Nigeria
Credit: Leondard Burt/Hulton Archive/Getty Images

contestants only to Miss World, although since 2007 it has also participated in the Miss Universe franchise.

Beauty pageants appeared briefly in Tanzania (then Tanganyika) during the late colonial period, when the British colony sent a representative to the Miss World contest in 1960 for the first, and only, time. Like all other contestants from British colonies participating in Miss World at that time, the Tanganyikan delegate was a white woman, named Carmen Lesley Woodcock. Tanganyika gained its independence from Great Britain the following year and held no more national beauty contests until 1967, when Theresa Shayo, a black woman, was the independent nation's first Miss Tanzania and its first representative to Miss World (see Figure 3.1). Within months of Shayo's participation, however, the Tanzanian government banned beauty pageants entirely, and the Miss Tanzania contest was not reinstated until 1994.

Tanzanian pageant phenomenology and the Miss World model of competition

Despite resistance, Miss Tanzania and its feeder pageants have become very popular. Since their reinstatement in 1994, pageants have expanded to occur annually in almost every region of the country.[4] A hierarchical structure divides competition into three major levels – *taifa* ('nation'), *kanda* ('zone') and *mkoa* ('region') (Figure 3.2). The top three winners of each regional competition progress to a zonal-level event, and the top three of each zonal-level competition continue to the national event. Dar es Salaam, the cultural and economic capital,[5] is treated specially; it is technically an *mkoa* – Tanzania's primary geopolitical unit – but each of its three districts, Kinondoni, Temeke and Ilala, counts as a *kanda*, and so sends its top three finishers directly to the Miss Tanzania competition. Furthermore, these three districts are further subdivided into subdistricts, each of which holds its own competition.

The pageant season lasts from mid-June to early September, and at each pageant, from poorly financed local competitions to the glamour of the season's culmination at the Miss Tanzania competition, a core formula prevails. Every pageant includes five segments in which the contestants appear on stage. The first is what is referred to, in English and Swahili, as the *opening dance* or *welcoming dance*. During this segment, contestants come on stage, usually wearing short skirts and tight t-shirts, and perform a choreographed group dance to a popular song. The second segment is the *vazi la ubunifu* ('creative wear') competition (Figure 3.3), during which the contestants introduce themselves one by one while modeling an original

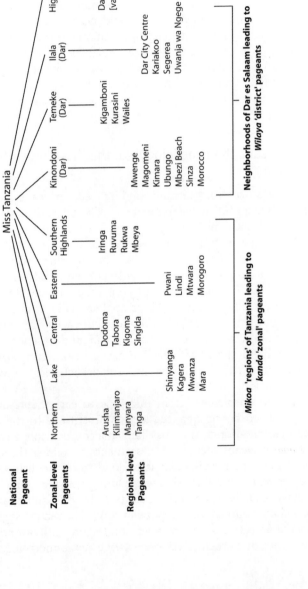

Figure 3.2 Miss Tanzania pageant hierarchy

MSHIRIKI Miss Tanzania 2003, Cleopatra Segumba Margareth Willson, akipita na vazi la ubunifu. (Picha zote na Athumani Hamisi)

Figure 3.3 Creative wear (from *Nipashe*, 27 September 2003)

design. These outfits are frequently made of local fabrics, such as *kitenge*, *kanga* or *batik*, which are crafted into modern and often revealing outfits. Following creative wear is the *vazi la ufukweni* ('beach wear') segment (Figure 3.4), in which contestants walk on stage wearing either a bikini top or a one-piece bathing suit, accompanied by a sarong or shorts. Next is the *vazi la jioni* ('evening wear') competition (Figure 3.5). In this segment, contestants model formal, often sequined and floor-length, dresses and high-heeled shoes. Following the evening wear segment, the top five contestants are announced and each of these finalists must answer a question, usually about topical social issues, for example 'What advice would you give to your friends and to society about AIDS?' (see Chapter 4 and below). From pageant to pageant, the order of these five segments is never altered, and the

MSHINDI wa tatu Miss Tanzania 2003, Nargis Mohammed, akipita na vazi la ufukweni.

Figure 3.4 Beach wear (from *Lete Raha*, 7–13 September 2003)

Washiriki walioingia hatua ya tano bora, kutoka (kushoto) ni Pilsner Ice Miss Tanzania 2003, Sylvia Bahame, Joan Cassian (namba nne Miss Tanzania), Nargis Mohammed (mshindi wa Tatu), Aneth Doto Nusurupia (mshindi wa pili), na Jacqueline Nathan (mshindi wa tano) (Picha zote na Athumani Hamisi).

Figure 3.5 Evening wear (from *Spoti Sterehe*, 7–10 September 2003)

segments are interspersed with various kinds of entertainment (see Chapter 6), as well as speeches and banter by hosts and special guests. The top finishers, announced in reverse order, take the stage, and finally the winner is crowned and takes her position on a throne. The outgoing beauty queen crowns the winner, while the two runners-up cluster around the new queen to pose for throngs of photographers and fans (see Figures 4.3 and 6.4).

In many respects, the formula used in the events corresponds to the norms of the Miss World competition, to which Miss Tanzania is sent annually. The particular competitive segments, interspersed with entertainment and MC banter, come straight from Miss World, and even the way in which winners pose for photographs shares a visual vocabulary with Miss World picture-posing. Many Tanzanians, and certainly many contestants, tune in annually to watch the broadcast of the Miss World contest and are familiar with the general expectations and structure of the events; contestants, judges, audiences and organizers are able to tap into this knowledge in their participation. Furthermore, pageant organizers rely on the expertise of national champions, having returned from the international competition, to share their experience and know-how with current competitors. Reigning and former Miss Tanzania crown-holders serve in an official capacity during the two to three weeks of training leading up to the national event. During this time, they coach contestants on all elements of the competition: how to walk the catwalk, how to dress and wear one's hair, and how to smile at the judges and audience. This instructor role of current and former beauty queens exists at all levels of the competition, with, for example, the reigning Miss Northern Zone, who herself would have had the opportunity to train under a former Miss Tanzania at the national competition, coaching this year's competitors in her home zone. The formula for the pageants, then, is passed down year after year through the ranks of outgoing beauty queens.

Nonetheless, while certainly the overall framework for the competitions in Tanzania is based on an international model, the ways in which this framework is realized takes on a palpably *Tanzanian* quality. These events unfold in local spaces, with local resources, under the tutelage of local experts and with the goal of choosing a local representative. What is more, some aspects of the international model are directly questioned for the relevance to Tanzanians, such as the issue of the swimsuit competition (see below). While globally oriented and informed, these pageants bear sometimes subtle, often taken-for-granted signs of being *Tanzanian* events in search of a Tanzanian representative. Sometimes, they also include self-consciously staged elements of Tanzanian nationalism. Indeed, every participating nation interprets the international pageant model to make local sense, and below I will give a brief case study of Miss India. In Chapters 5 and 7, I will draw a few other comparisons between Miss India and Miss Tanzania, which, as former British colonies in the global south, share certain compelling features in terms of the ways in which international beauty pageants are understood locally.

A Case Study: Miss India

In her analysis of the Miss India enterprise, Dewey (2008) discusses the ways in which that pageant allows spectators to envision themselves all as 'Indian', even in the face of vast cultural, religious, ethnic and linguistic differences, as well as striking class-based ones. Throughout the Miss India pageants, elements of performance, clothing and language are employed that conjure a sense of shared Indian culture and authenticity, giving legitimacy to the process as well as to the final product – a national delegate to the Miss Universe contest.

On stage, contestants pepper their English-language self-introductions with nationalist Hindi phrases such as, 'Tonight, bharat mata [Mother India] stands proud', inspiring the audience to applaud enthusiastically (Dewey, 2008: 215). During a group performance, contestants wear intricate saris. For many of the young women, it is the most challenging portion of the event, as they have never worn these heavy and constricting outfits before. In a reference to North Indian Hindu temples, an announcer credits 'the magic of Khajuraho' as inspiring the designs of the saris (Dewey, 2008: 218). And very dramatically, two singers – one Kannada-speaking from South India and one Hindi-speaking from Delhi – switch languages during a musical performance in a display of national cooperation and integration. This symbolic gesture also seems to perform the relative unimportance of linguistic and cultural differences within the Indian Hindu national imaginary, since these differences can be shed or exchanged at will.

In addition to enregistered emblems of patriotism and a culturally unified nationhood, such as saris, Hindi language and temples, new and emergent or entextualized emblems of a modern Indian identity work to connect together people across the vast country (cf. Agha, 2007). Dewey (2008) describes a rural pageant advertising campaign in which village women were given free samples of shampoo from Sunsilk, a corporate sponsor of the Miss India pageant. The Sunsilk campaign was successful in keying rural Indian women into the beauty contest and the presumptive benefits of the product, as it tapped into women's hair as a key component of Indian femininity across the sub-continent. Through aggressive advertising techniques, Sunsilk shampoo allowed rural women to imagine themselves as similar to those on stage, connected through their hair-grooming practices to an (urban, middle-class) ideal of feminine Indian beauty. At the same time, the campaign shamed rural women into questioning their own long-standing beauty regimes, which rely on natural hair-care products and less-frequent washing.

This example is enlightening for the current project in several ways. First, even in the face of vast linguistic and ethnic difference, there are nonetheless numerous widely recognized symbols of unified Indian culture that come into play in performing Indian national identity within beauty pageants; as I will discuss below, Tanzania has struggled for decades with defining a portfolio of national symbols. Second, the Miss India example makes clear that, in addition to the cannon of self-consciously (re)produced symbols, national symbols may also be emergent as well as commonplace or taken for granted. Third, the Miss India examples emphasize that national symbolism is strongly gendered, with enregistered symbols such as saris, as well as emergent ones such as Sunsilk shampoo, referencing a strictly feminine version of national identity. Finally, while within the realm of pageantry these symbols might seem relatively uncontested, many Indians do indeed question the validity of the kind of woman who is selected as Miss India to represent the nation, as evinced by the riots that took place in Bangalore in 1996 (see above). In the case of Miss Tanzania, even if feminin-ity is a critical component of national identity, just what constitutes the ideal Tanzanian woman, and the extent to which she may be represented by a beauty queen, is very much up for debate.

Tanzanian National Culture as Anti-culture: The Rhetoric of Miniskirts, Misses and Maasai

The disappearance of beauty pageants from Tanzania for almost 30 years is significant in that it showcases the connection between the state, the national imaginary and the female body. Following independence in 1961, and especially after the Arusha Declaration of 1967 (see Chapter 2), the socialist project pursued by the ruling TANU party sought to create a state based on equality for all and at the same time encouraged economic and psychological independence from the West (Blommaert, 1999a). The effort to achieve social equality focused on eliminating ethnic difference and, unlike its European and Asian socialist counterparts, only secondar-ily was concerned with class structure. A largely implicit ideal of gender equality was also part of this conception of socialism (but far from reality – see below, and Geiger, 1987). In this particular politico-ideological climate, beauty pageants – certainly as commercial and Western in nature, but also as events based on highlighting difference – could not exist.

Within this political framework, modeled on other socialisms such as those in China and the Soviet Union but also drawing on an idealized conception of indigenous African socialism, the Tanzanian state sought to create a 'national culture' in terms of which nation-building (*kujenga taifa*) could occur (Blommaert, 1999a). The concept of national culture incorporated two major strands. One strand, as indicated in a statement by the then President Julius Nyerere, was the project of 'seek[ing] out the best of the traditions and customs of all our tribes and mak[ing] them a part of our national culture' (quoted in Ivaska, 2002: 591). The other strand, which became more prominent in the later years of the 1960s, was based on 'the production of a self-consciously "modern" culture as a tool for national development' (Ivaska, 2002: 591). Overarching these two strands was a general desire, as stated in an important ministerial memo, 'to remove or lessen elements that are inappropriate in that they are shameful or disgusting for a condition of civility and modern development in general' (Ivaska, 2002: 591). National culture was a concept defined in the negative: 'Most people knew what it was not: it was not ethnic, not traditional, not western. But what it *was* remained unclear' (Blommaert, 1999a: 67).

In the late 1960s and early 1970s, the pursuit of national culture resulted in official bans on products and practices considered to be foreign, from tight trousers and skin-lightening creams to soul music and pornography; even indigenous but blatantly ethnic Maasai dress was forbidden, as it challenged the ideologies of ethnic homogeneity (Ivaska, 2002). But it was the products and practices concerning urban women that drew the most attention. The ban of miniskirts in 1969[6] was a hot topic in newspapers and women were attacked by groups of young men for their perceived fashion transgressions (Ivaska, 2002; Lewinson, 2000). It was in this same spirit that beauty pageants were outlawed, although, unlike the ban on miniskirts and other fashions, which reappeared within a year (Ivaska, 2002), the ban on the beauty pageants stuck.

It was clear by the late 1970s that the socialist project in Tanzania had failed, and while economic liberalization came in the early 1990s, the government still influences or controls certain aspects of social and cultural life, such as the themes and typologies of music, dance and theater performances (Askew, 2002; Edmonson, 2007), and the state still exerts some control over pageants as well. In 2002, the Parliament (*Baraza*) of the semi-autonomous and Muslim island of Zanzibar prohibited the competitions from taking place there. According to the Zanzibari Minister of Education and Culture, beauty pageants are irrelevant on the island, because 'all Zanzibaris are beautiful' (*Guardian*, 2003). These comments recall the ideal of equality that was a cornerstone of Tanzanian 'national culture' in the early years of independence. Zanzibar has historically been more politically leftist and radical than mainland Tanzania and it is of note that, unlike the mainland, Zanzibar still adheres officially to the political ideology that characterized a decidedly more socialist Tanzania of the 1960s and 1970s.

Tanzanian beauty pageants, though commercial, private enterprises, are monitored by the National Arts Council, BASATA (Baraza la Sanaa). The relationship between BASATA and the Miss Tanzania organizing committee is a knotty one. In some ways, the committee embraces this government partnership as a way of legitimizing the contests; the pageant's own official website states that BASATA 'has helped to restore its [Miss Tanzania's] credibility' (misstanzania.net). At other times, however, BASATA has made rulings that pageant directors have opposed. For example, BASATA has restricted the range of outfits that contestants can wear during the beach wear segment of the competitions; contestants may not expose their upper thighs and pelvic area – a highly eroticized part of the female body – and so they are required to wear a sarong or shorts on top of their bathing suits.[7] In 1998, all beauty pageants in the country were briefly banned again because a pageant director 'flouted rules and allowed the contestants of the Miss East Africa pageant to parade before judges in skimpy beach wear against state orders' (Odhiambo, 1999). While many Tanzanians agree that baring this part of the body is un-Tanzanian, organizers and contestants often take issue with this decision, arguing that the ruling is based on old-fashioned beliefs antithetical to the modern spirit of the pageants.

Here we see a state-level agency governing female decency in the name of protecting national culture. Yet, in keeping with Blommaert's (1999a) analysis that national culture has largely been defined in terms of negatives, the BASATA judgment does not give a concrete sense of what that culture actually *is*. Whatever it is, however, it is clear that an understanding of femininity and gendered dress and comportment are one of its cornerstones.

Miss Tanzania and National Culture

'Performing the nation': *Ngoma, kanga* and women's bodies

Though the creation of a national culture has always been elusive in Tanzania, symbols have emerged of collective Tanzanian identity, and many of these appear regularly within beauty pageants. These symbols orient audiences as well as participants to the local – national – side of the events. The infusion of a national symbolism into the pageants works to legitimize and ground the events within a national imaginary, a counterbalance to the Westernizing threat that the contests pose.

As discussed in Chapter 2, Swahili has been constructed as the national language and remains strongly symbolic of the nation, even though debate rages as to its place in education and as people doubt its viability in ushering in opportunity for Tanzania's citizens. In pageants, Swahili's symbolic role is largely implicit; government officials and special guests always address the audience in Swahili, and outgoing beauty queens also use Swahili to say their farewells. These participants' use of Swahili is critical, for referential as well as symbolic reasons; government officials and lower-level beauty queens are likely not fluent in English, and the same can be said of the audiences, for whom Swahili is simply the unmarked code. But in serving in some kind of parastatal capacity, these participants' use of Swahili is an expectation of the office, in practice if not in law. In contrast, among MCs and especially yet-to-be-crowned contestants, the importance of using the national language is, at best, secondary to the importance of indexing oneself as a cosmopolitan elite, so mixed Swahili–English varieties as well as versions of standard English become vital tools, as will be discussed in depth in Chapters 4 and 5.

Rather than relying on a strict canon of nationalist symbols in which Swahili is front and center, pageants – through many aspects of staging, performance and discourse – perform the nation in recognizable, but often emergent, ways. Askew emphasizes the emergent, fluid and contested nature of nationalism and its symbols, and states:

> Rather than an abstract ideology produced by some to be consumed by others, nationalism ought to be conceptualized as a series of continually negotiated relationships between people who share occupancy in a defined geographic, political, or ideological space. (Askew, 2002: 12)

'Traditional' *ngoma* dances have, since the independence era, been self-consciously constructed by the state as authentic symbols of the nation, even as they meld and blend elements from different ethnic traditions into distinct and widely recognized dances (Askew, 2002; Edmonson, 2007). These are the only state-sponsored fora for celebrating ethnic diversity, but since they are performed by trained dancers from various ethnicities (see Chapter 6), their divisive potential is thought to be nominal. Furthermore, new dance troupes emerge, and innovative dances surface, with the body of 'traditional' Tanzanian dance being constantly reinvented and reinterpreted. In pageants, *ngoma* troupes take the stage between competitive segments to perform these ubiquitous dances, a common feature of public gatherings. *Ngoma*, which often theatrically place women, with swaying hips and inviting smiles, as the subdued object of frenetic men's lust (Edmonson,

2007), are particularly noteworthy in the context of urban pageants, as they emphasize the disjuncture between the ideal Tanzanian woman – rural, full-bodied, voiceless, submissive and well behaved[8] – and the urban and socially dangerous young women on stage. But it is not an altogether unfavorable juxtaposition for contestants, who, in contrast to the dancers, appear as modern and educated bodies of the future (see below and Chapter 6).

Other symbols of the nation appear as well. In 1993, in a competition entitled 'In Search of a National Dress', Tanzanians selected the *kanga*, a two-part colorful cloth inscribed with Swahili proverbs at the bottom edge and worn by Tanzanian women across the country as well as across social classes (Askew, 2002). In beauty pageants, contestants often don *kanga* or similar fabrics that have been cut and crafted into stylish outfits to perform their opening number (see Figure 3.4). This dance, usually done barefoot, to an African pop or reggae song, incorporates a mélange of styles, including elements of Tanzanian dance genres and those from popular Bollywood films and contemporary Western dance. The result is typically a pleasant, if relatively sterile, performance that, while not overtly sexualized (unlike *ngoma*), is still alluring because of ample amounts of bare skin, swaying bodies and inviting smiles. The *kanga* are chosen because they are an inexpensive, creative and colorful solution to the task of costuming two dozen young women and because, even in their renaissance as dance attire, they invoke Tanzanian femininity.

Thus *kanga*, like *ngoma*, are both grassroots as well as state-supported symbols, a tension that results in a performative flux in the material substance of the symbols as well as in the nature of what exactly they symbolize. In the space of pageants, the *kanga* is the closest thing to national dress that contestants can wear, though wearing *kanga* in the body-draping fashion of everyday Tanzanian women would be contrary to the fashion-forward and Western orientation of the pageants. In wearing recrafted *kanga*, competitors embody a contemporary, urban, youthful and even Western version of Tanzanian femininity that works in the context of beauty pageants.

'From the Geneva of Africa': Tanzania, tourism and gender in the national imaginary

Another key way in which the nation is performed in pageants is through the discourses, symbols and imagery of tourism. Tanzania, home to Mount Kilimanjaro, the Serengeti, Zanzibar and Olduvai Gorge (called the 'Cradle of Mankind' for its paleoanthropological finds), is a tourist's dream, and 14% of the economy is derived from international tourism (Salazar, 2009).

Salazar (2009) describes how, during the Nyerere years, the socialist state vilified tourism on an ideological plane as capitalist imperialism, and on a pragmatic plane as dangerous in its capacity to draw Tanzanians' attention to great gulfs in wealth. Furthermore, it was thought to corrode the purity of rural areas, the location of the true Tanzania. Yet, since economic liberalization in the 1990s, Tanzania's official position on tourism, as with many aspects of national identity, has shifted, to one which embraces tourism for economic uplift and as a source of pride.

In multiple ways, tourism frames the happenings at and around the pageants, most visibly in the kinds of venues that house these events – typically mid-range tourist-class hotels, often serving a sizeable African clientele. Reminders of the cultural and natural beauty of Tanzania take form in tourist trinkets – Makonde tree-of-life statues and *tinga-tinga* paintings – serving as taken-for-granted backdrops to pageant happenings.

Pageant promoters describe a key function of beauty queens as 'goodwill ambassadors' and one of their chief responsibilities is to promote national and international tourism. In the weeks leading up to prominent pageants, contestants tour the region or the country to visit top tourist destinations, which the majority of Tanzanians have never seen. Newspapers draw public attention to these tours, with headlines such as:

Miss Tanzania beauties to visit tourist attractions. (Winfrida Ngonyani, *Business Times*, 20 August 2010)

Vodacom Miss Tanzania aspirants in Arusha tourist destinations. (*Guardian*, 25 August 2010)

TAZARA hosts Miss Tanzania for train ride. (*Daily News*, 16 September 2011)

TAZARA (run by the Tanzania Zambia Railway Authority) is a railroad line running from the port of Dar es Salaam to the central Zambian town of New Kapiri Mposhi. Sometimes referred to as 'the people's railway' (Monson, 2009: 37) or 'freedom railway' (Monson, 2009: 2), this railway line itself, a project funded by the Chinese during the Cold War, has long served in discourses of socialism and nationalism. By boarding the train, the contestants stand as an advertisement for the railway as a potentially glamorous alternative to other modes of transport and as a reminder of the railroad's role in building a national culture based on modernity, self-esteem and self-reliance.

The role of beauty queens in supporting national tourism is made explicit in the following excerpt from a newspaper report summarizing an interview with the Miss Tanzania pageant director:

> The Lino Agency Chairman and Organizer of the Vodacom[9] Miss Tanzania, Hashimu Lundenga, said that the camp is to support [the] local tourism sector in Tanzania by ... encouraging Tanzanians to be tourists by being proud of what makes Tanzania beautiful. (*Guardian*, 25 August 2010)

The director's statement suggests implicitly that contestants use their own beauty to draw attention to the nation's natural beauty and, indeed, that their feminine beauty is *part of* that natural, national beauty. The well publicized excursions are thus important for forging links between a Tanzanian modernity, Tanzanian femininity and the 'natural' symbols of the nation.

Within beauty contests, the importance of tourism as a source of regional and national pride as well as revenue is a recurrent theme. Question-and-answer competitive segments put forth tourism as a critical component of national identity and independence, with queries such as:

> If you were given a chance to boost the tourism industry, what would you do and why?

> In your view, what should be done to improve both local and international tourism in Tanzania?

> Mount Kilimanjaro is the pride for our country. What is your opinion?

Furthermore, though audiences are almost exclusively local, announcers issue welcoming statements befitting tourism brochures. In the following introduction at a Miss Northern Zone competition in Arusha, the announcer (the master of ceremonies, M) enumerates the various regions from which the contestants hail. As she mentions each region and its tourist appeal, the region's three representatives take the stage. Here, the connection between female beauty, natural tourist attractions and the nation comes to an explicit climax, as the women in trios present themselves on stage, all dressed in stylish *kanga* creations:

1   **M**:   Today we are going to have 12 participants.
2   From Geneva of Africa, this is Arusha.
           [Enter top three finishers from the Miss Arusha pageant]

3   From land of Mountain Kilimanjaro, Kilimanjaro.
    [Enter top three finishers from the Miss Kilimanjaro pageant]
4   From the land of Lake Manyara, this is Manyara.
    [Enter top three finishers from the Miss Manyara pageant]
5   And from the coast city of Tanga.
    [Enter top three finishers from the Miss Tanga pageant]
6   Three of these will go on to represent at Miss Tanzania
7   and with luck the Northern Zone will make Tanzania proud in Sanya.
8   So, I hope everyone will enjoy this show.

Each region has its iconic source of pride: for Tanga, it is the coastline; for Manyara, Lake Manyara; for Kilimanjaro, its famous mountain namesake; and for Arusha, the 'Geneva of Africa'. The last sobriquet was first used by former American President Bill Clinton, who, along with Nelson Mandela, visited the city of Arusha for the signing of the Burundi Peace Accord in 2000. Arusha at that time was already the headquarters of the United Nations International Crime Tribunal for Rwanda, and hence the reference drew the similarity between this African city and Geneva, Switzerland, home to one of the United Nations' four headquarters. The allusion also took into account the fact that, like Geneva, Arusha sits in a gorgeous natural setting, in the shadow of the famous Mt Arusha and Mt Kilimanjaro. By using the phrase 'Geneva of Africa', the announcer glamorizes and internationalizes the city, constructing it as a cosmopolitan capital befitting not only of a world-class beauty pageant but also of the business of international peace-making and development.

While the announcer's description of each of the four regions' top tourist appeal serves to highlight the tourism value of the Northern Zone in which they are located, her statement also emphasizes that these regions and tourist sites are simultaneously part of the value of Tanzania as a whole. She states that perhaps the winner that night will succeed in winning the Miss Tanzania crown, then go on to represent Tanzania at the Miss World competition in Sanya, China, in November. Furthermore, rather than using the women's names or titles, the announcer's proclamation with the appearance of each group on stage, 'this is Arusha' or 'Kilimanjaro' iconizes the women as, just like the tourist sites themselves, standing for the regions and, ultimately, for the nation itself.

The connection between tourism and beauty queens takes on a personal dimension when we also consider the fact that many contestants, especially those hailing from the tourist-dense area of northern Tanzania, express an interest in becoming tour guides. They enroll in one of several local tourism schools, which offer English language classes as well as courses in Tanzanian ecology, in the hope of securing a coveted position with a safari outfitter or tourist-class hotel. Furthermore, growing up in the midst of some of Africa's most popular tourist destinations, Arushans witness, if not personally interact with, the comings and goings of well-heeled international visitors who troll the city's dusty streets in search of souvenirs and adventure. Working in tourism not only would be a sustaining and cosmopolitan career, it also, for some young women, would offer an opportunity to meet wealthy foreign men who could whisk them from Tanzania. This is, of course, ironic, in that, rather than promoting Tanzania, many would-be tour guides seek instead to escape it (see Chapter 7).

Public education, national crises, and the worried face of cosmopolitanism

Many scholars have studied women's supposed role in educating and 'civilizing' a populace or a nation (e.g. Boddy, 2007; Kerber, 1980; see Chapter 5) and Banet-Weiser (1999) discusses the fact that this civilizing role is also a key function of beauty pageants in general. The Miss Tanzania official website (misstanzania.net) indicates that, among Miss Tanzania's duties, it is her responsibility to 'sensitize members of the public on issues that are detrimental to society such as HIV/AID, fight against drugs abuse, poverty eradication, gender equality, health, nutrition and environmental conservation'. Questions asked during the question-and-answer session concern issues of national interest and a successful contestant must speak confidently – even if briefly and without substance – on these topics. Typical questions include:

> In the recent budget, Tanzania has embarked on campaign to remove poverty. Tell us, in your view, what should be done to remove the poverty?

> Drug addiction is a critical problem among youth in our country. What is your solution?

> Juu ya maswala ya elimu Tanzania nini maoni yako?
> [Concerning the issue of education in Tanzania, what is your opinion?]

Contestants must navigate responses which show a progressive sensitivity to the less fortunate members of Tanzanian society. In doing so, they serve not only as educators but also as role models of feminine modernity, knowledgeable and articulate about matters of national concern. Questions frequently draw attention to very visible segments of society who are frequently the focus of popular attention – the homeless or destitute, drunks, as well as *vijana* ('youth'), who are often associated with petty crime and indolence – and responses emphasize a practical education that will remedy society and individuals' problems and that recalls the vision offered in the Arusha Declaration (see Chapters 2 and 5). Contestants also stress *kujitegemea* ('self-reliance') in overcoming adversity, but here it is a personal self-reliance, rather than the societal self-reliance stressed by Nyerere in which citizens should call upon their individual strengths and moral fiber to overcome temptation and adversity.

While the questions and responses are framed within a national understanding of societal scourges and solutions, this segment of the competition also allows contestants to capitalize on what Hannerz (2004) has called 'the worried face of cosmopolitanism', or 'cosmopolitics' (Hannerz, 2005), by displaying their knowledge of and engagement in international causes, ones which just happen also to be in their own backyard. In the following response, the contestant addresses the issues of gender equity and the abuse of women, relatively new social agendas in Tanzania:

> Asante sana kwa swali lako, na ninajibu kama ifuatavyo. Kama nitapewa nafasi ya kubadilisha kitu chochote katika maisha yangu ni ningependa kubadilisha unyanyasaji wa wanawake kwani unyanyasaji wa wanawake ni tatizo sugu katika nchi yetu na pengine. Pia, ningeomba serikali itashauri wanawake wawe sawa wawe na haki sawa na waume. Asante.
> [Thank you for your question and I will answer as follows. If I would be given the chance to change something in my life, I would like to change the abuse of women because the abuse of women is a chronic problem in our country and elsewhere. Also I would to ask government to advise women to be equal, to have equal rights with men. Thank you.]

Although the question asked was personal in nature – 'If you could change one thing in your life, what would it be and why?' – the contestant instead offers an impersonal response that allows her to show off her education, expertise, and worldliness (see Chapters 4 and 5). The contestant firmly places the issue of the abuse of women as 'a chronic problem' in Tanzania, positioning the state as an important actor in forging equal rights. At the same time, she taps into international discourses of human rights and gender equity, the kinds of agendas that beauty queens worldwide adopt as their official platforms. In stating that such abuse is 'a chronic problem in our country and elsewhere', the contestant explicitly makes reference to the connection between Tanzania and the rest of the world in the fight against inequality and abuse.

Perhaps more than any other, the topic of HIV/AIDS allows contestants to perform their own cosmopolitanism, even when, as in the case above, the question does not explicitly concern the issue. Contestants successfully place the disease, as well as themselves, within a cosmopolitan framework as well a national one. They frequently repeat the English catch-phrase, 'AIDS kills', which allows them simultaneously to reference their knowledge of the devastating effects of the disease, their own education (see Chapter 5) and their own personal awareness of this international HIV/AIDS awareness slogan.[10] Likewise, the frequent mention of the word 'condom' signals a particular kind of Tanzanian positionality in which speaking openly about AIDS, sex and prophylactics marks one as urban and educated, at the same time that it likely references well known and successful HIV/AIDS education programs such as the ABC (Abstain, Be faithful, Condomize) initiative in Uganda, in which condom use is a critical component. The explicit mention of condoms in Tanzanian beauty pageants serves as a reminder that, while drawing on global discourses, values and tastes, cosmopolitanism is also realized in locally relevant ways. Banet-Weiser (1999) discusses the fact that, in Miss America pageants, contestants have been overtly reprimanded for their use of the word 'condom' in addressing the question of HIV/AIDS because it brings to mind the act of sex within a cultural context in which abstinence is often configured as the sole acceptable preventive measure against the disease.

Despite the historically taboo position of HIV/AIDS in Tanzanian society (Setel, 1999), other public voices have taken on the role of HIV/AIDS edutainment in Tanzania, especially since 1999, when the government declared it a national crisis. Theater troupes perform plays (Edmonson, 2007) and hip-hop artists compose songs about the disease (Higgins, 2009). Billboards advertise condom use to urban youth (Higgins, 2009). Yet contestants' educative role differs, in that they figure themselves within a framework of cosmopolitics, especially in terms of language use. Unlike theater performers, musicians and advertising campaigns, which primarily use various codes of Swahili, contestants' speaking English allows them to draw parallels not just in message but also in medium with like-minded others (especially beauty queens) worldwide (cf. Besnier, 2002; see Chapter 4). Furthermore, contestants' use of direct (technical) and lexically pure language (see Chapters 4 and 5) stands in contrast to the circumlocutions and slang often utilized in other, less cosmopolitan, public contexts to discuss the disease and related issues (Higgins, 2009; Stambach, 2000a). Indeed, the latter highly local ways of speaking and discussing HIV/AIDS are, by design, meant to index a local problem and local categories of people who must manage the disease, its trajectories and its repercussions. Instead, contestants' more standard, and especially English, language use implicitly contextualizes local problems within an international framework.

But contestants' and beauty queens' presumed educative role is not just didactic and it is certainly not understood by the public solely in terms of cosmopolitan imaginings. Rather, part of their role as educators is to embody locally desired qualities and behaviors in their daily public lives, to serve as role models for a particular version of the modern Tanzanian woman. Their behavior is well monitored by the media and hence subject to analysis and critique. For young women in the city, this scrutiny puts them in a problematic spot, as I will discuss in the following sections.

Sex in the City

'Loose' women, materialism and modernity in urban Africa

Across the continent, a broad suspicion of city-dwellers dates to the colonial era, when many Africans and colonial officials alike considered the migration of Africans to cities as a threat to patriarchies, gender roles, religious and ethnic practices, and economic activities. Administrators also saw African urbanity as a menace to colonial rule (Ferguson, 1999). During that time, an understanding of unmarried urban women arose as a particularly dangerous category, a category who threatened, through their perceived unbridled sexuality – and through their earning potential – to undermine masculine African authority (White, 1990). While a cottage industry of female sex work did indeed arise in urban areas during the colonial era (Hunt, 2005 [1991]; Van Onselen, 1982; White, 1990), single female city-dwellers in general became stereotyped as prostitutes. In her study of morality in Belgian Africa, Hunt gathered oral histories of older urban women in Swahili-speaking Eastern Congo; according to one of these women, 'They [we] were all considered prostitutes.... Be you a *malaya* [prostitute], be you not, but so long as you were without a husband you were generally considered a *malaya*' (Hunt, 2005 [1991]: 57).

Certainly, the label of 'prostitute' had sticking power because there were relatively few single women in the city and prostitution was a fairly visible profession for some of them (White, 1990). Furthermore, people wondered how else a woman without a husband would support herself, if not through prostitution. But in addition, because some women – prostitutes or not – acquired wealth through their entrepreneurial activities, the label cast them as social pariahs for disrupting traditional lines of authority and wealth accumulation through their own financial and personal independence (White, 1990). While this stereotype erases the presence of women who were not engaged in such professions and essentializes those who were in terms of their sex roles (Haram, 2004), it is nonetheless one that perdures across East Africa today (Davis, 2000; Swilla, 2000; Wallman, 1996).

Apart from being stereotyped as prostitutes, urban African women have often been associated with loose morals, frequently in conjunction with a perceived desire for material possessions and cosmetics, thought to be obtained through sexual exchanges. In the context of 20th-century Zimbabwe, Burke tells us that:

> many African men have regarded cosmetics as the material expression of their fears about women's mobility and women's power. The stereotype of the socially destructive woman, the woman who defies patriarchy and its rules, has long had great currency among Zimbabwean men. Such a woman has usually been seen as urban, often as a prostitute, and frequently has been described as a social climber obsessed with 'modernity'. (Burke, 1996: 196)

Similar linkages of modern, Western feminine cosmetics and clothing with moral laxness have repeatedly been noted across Africa and throughout the 20th century and into the 21st (Burgess, 2002; Ivaska, 2002; Stambach, 2000a, 2000b). Thomas gives evidence that young women in 1930s southern Africa who self-styled as 'modern' using cosmetics, hairstyles and clothing did so at the expense of being labeled as 'girls of low morals' (Thomas, 2009: 50). Pierre (2008) describes the association in urban Ghana between prostitutes and skin-lightening regimes, and her analysis hinges on framing these products in terms of tensions between local and global meaning attributions. While Western-style cosmetics and clothing have been embraced by young urban women as indices of a modern lifestyle, this desire has also earned them a reputation for moral turpitude and prostitution, fueled by a belief that such products not only are payment by men, but are also necessary for luring the men in the first place. In other words, if a woman adorns herself with modern cosmetics and clothing, she is likely not only seeking a man but must already have a man who has provided these things for her.

Other studies have been careful to understand transactional sex as socially distinct from prostitution (e.g. Cole, 2004; Hunt, 2005 [1991]; Masvawure, 2010; Naidoo & Misra, 2008; Nelson, 1987; Wojcicki, 2002). On the Zambian Copperbelt, Ferguson (1999: 186) describes 'a continuum of forms of heterosexual relationships', from one-night tricks to committed marriages, all of which were characterized by some kind of money–sex exchange. Likewise, in

South Africa, Hunter describes how, in relationships involving transactional sex, 'participants are often constructed as "girlfriends" and "boyfriends" … and the exchange of gifts for sex is part of a broader set of obligations that might not involve a predetermined payment' (Hunter, 2002: 101). Hunter (2009) emphasizes the practical side of such exchanges; in a context of high unemployment, men are increasingly unable to offer bride price and marry, leaving women unmarried and seeking financial and emotional support from multiple men. The willingness of a man to commit material resources is a sign of his emotional commitment to her.

In sum, the combination of gender, single status, urban space and Western products and fashions points to a complex network of practices and beliefs concerning women's sexual behavior and moral character. In many parts of Africa, more and more urban African woman are single, pursuing lives they view as modern (Antoine & Nanitelamio, 1991; Haram, 2004). Yet, even as their educational and career options improve at least marginally (see Chapter 5), the common framing of their desire for independence and modernity in terms of sexual prowess continues to hold sway.

Tanzanian beauty contestants and *utovu wa nidhamu* ('lack of good behavior')

Tanzanian beauty contestants, as the self-styled embodiment of modern Tanzanian femininity, stand in a dichotomous relationship with a conception of rural Tanzanian women. Rural women have long been understood as the locus of true, traditional and hard-working Tanzania, to the extent that city-dwelling women in Tanzania:

> serve as the inauthentic urban migrants since postcolonial nationalist discourse situates the authentic woman as rural and traditional. Within this framework, the village serves as an object of precolonial pride when associated with womanhood. (Edmonson, 2007: 88)

McClintock argues that this linkage is characteristic of the postcolony more generally, in which women are the 'atavistic and authentic body of national tradition … embodying nationalism's conservative principle of continuity' (McClintock, 1995: 359). And while women belong in villages, men's natural place – in postcolonial Tanzania – is the city. The 1967 Arusha Declaration naturalizes these associations:

> The energies of the millions of men in the villages and thousands of women in the towns … are at present wasted in gossip, dancing and drinking. (Nyerere, 1968: 245)

State-level and state-affiliated groups not only explicitly voiced this perspective, they – along with like-minded citizenry – also attempted to regulate the physical movements and fashion choices of women within the city, in the name of fostering this gendering of national culture (Ivaska, 2002; see above).

Yet there were oppositional discourses arguing for the viability of 'urban respectability' (Ivaska, 2002: 593; see also Burgess, 2002). The ban on miniskirts and the assaults carried out on women 'guilty' of violating the interdiction spurred an active debate in local newspapers concerning alternative interpretations of urban female types, as enregistered especially through their fashion choices. One contributor drew readers' attention to 'the beautiful image of our ... well-dressed girls emerging from offices with their purses' (quoted by Ivaska, 2002: 602). Others pointed to the practical choices of short skirts rather than the national female dress – the long, wrapped *kanga* – because of the fact that miniskirts were inexpensive and facilitated movement around the city, to and from work on buses. Modern-dressed women could be seen, rather than as prostitutes, as being as practical, frugal and hard-working as their rural counterparts. Ivaska thus states that:

> the mini-skirt ... also stood for other urban 'types' and tropes: the secretary, the schoolgirl, the girlfriend of the 'sugar daddy'. These were ambiguous figures, which, while often conflated with that of the prostitute, were also subject to struggles to define new and viable – sometimes even respectable – urban identities for women. (Ivaska, 2002: 598)

In her study of education and gender in the Kilimanjaro region of Tanzania, Stambach (2000a) describes such differing conceptions of urban women as envisioned by secondary school girls and other community members. These girls conceptualized the lure of the city in terms of an urban–rural dichotomy of oppositional types of Tanzanian femininity which allowed them to envisage a better life for themselves afforded by their education. *Dada wa mjini* ('city sisters') refers to the schoolgirls' ideal feminine type, their dream of a financially independent 'modern' and urban woman, with fashionable clothes, and a home and a career of her own. In contrast, *mama wa nyumbani* ('stay-at-home mothers') refers to a 'traditional', rural lifestyle in which motherhood, household duties and *kanga*, as well as subjugation by men, are defining characteristics. To be a *dada wa mjini*, one must have attained a relatively high level of education, necessary for securing sustaining, respectable employment. While education is highly sought after for boys as well as girls, parents and members of the community have mixed feelings about the effects of the girls' education, which is seen to fuel the desire for independence, mobility and modern style choices.

Beauty contestants, as quintessentially modern, educated and independent women in the city, are subject to many of the same tensions about the nature of Tanzanian femininity and, indeed, Miss Tanzania is considered by many to be a role model for *dada wa mjini* (see Ekström, 2010). There is a strong suspicion – on individual and societal levels – of these young women, a suspicion that centers around their moral, and especially sexual, essence. Middle-class Tanzanians regularly refer to beauty contestants as *malaya* ('prostitutes'), even while they eagerly await the next pageant. Popular newspaper reportage is pervasive during pageant season, with contestants treated as celebrities and pageants themselves covered in great detail. Reports thrive on tales of contestants' shenanigans and frequently allege contestants' *utovu wa nidhamu* ('lack of good behavior') in terms of sexual and anti-social activities, with the implicit insinuation that, as unmarried adult women in the city, their behavior is not kept in check by masculine authority. For example, the headlines in Figure 3.6 announce: 'We don't

Figure 3.6 Headlines purporting *utovu wa nidhamu*: (a) 'We don't want prostitutes in Miss Tanzania' (from *Sani*, 8–15 July 2003); (b) 'Angela Damas, why have you been this way?' (from *Panorama*, 15–21 July 2003)

want prostitutes in Miss Tanzania' and 'Angela Damas [Miss Tanzania 2002], why have you been this way?' Similar headlines have included:

Miss Ilala: mimi si kilema, ni mikogo. (*Majira*, 6 August 2003)
[Miss Ilala: I'm not ignorant, it's pride.]

Angela, Mbiki ndani ya chungu cha moto! (Dotto Mwaibale, in *Ijumaa*, 18–24 July 2003)
[Angela, Mbiki given harsh warnings!]

These headlines illustrate both the popularity of beauty pageants – a topic worthy of taking a lot of ink – as well as their location outside of broadly accepted cultural norms, a tension that highlights a struggle of modern Tanzanian women today. Contestants are commonly also accused of buying favor with judges, exchanging sex for their vote. References are typically veiled, as in the following newspaper report about a regional winner advancing to the next level:

Rumors of corruption in the pageant's officials do not dampen her hopes for glory. She says speculations of corruption in the whole competition for Miss Tanzania are false. By her accounts, competitors are not asked to do anything unbecoming to win the title. (Joel, 2011)

Yet it is not typically the judges who bear the blame, but rather the young women, who, through their behavior and clothing, are seen not only as responsible for luring the men but also for more generally driving cultural decline. The connection between fashionable clothing and moral turpitude has two sides: on the one hand, people assume that the only way a young woman could acquire an array of stylish clothing is through the help of a sugar daddy; on the other, young women are blamed for luring men into un-sanctioned sexual relationships through their self-adornment. A newspaper headline states:

U-miss na uchangudoa haviko pamoja!! (*Panorama*, 29 July–4 August 2003)
[The misses competitions and prostitution are not the same thing!!]

Though the headline indicates a defense of pageants and their contestants, the text goes on to say:

These beauty queens are very important to educate society but instead, they are using their celebrity status to track down men who have a lot of money in order to get rich quick. (*Panorama*, 29 July–4 August 2003)

Indeed, a discourse of 'spoilt girls' characterizes much reportage and discussion of Tanzanian pageants and beauty queens, with an understanding that it is only spoiled, or sexually corrupted, girls who enter the events, or else that they become spoiled through the process of competing. According to one contestant interviewed by a newspaper reporter:

'They [my parents] advised me to forget the competitions at least for now and concentrate on my studies first', she explained. 'They disliked the dress the girls wear and said it was a sport that spoiled a girl...'. Although the parents argued that a beauty contest was not 'good for our culture', they eventually relented to her pleas to participate. (Joel, 2011)

A newspaper interview with a Miss Tanzania crown-holder similarly stated:

Contrary to the belief that it is only the spoilt girls who go for the contest, Genevieve says she has learnt a lot during her time as Miss Tanzania.
    'I must admit that it was really difficult to convince my parents ... to go for the contest due to the negative publicity that some of the beauties had generated in the recent past. I assured [my father] that I would not change my behaviour and I have proved that', she says. According to the tall beauty, she enjoyed her time as holder of Miss Tanzania crown, calling on parents to allow their daughters to contest in the competition. (Owere, 2011)

While many of these judgments unfold within discourses of what it means to be 'Tanzanian', religion also factors into understandings of contestants' *utovu wa nidhamu*. Stambach (2000b) describes the attitude of Tanzanian born-again Christians – a fast-growing segment of the population – towards young women and modern dress and cosmetics. According to Stambach, born-again Christians consider young women who dress in contemporary fashions as morally distracted, needing instead to devote that attention to God. And for many Muslims, Western female clothing has long signaled indecency and dishonor. Speaking of 1970s Zanzibar, Burgess (2002) says that:

If the Muslim veil awarded women virtue, distance, and integrity, what could have been more of an affront to these traditional dress codes than the miniskirt? This was construed as a piece of highly eroticized public display, a violation of norms of bodily decorum. (Burgess, 2002: 302)

Such associations with Western fashions linger, and Zanzibar is the only political unit within Tanzania that does not send delegates to the national competition. According to a Zanzibari minister, 'We don't need beauty parades in Zanzibar and Pemba ... after all that does not augur well with our culture and history' (*Daily Times*, 2003). Yet less conservative Muslim women hailing from Dar es Salaam and other mainland coastal cities with significant Muslim populations regularly compete, so it is usually more traditionalism or social conservatism, rather than religion *per se*, that constructs opposition to pageant participation.

For many Tanzanians, beauty contestants and queens represent the epitome of menace posed by urban single women. Women's competing in pageants signals a quest for independence and their use of their bodies in competition further sexualizes these efforts. But while citizens lambaste contestants and the entire pageant enterprise, many are simultaneously obsessed with them. In part, it is a pop cultural fascination, or a lurid obsession, but for a significant portion of citizens it is also a matter of national pride. While people may question contestants' morality, they nonetheless seek a representative who is suitable and respectable, and they express a genuine desire for this representative to perform well at the Miss World competition, much as with sporting competitions (see Chapter 7 and Higgins, 2009). Furthermore, contestants represent what is, to some, a legitimate feminine type, a genuine role model of urban respectability for young women across the country. Pageants and their contestants take place within discourses about the nation, even as they challenge just what that nation and its symbolism are.

Namba Moja or *Namba Nane*: English Figures and African Beauties

By choosing a symbol for the nation in the unambiguous form of a single woman, national beauty pageants across the world bring to the surface personal and societal ambivalence about modernity, progress, tradition, femininity, ethnicity and global integration, all within the framework of a firmly felt yet never stagnant national identity. Banet-Weiser (1999) describes this tension:

Within the site of the beauty pageant, the opportunity arises for the presentation – or the invention – of a national crisis and also for the possibility of containment or conversion. This promise, or these conditions of possibility, are offered through the vehicle of the female body, which comes to 'represent' nationalism in terms of a particular image of femininity. This same female body, however, also 'represents' the nation in terms of a particular culture or community. (Banet-Weiser, 1999: 7)

Stemming from these national pageants, alternative pageants emerge which seek to promote other local femininities that may stand in contrast to that which is celebrated in prominent national pageants. For example, Miss Chinese Jamaica seeks to legitimize the Chinese community as truly Jamaican while also ethnically and culturally unique (Barnes, 1994); Guatemala's Maya Queen (McAllister, 1996) celebrates the feminine beauty of its inhabitants' indigenous origins; Besnier (2002) describes transgendered beauty pageants that strive to celebrate and normalize that marginalized community in Tonga.

In Tanzania, the very visible presence of the Miss Tanzania beauty pageant has encouraged the establishment of other beauty pageants that celebrate different types of beauty and values. Higgins (2009) discusses several Afro-centric pageants which promote 'authentic', 'traditional' or 'local' femininity, such as Miss Bantu, Miss Swahili and Jimama. All of these pageants encourage or require Tanzanian clothing, such as the draping *kanga*, the Swahili language, and untreated skin and hair. Furthermore, it is an 'African' or 'Swahili' body type they look for, in particular a large and shapely rear end. Leseth (2004) discusses the local category of *namba nane* ('number eight') bodies, those which are curved like a number eight and linked with the Afro-centric identities of women who might participate in a Miss Bantu contest. In contrast, she describes *namba moja* ('number one') figures, straight and thin like the number one, iconic of Western-oriented identities and often used to describe beauty contestants participating in the Miss Tanzania circuit. While a *namba nane* body is often understood in terms of 'traditional' values and knowledge, versus the modern values and knowledge of *namba moja* bodies, *namba nane* women can also be urban and modern; indeed, alternative pageants, like the mainstream pageants that are the focus of this study, are exclusively held in cities and draw upon an urban population as participants, judges and audiences. *Namba moja* and *namba nane* body types thus bring up a different dichotomy of Tanzanian femininity, not necessarily of rural versus urban but rather of African versus Western. These contrastive types are sometimes also described with the dichotomous terms *African beauty* and *English figure* (Leseth, 2004; see also Leseth, 2010). The terms reveal a certain bias, in the sense that *African beauty* is a positive valuation of the entire person, while *English figure* is at best a neutral description, focusing exclusively on the woman's physicality, as defined most clearly by its foreignness.

While Afro-centric contests and their supporters in Tanzania sometimes claim superior cultural authenticity over national pageants, Higgins argues that discussion surrounding these pageants more often than not concerns a 'multivocal and multimodal representation of womanhood' (Higgins, 2009: 90). Higgins describes a newspaper cartoon depicting a fictional beauty contest that pits the two types of beauties against each other. The women are to compete with their distinct skill sets and knowledge bases, and the MC finally declares it a tie. This judgment conveys the idea that there is room for more than one understanding of Tanzanian femininity.

Yet Higgins (2009) points out that, unlike Miss Bantu and similar pageants, the Miss Tanzania pageants offer far more in terms of material reward and, as I will argue in subsequent chapters, are conceived by contestants as an avenue for escape. Although competing in the Miss Tanzania circuit threatens young women with the label of prostitute, it also lures them with cash, prizes and mobility far exceeding what is offered by alternative, Afro-centric pageants. Indeed, what pageants such as Miss Swahili offer in respectability, Miss Tanzania offers in shillings, a fact that, for many young women, makes the sacrifice of reputation well worth it. Thus, though these are indeed 'multivocal and multimodal' conceptions of Tanzanian femininity, they are not equal conceptions. Rather, it is the Western-oriented *namba moja*, English figure, *dada wa mjini* type that is rewarded materially and whose very value is considered to be its foreign-ness, its appeal extending beyond a purely local setting. And as *namba moja* figures are also linked with the English language, while *namba nane* figures are linked with Swahili, we return to observations made by Blommaert (2010) regarding the sociolinguistics of mobility; semiotic resources – including, but not limited to, language – are nested within scalar hierarchies that make some of these resources more broadly valued, and more broadly rewarded, than others.

Conclusion

The tensions around pageants reflect rapidly changing urban life in Tanzania. Ambivalence about the relative benefits of capitalism and socialism, about government control of cultural aspects of social and economic life, about changing gender roles and about the balance between Tanzanian 'tradition' and Western influence, coupled with ever-increasing class differences, are part and parcel of day-to-day life in Tanzanian cities. While debate swirls on newspaper pages and on citizens' lips about the relevance of pageants and the character of its participants, the selection of a beauty queen offers a temporary resolution to these ambiguities, presenting a concrete example of what is good, modern and moral about Tanzania's young urban women.

Of course, it is clear that Nyerere's sentiment many years ago about the unsuitability of women to the city, as echoed in the negative reportage of contestants' *utovu wa nidhamu*, remains true for many Tanzanians today. Creighton and Omari have argued that women in Tanzania 'are seen ... as embodying tradition and having a particular responsibility for preserving its more desirable features' (Creighton & Omari, 2000: 11).[11] Indeed, the anxieties felt by 'anti-mini militants' (Ivaska, 2002) in the 1960s and voiced by those opposed to pageants today manifest a fear that, through their embrace of modernity, women may corrode Tanzanian culture and, in particular, the power structures that benefit the patriarchal status quo.

But within pageants, young women are presented as hope for the future, important not for their role in *preserving* aspects of traditional, rural culture but in *changing* Tanzanian society, as educators, role models and shepherds of future generations, towards a 'modern' sensibility. In the pageant spectacles themselves, this role is naturalized largely through enactments of 'banal nationalism' (Billig, 1995), making implicitly evident to spectators that what they are observing indeed has something important to do with the nation, even in the pageant's 'foreign' packaging and its position as a rung on the Miss World ladder. Such banal nationalism helps construct pageants as a national endeavor, the mission of which is, in part, to choose a woman who represents *all* Tanzanian citizens, even in her dissimilarity to *most* Tanzanians.

This perhaps surprising faith in these young women – given the context overviewed in this chapter – is indeed significant, and I argue that it is not completely restricted to the confines of the pageant spectacle. Rather, in part, it is linked with a more broadly held conviction among some that young women, at least in their capacity as likely future child-bearers and child-rearers, hold the keys to Tanzania's future (see Chapter 5). Furthermore, in light of the many young women seeking independent lives in the city, beauty queens can serve as another example of the decades-old quest for 'urban respectability' for Tanzanian women (Ivaska, 2002) and, to be sure, are role models for many young women today. At the very least, contestants themselves have some faith in their own abilities to effect change in their roles as beauty queens, even if it is only in constructing modern and independent lives for themselves. In the next two chapters, I discuss the centrality of Swahili and English – as idealizations, as registers and as resources – in determinations of contestants' worthiness as crown-holders; in formulations of human value as produced by educational, socioeconomic and geographic difference; and in attempts at realizing the life changes that these young women seek.

Notes

(1) On the other hand, national identity has often been understood within scholarly inquiry in masculine terms (e.g. Anderson, 1983; Hobsbawm, 1990).

(2) Data from the preceding sentence and following paragraph were collected from participant rosters and photographs of contestants posted on www.pageantopolis.com and www.globalbeauties.com, two comprehensive websites on worldwide beauty pageant history and lore.

(3) The American delegate to both Miss World and Miss Universe is called Miss USA. Miss America is a domestic competition that does not participate in an international franchise.

(4) Only the semi-autonomous and Muslim island of Zanzibar does not participate.

(5) The centrally located city of Dodoma is officially the nation's capital, and it is home to key governmental and administrative activities. However, as a much smaller and less connected city, it in no way competes with Dar es Salaam in terms of its national and international prominence in matters of arts, finance, education, business, diplomacy, tourism and the like.

(6) The ban of miniskirts as well as of other kinds of clothing and products was put into effect by the Youth League of the ruling party, TANU, under the name 'Operation *Vijana*' (*vijana* is Swahili for 'youths') (Ivaska, 2002).

(7) The controversial and titillating reputation of the beach wear competition can be seen in following excerpt, just one of scores of similar references in the media: 'walionekana kushangiliwa sana kila walipopita jukwaani kuonesha mavazi yao likiwemo lile vazi maarufu la ufukweni na la ubunifu na vazi la jioni' ('they [the audience] cheered wildly each time they [the contestants] walked on stage to show their outfits, the famous beach wear outfit, the creative wear and the evening dress' (*Kiu*, 14–17 July 2003).

(8) However, it is not accurate to see *ngoma* exclusively as subjugating women. Askew (2002) points out that *ngoma* have been used by women to resist their domination and to participate, through dance, in political life, and Geiger (1987) discusses the role of all-women *ngoma* societies in empowering women to express political and nationalist principles.

(9) Vodacom, a pan-African mobile telecommunications company, was the sponsor of the Miss Tanzania pageant for several years.

(10) The phrase 'AIDS kills' has come under international critique in recent years for its reliance, likely ineffective, on fear tactics to curb the spread of the disease (e.g. Olatunji & Robbin, 2011). Ironically, contestants' use of the phrase 'AIDS kills' to place themselves within a global cosmopolitics could actually signal, to a particular cadre of well informed spectators, their ignorance of such matters.

(11) Lewinson offers a similar observation that 'feminine actions embodied aspects of "traditional" Tanzanian culture which the state wished to preserve' (Lewinson, 2000: 271).

4 'I Am Very Good at Expressing Myself, Especially in English': The Packaging of Privilege in the Making of Tanzanian Beauty Queens

Salha answered well the question with great confidence in English and made thousands of beauty pageant fans to cheer her. The move made fans to predict to her that she would be the top queen in the contest.
Newspaper report describing the performance of winning contestant Salha Israel at the Miss Tanzania 2011 competition, in *The Citizen* (12 September 2011)

In this chapter I discuss the ways in which successful contestants emerge, through clusters of linguistic and non-linguistic behaviors, as Tanzanian beauty queens. Beauty pageants are events in which value judgments of all kinds are central to determining a winner. Judgments about how she should dress, smile and wave, about the color and condition of her skin, teeth and hair, about the shape of her body and the way she moves it, all go into decisions about who should be crowned. These decisions, while often informed by international standards, are never appropriated wholesale but instead must make local sense to contestants, judges and audiences alike. Perhaps few things are more local – yet often more taken for granted – than ideas about how a contestant should speak on stage and which languages or registers are appropriate for the context. Not only should a beauty queen look a certain way, but she should speak a certain way as well.

While, on the surface, these events are lighthearted forms of entertainment, Tanzanian beauty pageants, like similar competitions worldwide, reveal, through their orientation to self-conscious performance and appraisal, manifold ways in which semiotic behavior is taken to stand for differentially valued types of people within broader swathes of society (Besnier, 2002; Ballerino Cohen *et al.*, 1996b; Schulz, 2000). In the present case, the patterns of self-presentation and evaluation that unfold within these events reflect cultural beliefs about language and other symbolic material as indices of personal worth, especially as reflections of urbanity, education and elite status.

Tanzanian beauty pageants exist within a multi-tiered hierarchy (Chapter 2), which structures not only the advancement of contestants through the competitive process, but which also regiments the people who compete, observe, judge and win at these events. Although discourses and official policy concerning the desirable qualities of a successful beauty queen remain constant across levels and cities, the instantiation of these qualities varies significantly between Dar es Salaam and its satellites. In other words, the materiality of what constitutes a beauty queen changes as contestants move up the pageant hierarchy and towards Dar es Salaam. But rather than a case of provincial contestants attempting, yet ultimately failing, to achieve a national standard more fully realized by contestants in Dar es Salaam, I argue that provincial contestants engage in a vernacular cosmopolitanism, while often Dar es Salaam contestants orient around a more globally informed cosmopolitan style and sensibility. It is only when the two kinds of contestants come together that these different orientations are revealed as unequal rather than parallel, at least in terms of facilitating opportunity.

In particular, this chapter will highlight the emergent nature of what it means to 'speak a language' (Blommaert et al., 2005; see Chapters 1 and 2) for contestants who are able to manipulate fragmentary English knowledge in order to present themselves in the most positive light. From this perspective, the very notion of 'bilingualism' or 'multilingualism' should be reframed into one of *truncated multilingualism*, so that 'full competence in different languages' is not the concern, but rather 'linguistic competencies which are organized topically, on the basis of domains or specific activities' (Blommaert et al., 2005: 199). This view helps to recast what has been labeled, for example, 'broken English' as a viable mode of communication within certain contexts. In the present case, these 'truncated' registers serve as an index of education and as evidence of being worthy of wearing the crown.

But there are limits to such tactics as one attempts to rise through the ranks, when contestants find that not only their linguistic but also their style choices mark them as unrefined. While contestants across the country enjoy pageants in part as a creative engagement with the aesthetics of the broader world, the ways in which they are evaluated reflect the realities of a steeply unequal society, in which access to opportunity, privilege and symbolic capital – of both the linguistic and the non-linguistic varieties – is concentrated within a very small geographic and social space.

'And the Winner Is...': Linking Linguistic with Non-Linguistic Signs in Contestant Evaluation

Three orienting concepts

To understand the ways in which contestants are differentially evaluated, I will employ three interconnected concepts – metasemiotic scheme, indexical (non)-congruence and social domain – put forth by Agha (2007). These tools point to several aspects of pageant evaluation and success: how audiences and judges link linguistic and non-linguistic signs as belonging together and as standing for types of persons; how audience reactions guide the researcher to ideologies about language and other culturally held beliefs about personhood; and how different sets of competitors, audiences and judges interpret norms for onstage behavior in different ways. More generally, these concepts help shape an understanding of the patterning of pageant outcomes as a reflex of broadly held beliefs about language, education and status in urban Tanzania.

The first concept, metasemiotic scheme, concerns the fact that, in social interactions, we link linguistic signs and behaviors with a wide variety of non-linguistic ones, as comparable and belonging together. Agha (2007: 23) gives an example of a very codified metasemiotic scheme, that of the Javanese aristocracy, for whom a specific and intricate set of restrictions guides a range of cross-modal behaviors. From hand movements and manner of dress to language (the famous Javanese speech levels), diverse behaviors have, when used together, comparable value in their ability to index the aristocratic status of the speaker.

So what happens when a sign (an outfit, a gesture, a word, a pronunciation) does not fit with the unfolding metasemiotic scheme? Agha (2007) describes this as 'indexical non-congruence', the second of the concepts informing this analysis. Indexical non-congruence refers to a mismatch between co-occurring signs otherwise understood to be part of a particular metasemiotic scheme. While indexical congruence is pre-supposed, the unmarked sign combination for a particular context, indexical non-congruence can either be performed to create particular effects, or it can be inadvertent. In the present case, pageant judges and audiences indicate their interpretation of elements of contestants' onstage behavior as congruent or non-congruent, and hence whether the contestant herself is a suitable crown-holder.

The third concept is that of 'social domain' (Agha, 2007). The interpretation that a particular sign is non-congruent depends, crucially, on the social domain of evaluators. Linguistic registers exist only insofar as there is a group of people – a social domain – who regularly recognize a specific bundle of features as having a particular social value. The notion of social domain is thus related to the seminal yet fluid notion of speech community (e.g. Bloomfield, 1935; Dorian, 1982; Labov, 1972). Both concepts hinge on an understanding of language and linguistic signs as only meaningful insofar as there are particular groups of people who share or coordinate modes of communication and interpretation. Yet the notion of social domain is distinct, in a few ways. First, Agha uses the term 'social domain' to pertain primarily to register formation, as he considers registers to be central in constituting social life (Agha, 2007: 183). In contrast, a speech community can be governed by any sociolinguistic variation. Second, as overviewed in Duranti (1997) and Morgan (2004), the term 'speech community' can have a wide variety of meanings, some of which may not reflect the fluidity and reflexivity that are key to Agha's formulation, instead sometimes construing community boundaries, as well as register formations themselves, as at least somewhat pre-determined and rigid.[1] Third, while 'speech community' traditionally includes speakers and evaluators in the same frame (e.g. Labov, 1966), 'social domain' distinctly refers to evaluators, while 'social range' refers to sign users, a distinction thus emphasizing the lack of complete overlap in language use and evaluation (Agha, 2007: 121). Finally, although proponents of the ethnography of communication, the approach that popularized and modernized the concept of speech community, acknowledged long ago that non-linguistic signs are often linked with linguistic ones and are central in interpreting language use (e.g. Hymes, 1964), the notion of speech community does not readily accommodate that fact. Social domain, in contrast, not only concerns register formation but also the formation and interpretation of metasemiotic schemes:

> A register's tokens are never experienced in isolation during discourse; they are encountered under conditions of textuality (co-occurrence) with other signs – both linguistic and non-linguistic signs – that form a significant context, or co-text, for the construal of the token uttered. (Agha, 2007: 148)

Language and non-language are thus inextricably linked into meaningful social units.

These analytic tools support an understanding of language ideologies as overt, that is, as observable by the analyst in one way or another (Agha, 2007). Sometimes these observations come in explicit form, such as in interviews and other meta-commentaries. In other cases, these observations come in implicit form, such as in the patterning of languages, codes, grammatical structures or other symbolic material, across settings, persons and places. Critically, this perspective recognizes the fact that language users are able to identify or characterize some aspects of language more readily than others (Silverstein, 1993) and directs us away from the polarization of ideologies as either implicit or explicit, a tension overviewed by Woolard (1989).

Audiences and indexical non-congruence

While contestants are pageants' *raison d'être*, the events are made up of ensemble casts that include masters of ceremonies, performers, special guests and judges. Crucial in shaping the events are audiences. Folklore and performance studies (e.g. Duranti & Brenneis, 1986; Hymes, 1975) and work on conversational structure (e.g. Goodwin, 1986) have demonstrated the importance of the role of the audience in co-constructing the events they observe or listen to. Scholarship on African oral and popular culture has likewise highlighted the role of audiences as a key constituent of perform-ances (Barber, 1997; Finnegan, 2007).

In the present case, audiences – enthusiastic, loud and honest, often with the aid of inexpensive beer and wine – contribute greatly to the events. These are not crowds gathered to appreciate high art or some other serious spectacle, and they are at least as entertained by mistakes as by flawless per-formances. Audiences may react to the physicality of contestants, showing approval or disapproval of a dress, hairstyle or walk. At other times, they react to the content of contestants' speeches, an example of which will be given in Chapter 5. From time to time, audiences also give feedback on the linguistic form of contestants' speeches. If a contestant speaks for too long, audiences heckle her off the stage. If she mumbles or makes certain kinds of grammatical mistakes, they may sneer. And when audiences react, contest-ants adjust their own behavior; they are trained to pause and smile when audiences cheer approvingly, but in the case of negative reactions they may become rattled, continuing to tumble into disgrace.

Several studies (e.g. Errington, 2000; Haney, 2003) have explored ways in which audiences offer the analyst insight into local conceptions of what is good, bad, beautiful, ignorant and so forth, and how these judgments are linked with perceptions about language use. Here, the notion of indexical non-congruence (Agha, 2007) is useful in examining how audiences evince these local conceptions. Furthermore, any determination of non-congruence is necessarily linked to the social domain of evaluators (Agha, 2007). In this chapter, we will see that what one audience – or set of judges – as a social domain, finds laudable, another will find laughable. What is congruent and felicitous for one group is non-congruent, an utter embarrassment, for another. Furthermore, metasemiotic schemes are ordered hierarchically, both geographically and socially, and both of these hierarchies will reach their pinnacle in Dar es Salaam. What counts as good or worthy or competent in one contest becomes embarrassing, out of place and subject to ridicule in another, in ways that reflect more general social categories.

Metasemiotic Scheme for Tanzanian Beauty Queens

The Miss Tanzania committee requires that competitors at all levels meet some basic standards. They must be 24 years old or younger, childless, unmarried and have completed at least Form 4 education (approximately grade 10). Furthermore, and following international standards for beauty queens, they strongly recommend that contestants be tall (at least 5 feet 9 inches, or 175.3 centimeters) and slim, though pageant organizers frequently stress that *anyone* is able to compete. Other features are also highly valued and the focus of a good deal of attention, in particular, healthy teeth and clear skin – without blemishes or signs of chemically lightening. Though not usually mentioned, naturally light skin and long, straight(ened) hair are also strongly preferred.

In reality, these standards and preferences are often relaxed at the local level in order to have a sufficient number of competitors, because stigmatization of the events and of their participants can deter many potential participants. Some requirements are more overlooked than others; for example, while shorter and darker contestants appear (and succeed) with relative frequency, one rarely sees heavy contestants. Although contestants with known children or husbands will be immediately disqualified,[2] the educational requirement is regularly overlooked. In fact, pageant organizers comment that the biggest challenge is finding contestants who have completed Form 4, and some admit to relaxing this rule informally in order to have enough participants.

In addition to official and prominent preferences and requirements, other qualities emerged in offstage interviews as central to a Tanzanian beauty contestant's success. Contestants stressed that they should dress stylishly, but not overly provocatively or garishly. They repeatedly emphasized to me the importance of walking like a model, or *kujyata*, a leggy gait that at once conveys both nonchalance and poise on the catwalk. It is a walk they practice in preparing for competition, but which many also try to employ in their daily comings and goings to signal their modern, cosmopolitan orientation (see Leseth, 2010). But more than any other feature, contestants stress the importance of 'confidence' – expressed with the English word even when speaking Swahili – as manifested through smiling, eye contact with judges and the audience, and standing up straight. According to one mid-level contestant:

> Uwe na ufahamu na uwe na *confidence* yaani usiogope na uwe mchangamfu ... huwezi kufika Miss Tanzania ukiwa na ule uogauoga.... [You have to have awareness and *confidence*. That is, don't be afraid and be charming ... you cannot become Miss Tanzania if you are nervous....]

Confidence is considered to be a quality gained as a girl becomes a woman; while shyness is valued in a girl, it is not valued in a woman, who should carry herself with self-assuredness (Taylor, 2008). This sentiment is realized in the pageant data; a contestant who appears to lack confidence, by slouching, hanging her head or walking poorly, will stand little chance of success and might be the recipient of lively audience critique.

Contestants also speak in these competitions and so, bundled with expectations for dress, body and comportment, are ones for language use. While, in offstage interviews, contestants and pageant organizers did not spontaneously mention language as a central quality of Miss Tanzania, when pressed a bit they did mention aspects of language and communication that were relevant. As with their physicality, contestants should exhibit confidence in their speech, but without showing pride. This means speaking loudly but not too loudly, for long enough but not too long, and stating one's accomplishments without bragging. In addition, participants emphasized the importance of using a *fasaha* or 'pure' register on stage, a topic about which I will elaborate below.

Bundled together, these linguistic and non-linguistic features index a worthy Tanzanian beauty queen. Some features, such as height, are less potent and unlikely to draw overt attention or make a difference for pageant success. But when a contestant appears to lack confidence, wears an inappropriate outfit or has an unflattering walk, she quickly garners audience ridicule and stands little chance of being selected by the judges as the winner. Language has, perhaps more than any other characteristic, the ability to make or break a contestant's success, and it is to this topic that I now turn.

Maksi Ni Moja ('The Score is the Same'): Swahili and English as Equal?

Swahili and English are the official languages of all Tanzanian beauty pageants, as they are the official languages of the country. Yet, like most Tanzanians, the majority of contestants are not able to speak fluent English, despite having achieved a relatively high level of education in English-medium schools (see Chapters 2 and 5). But even though they may not be fluent in English, it is not true that contestants do not know any English at all. As overviewed in Chapter 2, other registers involving English are in broad circulation in Tanzania. Contestants, like urban youth across the country, devour American music and devote themselves to memorizing the lyrics, which are published in entertainment newspapers. These popular newspapers themselves often employ a wide range of English language material, as do street and business signs that are part and parcel of the urban landscape (Blommaert, 2005; Higgins, 2009). This familiarity with English supplements whatever elements of standard English contestants have acquired through their many years of exposure in school. Ultimately, it is this knowledge of English, accessed through formal and informal contexts, that, while in some estimations not amounting to fluency or 'complete' knowledge, allows many contestants to win pageants.

Contestants have one or two opportunities to speak on stage, with their first chance coming near the beginning of the competition, during the 'creative wear' (*vazi la ubunifu*) segment. During this segment, each contestant walks the catwalk dressed in an outfit of original design and delivers a brief self-introduction, including name, age, educational background and hobbies (see Chapters 3 and 5). Following the 'beach wear' (*vazi la ufukweni*) and 'evening wear' (*vazi la jioni*) segments and interspersed with guest performances, the top five finalists are announced and have a second chance to speak, during the question-and-answer (Q&A) session. In this segment, each contestant responds to a question on a pertinent social issue, such as AIDS, education or poverty, while still dressed in an evening gown. The master of ceremonies (MC) begins each question by asking the contestant about language use: 'Ungependa kutumia lugha gani, Kiswahili au Kiingereza?' ('Which language would you like to use, Swahili or English?') The contestant responds in either English or Swahili and then the MC asks the actual question in whichever language the contestant chooses.

This metalinguistic query of 'Swahili or English' reflects two aspects of language ideology in Tanzania. On the one hand, the 'Swahili or English' question highlights the public invisibility of local ethnic languages, in the way that Spitulnik (1998: 166) points to for language use at Radio Zambia, where 'the code [or codes] chosen indexes the codes not chosen'. As I will overview in Chapter 6, despite Tanzania's tremendous linguistic diversity, there was not a single instance of a local ethnic language used by any pageant participant across the fieldwork data, except for infrequent artistic contexts. While there are certainly some practical reasons for this absence, there is also an ideological level to the explanation, whereby these languages have been constructed as codes of the home and village (Blommaert, 1999a), ideologically removed from public life through the semiotic process of erasure (Irvine & Gal, 2000). Since this ideology is naturalized, it is only inadvertently that the 'Swahili or English' question rules out these languages as possible mediums of response.

The 'Swahili or English' question serves also to highlight a second aspect of language ideology in Tanzania, according to which, in official discourse, Swahili and English are configured in an egalitarian relationship, a kind of 'separate but equal' framework, within the public sphere. In this framework, the two languages are constructed as parallel choices of identical value, either of which will serve contestants well. Indeed, while Swahili is the national language and bears some of the symbolic load that such a status carries (see Chapter 2), English and Swahili together are Tanzania's co-official languages and are represented in official discourse as equivalent: the national website is available in English or Swahili, passports are translated into both languages, as are certain official documents; road signs are often written in both languages. Of course, this perspective on translatable equivalencies hinges on a purely denotational view of language, leaving most matters of semiosis aside (Silverstein, 2003b).

In off-stage interviews, pageant participants reflected this ideology and insisted that a contestant's choice between Swahili and English is personal and bears no consequence.[3] Rather, they say, what matters in the eyes of the judges is that one speaks well, whichever language one chooses. Grace, a regional-level contestant, put it this way:

> Pia Kiingereza unaruhusiwa na Kiswahili unaruhusiwa; jinsi mwenyewe utakavyopenda. Kwa sababu wanasema kama utajibu Kiingereza lakini mtu mwingine ana uzoefu zaidi wa kujibu kwa Kiswahili, anaweza kujibu maswali vizuri. Na mtu mwingine anaweza kuongea Kiingereza akajibu vizuri maswali hii inatokana na jinsi mtu mwenyewe alivyo.
> [You are allowed to speak English or Swahili; it depends on how you prefer to express yourself. Because they say that if you answer in English but another person has more experience answering in Swahili, then she [the latter] can answer the questions well. And [if] another person can speak English then she answers the questions well, so it depends on the person.]

This contestant indicates that one should choose which language to use based on *uzoefu* ('experience') and that a contestant is better off speaking Swahili well than English poorly. Competing in the same contest, Esther offered a similar opinion:

It doesn't matter [which language you speak]. You may speak in English, but you haven't answered the question well. Or someone speaking Swahili and she answers the questions well.

Later in the interview, Esther explained that since the two languages are 'equal', she prefers to use English, with which she is more comfortable. On the other hand, Gloria used the same equality reasoning, which she encapsulated with the expression *maksi ni moja* ('the score is the same') to explain her choice of Swahili:

> Ukiongea Kiswahili na ukiongea Kiingereza maksi ni moja kwa hiyo ni uamuzi wako uongee Kiswahili au English. Lakini ukiongea Kiingereza maksi ni ile ile, kwa hiyo mimi napenda sana kuongea Kiswahili.
> [If you speak Swahili or English the score is the same, so it is your choice to speak in Swahili or English. But since if you speak English the score is alike, I really prefer to speak Swahili.]

A few contestants did express the belief that one's choice of language might have an influence on the judges or, more specifically, that speaking English might serve a contestant better than Swahili. One was actually a former contestant who made it into the top ten at the Miss Tanzania contest the year before. She framed the issue around the Miss World contest:

> Yes, I think it's good [to speak English], because when you go to Miss World, a lot of them, they speak in English. Swahili is not, *yaani, wachache – wengi hawajui Kiswahili, lakini Kiingereza* [that is to say, few – lots of people don't know Swahili, whereas English], at least they understand English.

For this contestant, English matters only insofar as it can facilitate communication at Miss World, where hardly anyone speaks Swahili. Another contestant also brought up the language issue vis-à-vis Miss World, but instead argued that 'I don't think of that [English matters], because even if you use Swahili [at Miss World], there are translators'. Both of these contestants constructed their responses exclusively in terms of the referential function of language – the comprehensibility of Swahili and English to non-Tanzanians.

Only one contestant, who grew up in Kenya, gave an explanation involving a non-referential function of language:

> [English is] something a little bit different. You know, people always speak Kiswahili, so when you speak in English, it's a little bit … different.

Coming from Kenya, where access to English is less steeply hierarchical than in Tanzania, she perhaps had experienced the positive effects of being a strong speaker of a standard variety of English in Tanzania.

In fact, the *maksi ni moja* ('the score is the same') vision of linguistic equality professed by most contestants (as well as by pageant organizers) and implicitly communicated in the 'Swahili or English' question beginning each Q&A session is quite illusory. Although most *contestants* used Swahili on stage – 108 out of 153 recorded instances of onstage speaking by contestants were in Swahili – *winners* overwhelmingly spoke English. In the eight pageants considered in this chapter, six first-place finishers spoke English in their self-introductions. In contrast, English was used by only two second-, third- and fourth-place finishers, respectively. Likewise, six of eight pageant winners spoke English in their Q&A sessions, as opposed to only three second- and third-place finishers, and two fourth-place finishers. The Kenyan contestant, thus, was on to something when she remarked that English carries more weight by being 'something a little bit ... different'; while her explanation is not the whole story, it does hint at the ideological, rather than purely denotational, level of language use in Tanzania, and perhaps her status as an outsider gave her this fresh perspective. Such preference becomes even stronger when rising through the pageant ranks. In newspaper coverage of the just-crowned Miss Tanzania 2009, a reporter commented on the winner's choice of language:

> Miriam, who triumphed over 28 other aspirants for the ultimate prize and acknowledgement in beauty glory, also becomes the second Miss Tanzania to answer a question in Kiswahili since the event was introduced in 1994. The first one was 1994 victor Aina Maeda in 1994. Subsequent winners in the interim had answered questions in English. (Ogot, 2009)

This report gives a longitudinal glance at language use at the pageant pinnacle, where only two of the 16 Miss Tanzania winners between 1994 and 2009 chose to speak Swahili rather than English in delivering their responses. This statistic is a stark indication that English and Swahili are not equal, and that the vision of *maksi ni moja* does not hold up. For ambitious beauty pageant contestants, English is undeniably better.

Audience reactions lend further support to the observation that language choice is, despite discourses to the contrary, a value-laden aspect of the competition and that English sets the speaker apart from her Swahili-speaking opponents. When a contestant announces in the Q&A segment that she will use English, audiences often react positively by cheering the contestant on. In contrast, a contestant who announces her intention to speak Swahili receives no audience response, as that language is expected and unremarkable.

The competing language ideologies seen here – one of language equality and the other of English superiority – are historically contingent as well as subject to reinterpretation and revision (cf. Spitulnik, 1998). As overviewed in Chapter 2, Swahili remains emblematic of Tanzanian unity and distinctiveness (see also Chapter 6), and the MC's 'English or Swahili' question posed to contestants seeks to construct Swahili as a language that can stand alongside English in all sorts of formal, public and high-level communicative settings. Furthermore, the official sanctioning of Swahili in these pageants, which take part in a transnational rather than purely local hierarchy of events, is of particular symbolic importance. Pageant participants' expression of the equality between these two languages conveys, then, an entrenched ideology of the goodness and viability of Swahili vis-à-vis English.

Yet this ideology of equality is at odds with other findings from this study and, ultimately, the professed equality remains elusive. Not only do contestants go to great lengths to use English rather than Swahili on stage, but judges and audiences alike often reward them for it. It is well documented that English today has come to represent not colonial oppression but rather education, success and opportunity, as well as a connection to the rest of East Africa and the world and is, as such, highly coveted as a commodity and a symbolic resource (see Chapter 2). While Swahili dominates in daily communication and in many public fora, and remains a symbol of nationhood, in practice it has become largely sidelined in favor of some variety of English in elite institutions such as education, as well as in globalized or cosmopolitan settings such as beauty pageants.

Ufasaha: Language Purity, Non-Standard English and Pageant Success

While denying the advantage of speaking English over Swahili, contestants state that what matters instead is that one speak *well*, whichever language one chooses. Contestants expressed repeatedly the importance of their speaking during the competitions in a way that is free of *kuchanganya* ('mixing') – that is, speaking Swahili without English, or English without Swahili. Like standing up straight and smiling, this was an aspect of their performance of which contestants were very aware. A successful contestant explained her view of why one should avoid mixing:

Unatakiwa ukiongea Kiswahili uongee Kiswahili fasaha kinachoeleweka na kama ukiongea Kiingereza uongee Kiingereza fasaha kinachoeleka....
[If you want to speak Swahili you have to speak a pure Swahili that is understandable, and if you speak English you have to speak pure English that is understandable...]

This contestant's choice of terminology to describe this way of speaking is significant. Instead of using the adjective *sanifu* ('standard'), she describes the target register as *fasaha* ('[stylistically] pure'; *ufasaha*, 'purity of language' or 'eloquence'). Although the two terms are similar, *sanifu* emphasizes normativity over purity, while *fasaha* emphasizes purity over normativity. As is characteristic of pure registers cross-linguistically (e.g. Álvarez-Cáccamo, 1993; Kroskrity, 1998), achieving this purity is considered difficult and Blommaert (1992: 61) notes that even for university faculty, 'Speaking "pure" Swahili seems to require special attention and effort'. In conversational settings, speaking Swahili without substantial English borrowings is not only difficult but also sometimes undesirable (see Higgins, 2007). Indeed, contestants' casual speech is a typically a register of fairly standard Swahili sprinkled with idiosyncratic English loans, as in these off-stage interview excerpts:

Kwa hiyo ndio maana nikaenda kushiriki na kweli nikashinda nikawa the winner.
[That's why I just went and tried and I won, I was the winner.]

Nilikuwa kwenye camp nilijua nitashinda kwa hiyo nilikuwa yaani na confidence....
[When I was at the camp I knew that I would win, I mean I had confidence....]

Kuwa mrembo unatakiwa uwe na experience usiogope.
[To be a beauty queen you must have experience, you can't be afraid.]

It is a register that, in its hybridity and relative standardness, reflects contestants' urbanity and the fact that they have obtained a certain level of education, affording them both standard Swahili as well as a broad knowledge of the English lexicon. In fact, contestants stress the difficulty of *fasaha* Swahili, as it differs from how they usually speak, and they signal this difficulty in choosing their onstage language variety:

yaani ndio naweza kuexpress zaidi kama nikiongea kwa Kiswahili ... kwa hiyo saa nyingine watu wanauliza swali halafu nikaanza kutafuta maneno yaani kutengeneza sentesi iwe <u>straight</u> halafu niongee nisiwe nimechanganya vitu. Lakini kwa Kiingereza niko <u>free</u> zaidi na ninaweza kujieleza vizuri zaidi

[that is, I can <u>express</u> myself more [in English] than if I speak in Swahili [during pageants] …. That's why sometimes people ask me questions then I start to look for the words, I mean, to make a sentence be <u>straight</u> [without codeswitching], then I speak and hope I don't mix things up. But with English I am more <u>free</u> and I can express myself much better.]

This contestant, who was not a fluent English speaker, articulated her choice of English as one that allows her to be 'more free'. This explanation addresses the difficulty of speaking pure Swahili at the same time that it reproduces a school-based ideology that speaking 'purely' is a matter of referential transparency. Yet her statement also likely masks more strategic reasons for choosing that language, a largely unarticulated knowledge among pageant-savvy contestants that speaking English gives one a competitive advantage.

Overall, contestants are adept at this definition of 'speaking well', with instances of codeswitching, in English or Swahili, quite rare on stage. Indeed, in most cases, winning contestants produce a wonderfully appropriate and indexically powerful, even if non-standard and non-fluent, register of English. Yet this interpretation of 'speaking well' is very distinct from a normative understanding of 'standard' or 'fluent' *sanifu* speech. Because questions for the Q&A session are frequently distributed in advance, many contestants rely on memorization in order to deliver their responses in English. Contestants are also able to memorize their self-introductions, and the result of both is often English statements with grammatical and lexical oddities, delivered in a stilted style. Usually, however, this linguistic performance works; contestants who choose to use English onstage consistently win over those who speak Swahili.

The following contestant response at a regional-level pageant in the northern city of Arusha illustrates the successful use of English by someone who, as confirmed by my interviews and interactions, was not a fluent English speaker. The contestant had already won a regional competition and would go on to win this zonal-level event, and would also place highly at the Miss Tanzania pageant later in the season. The contestant was asked, 'If you could change anything in your life, what would it be and why? Explain.' She answered:

Thank you for your good question. If I have to change anything in my life, I would have like to change the position of being sexually abused. Sexually abused are the most people who are forgot in the society and those people are even mostly abandoned in our society. They just see them like they are not the normal person, they just leave them like they don't have the real courage, but I want the society to see that they are the people like others and what happened in their lives, and what happened in their lives, they didn't plan it. It just happened like a mistake. So I would like the society to take them, to give them the courage, to make them see that what happened, it happened, to them to make them focus on their future and forget the past. That is all to understand. Thank you so much.

The response is full of grammatical, lexical and pragmatic oddities, yet the contestant delivered it in a poised and confident manner, and it 'counted' as a good response as evinced by the audience's enthusiastic cheers. No one seemed bothered by its deviation from standard English, or by the fact that the contestant forced her prepared English, cosmopolitan response about sexual abuse to fit the question she was asked. What the contestant did right, linguistically, was to speak purely. Here, as in other competitions, it is the focus on *fasaha* rather than *sanifu* speech that led audiences and judges to interpret many English responses as good. Especially at lower-level, provincial competitions, judges – typically local businesspeople and politicians – may not be fluent English speakers and the same can be said of audiences. Often there are two MCs, one of whom has the role of translating English into Swahili for the majority who do not understand English. To these people, a contestant who seems to speak English well, with the right trappings and no obvious Swahili mixing, has spoken English well. English then becomes as much a tool for indexing the speaker as the kind of person who speaks English – a learned elite – as for communicating referential content.

But using English does not miraculously lead one to victory regardless of all other factors. Competing against the contestant above were two others who spoke English, both more fluently than the contestant who won. Of these two, one was eliminated before making it into the top five. Although her English was strong, she made the mistake of speaking for far too long in her self-introduction, until she was booed off the stage with 'Stop, stop, *basi* ['enough']!' This mistake marked the contestant as arrogant and lacking in poise, and hence unqualified to advance. The second English speaker made it into the final five but suffered from the opposite affliction; while her English was good, focus groups that I conducted during my fieldwork commented on her lack of confidence, signified by the way she tilted her head to the side and down when she spoke, rather than holding it high. She also wore an outlandish outfit during the creative wear segment that prompted giggles from the audience.

The winning contestant had other qualifications: she was tall, trim, light-skinned and poised, and she delivered a politically trendy Q&A response addressing women's rights. She did not, however, stand out from other, Swahili-speaking contestants, apart from her use of English. When considering the patterns of success across pageants, then, it is not the case that English use is a free ticket to victory; rather, it gives one a substantial edge. However, at higher levels of competition, it may become a requisite for the crown.

The Pageant Hierarchy and Rising Standards of Spontaneity and Purity

In Chapter 3, I overviewed the pageant hierarchy and illustrated the fact that Dar es Salaam is treated like a higher-level unit than its actual status. This special categorization of Dar es Salaam reflects the city's strong influence on the pageant world, a result of the fact that it is, more than just the nation's biggest city, the epicenter of the country, where Tanzania's social, cultural and economic capital is concentrated.[4] Many people believe that contestants from 'Dar' are preferred as Miss Tanzania, a suspicion confirmed by the fact that 13 of the 19 winners of the national crown, between 1994 and 2012, were indeed from the capital city. What most people do not recognize, however, is that it is not a blind loyalty to the capital city and its inhabitants that leads to this partiality. Rather, it is a preference for an elite, globally oriented contestant who manifests her privileged upbringing through a range of bundled symbolic behaviors, and such people and resources are much more prevalent in Dar es Salaam than elsewhere in the country. The city is home to an impressive number of public and private secondary and post-secondary institutions and to the country's flagship university. It is also the center of national and international business, diplomacy and aid, and a launch-pad for tourists heading to destinations across the country and region. More of its residents are mobile, cosmopolitan and accepting of beauty pageants, leading to a larger pool of qualified contestants. It is not the case at all that every Dar-based competitor is elite, but rather that there are more such competitors in Dar than anywhere else.

What is more, even within Dar es Salaam, there is a perceived hierarchy among its three districts, with Ilala thought to be particularly productive in terms of Miss Tanzania crown-holders, followed by Kinondoni and then Temeke. Though not completely accurate – five Dar winners have hailed from Ilala, five from Kinondoni and three from Temeke – this ranked understanding of Dar's districts reflects a widespread conceptual mapping of the city, according to which Ilala, or 'downtown Dar', is the very center of the city's wealth, the most connected to international networks of finance, fashion and mobility. Even Miss Tanzania 2009, Miriam Gerald Martin, from the western city of Mwanza, told reporters upon her crowing, 'I am very happy to win this title, which, much as I was earnestly dreaming of, seemed a far-fetched dream. I feared Miss Ilala contestants mostly' (Ogot, 2009).

Throughout Dar, it is not just that competition is stiffer; each event as a whole becomes more elite and status-conscious. Judges in Dar, and especially at the national competition, are also more prominent people, and often include the chief executives of corporations, senior government ministers and popular entertainers. The audience members are wealthier, as the exorbitant admission prices at the Miss Tanzania event (10 times the ticket price – Tsh5000, or about US$5 – of lower-level competitions) select for a more elite group. At most competitions a contestant's shortcomings in standard English are not noticed and local versions of international fashions tend to appeal to spectators. But in Dar es Salaam, and especially at the Miss Tanzania competition, the expectations for language and dress shift to a more international model.

Consider the following passage, taken from a prestigious zonal-level competition in Dar es Salaam. The excerpt begins just after the contestant has announced her intention to use English for her response. M, master of ceremonies; C, contestant; A, audience; A1, individual audience member.

```
1   M:  Aiysha/ If you were given a chance to change one thing in
2       your life, what would it be and why/explain//
3   C:  Thank you judge for your good question/
4       If I were given the chance .. to change one thing in my life,
5       I would like to change- .. I would like to be .. uh .. Miss World,
6       because .. =no Tanzanian lady ... at <2> at <2> at this moment
7   A:                =HHHHHHHHHHHHHHHHHHHHHHHHHHHHHHHHH
8   C:  == =achieved the Miss World/ and that would give=me enable ..
9   A:      =HHHHHHHHHHHHHHhhhhhhhhhhhhhhhhhh=
10  C:  ==to .. fight with HIV AIDS {[ey'dis]} = in ( )//
11  A1:                          =AIDS{[ey'dis]}HHHH
12      hoo = hoo hoo hoo =
13  A:      =HHHHHHH =HHHHHHH=HHHHHHhhhhhhhhhh
14  M:          = Asante sana =
                'Thank you very much'
15      <3>
16  C:  [turns to walk off stage, normal procedure following response]
```

In this excerpt, there are two points at which the audience erupts into derisive laughter, and both of these concern the contestant's perceived lack of linguistic expertise. The first eruption (lines 7, 9) is triggered by the contestant's attempt to reframe the question – 'If you were given a chance to change one thing in your life, what would it be and why?' – into another one for which she had likely already rehearsed the answer. This shift occurs after the contestant repeats the question (line 4) at the beginning of the response, but in line 5 stops herself: 'I would like to change-' is then reworked into 'I would like to be .. uh ..'. The contestant has thus clumsily recast the question to which she is responding into another common pageant question, something like 'What would you do if you were to become Miss World?' The pageant-savvy audience sees through her flimsy effort to insert a memorized response to a different question into the answer slot. In attempting to present herself as a fluent speaker of standard English, the contestant has instead, through her inability to answer spontaneously, indexed herself as a linguistic phony. Recall, however, that it is a strategy that worked for the contestant in the Arusha competition described above.

Just after the laughter and hooting dissipate (line 9) the contestant makes another mistake, this time shattering the illusion of *ufasaha* that is so important to onstage speech. In line 10, she pronounces 'AIDS' with an epenthetic vowel – [ey'diz] – upon which one member of the audience mimics the pronunciation and then falls into a fit of laughter and derisive noises (lines 11, 12), obscuring the contestant's last words. The isolated reaction is immediately followed by a more general audience outburst of uproarious laughter and hoots (line 13). The MC mercifully draws the segment to a close and the contestant walks off stage according to custom.

At first glance, the reaction to this pronunciation is surprising. Throughout this response, grammatical oddities, such as 'give me enable' (line 8) and 'fight with' (line 10 – a calque from Swahili *kupigana na*, 'to fight with') – as well as awkward pauses (e.g. lines 4 and 5), passed without comment from the audience, while the mispronunciation of AIDS was hugely salient to the crowd. This particular feature – an interconsonantal epenthetic [i] – is a very common, typically unremarkable characteristic of English spoken in East Africa, resulting from the preference to avoid consonant clusters in Swahili. In fact, in this same contest, another contestant made a similar 'mistake', pronouncing 'guests' as [gɛst'iz]. As we might expect, the pronunciation received no reaction at all. So why, then, did [ey'diz], but not [gɛst'iz], nor other grammatical peculiarities, evoke such a strong reaction? The reason is that, unlike 'guests', 'AIDS' (and HIV/AIDS) functioned here as a register shibboleth (Silverstein, 2003b). It is a word that is frequently used in urban Swahili, in lieu of the standard Swahili word *UKIMWI*, and even when speaking Swahili, the term is normally pronounced approximately as it is in standard English – [eydz] not [ey'diz]. In mispronouncing the word, the contestant broke the frame of *ufasaha* not by lexical but rather by phonetic interference, by importing a Swahili pronunciation into a particularly salient English word. Furthermore, AIDS refers not only to an immense social problem, but also to a politically fashionable social agenda. Talking openly about AIDS is progressive in Tanzania and stands in contrast to the more traditional approach of suppressing discussion of it (Setel, 1999). The contestant's failure to produce the accepted pronunciation of this well known word thus both foregrounded to the audience her discomfort with English and also suggested to them that her interest in the disease was disingenuous (had it been authentic, surely she would be able to say the word right!).

Both audience outbursts, then, were fueled by the same comedic ineptitude and fraud. The contestant tried to dupe the crowd into believing, through use of English, that she was a member of an educated and progressive elite, but instead she succeeded only in indexing herself as the opposite: averagely under-educated, not to mention foolish. It is an interpretation that is really Dar-specific, as these same kinds of mistake occur frequently at pageants throughout the country yet go completely unnoticed.

'Does She Keep Her Toothpicks in There?' The Transformation from Beauty Queen to Bumpkin in Tanzania's Pageant Circuit

In the previous section, we saw an example of a less elite contestant ridiculed by members of a largely elite audience. From the same city and perhaps even the same neighborhood as the majority of the audience, the contestant's truncated English register indexed her as a phony, at least to some of the more educated spectators. But we can also consider what happens to provincial contestants when they arrive in Dar for the national competition. Any time a contestant advances from a local competition to a higher-level event, she faces more competition in terms of having more challengers who are of the same caliber as herself. But once a winner advances from the zonal competition to the Miss Tanzania event, she often encounters a different kind of competitor altogether. Young women living on the fringes of small, insular cities find themselves competing next to those who have traveled outside of Tanzania and East Africa, who have attended international English language schools, who are university students studying law or business, or who are the children of established members of a wealthy and well connected urban elite. The experiences, skills and worldview of many competitors from Dar are often very different from those of contestants hailing from the provinces, and these differences inform the qualities of a desirable contestant. While sometimes a provincial contestant does well at Miss Tanzania, young women from outside of Dar often feel sorely out of place. How they dress and fix their hair, how they move, smile and speak, all are subject to reinterpretation at the national event, a process which reconstrues what had been successful traits as, instead, indexical of lack of sophistication, education, style and know-how.

For example, contestants in the provinces and in Dar es Salaam often have distinct means of securing competition outfits and these methods are themselves indexical of crown-worthiness. During the creative wear segment of the competition, contestants often mention who designed their outfit as part of their self-introductions. Outside of Dar es Salaam, the designer is nearly always themselves. The fact that a contestant designed her own outfit, rather than relying on the creativity of a tailor or a family member, is a source of pride and signals her creative abilities and awareness of cosmopolitan fashions. Those who do not design their outfit often omit this information from their opening remarks. In contrast, it is very common in Dar es Salaam for contestants to commission a dress from a local designer and to declare the, typically one-word, name of the designer during their self-introduction. Compare the following two self-introductions, the first from a mid-level contest in Arusha, and the second from a mid-level contest in Dar:

> Habarini za jioni mabibi na mabwana. Jina langu naitwa Rachel Joel. Nina umri wa miaka ishirini. Napendelea kusoma vitabu. Vazi hili nimelibuni mwenyewe. Ni Miss Tanga. Asanteni.
> [Good evening ladies and gentlemen. My name is Rachel Joel. I am 20 years old. I enjoy reading books. I designed this outfit myself. I am Miss Tanga. Thank you.]

> Good evening ladies and gentlemen. My name is Mary Samson. I am 21 years old. My hobbies are reading, exercising and meeting new people. My dress was designed by Diana. In the future I would like to be a sociologist. Thank you.

In addition to delivering a sophisticated, English-language speech, the Dar-based contestant gives the name of her designer, Diana. It does not matter whether spectators are familiar with the designer; name-dropping serves the purpose, along with other signs, of signaling the contestant as elite, fashionable and in-the-know.

Yet certain designers, at the highest levels of competition in Dar, are indeed renowned among contestants, judges and pageant-savvy spectators, and contestants who wear such designers' creations often win the competition. Tanzanian designer Mustafa Hassanali is the most sought-after designer for the evening gown segment of the event, after he designed the dress of the Miss Tanzania winner in 1999. Several winners since then have worn his creations during the evening wear segment and wearing a Hassanali gown is an immediate sign to fellow competitors that a contestant is a serious candidate. Furthermore, Hassanali's evening gowns are typically innovative, as his designs are oriented towards the international, high-fashion scene. Often they are sari-inspired designs, or they may include motifs inspired by ethnic dress but played out on an *haute-couture* canvas (Figure 4.1). These gowns include luxurious draping, multiple fabrics and asymmetric lines, dresses the likes of which are not seen in pageants outside the capital. Hassanali, like other well known Tanzanian fashion designers, are almost exclusively based in Dar es Salaam, and their designs are out of reach both financially and geographically to provincial contestants. The provincial contestants competing at the Miss Tanzania competition had

Figure 4.1 Evening gown by Tanzanian designer Mustafa Hassanali

not heard of him, and they repeatedly described the Hassanali worn by a particular finalist with phrases such as *halivutii* ('it is not attractive') and *si kitu maalum* ('it's nothing special').

Contestants competing at lower-level competitions acquire their evening gowns through a variety of means. Often, a primary pageant sponsor will be a wedding gown outfitter that donates or rents for a small fee formal attire to the contestants or the pageant organizers. Some contestants will have a dress custom-made by a tailor, which can be itself a sign of prosperity and taste. These dresses are standard, floor-length gowns, elegant and modern but not cutting-edge or innovative from an international fashion perspective; they are often in a fabric bedazzled with bright sequins or giving the effect of bead-work. Shoes are also a focal point. In lower-level pageants dress shoes often either are *mitumba* (secondhand clothing)[5] or are borrowed or rented from a pageant sponsor or a friend. While always in good condition and reasonably stylish, it is not uncommon to see young women wearing shoes a size or two too big or small. I never saw such compromise at lower-level Dar pageants, where contestants are not necessarily wealthier but have access to different ideas and a wider variety of products.

At the national pageant, such geographical differences in fashion access and preferences sometimes become apparent. A contestant who had been successful in her hometown might recycle certain elements of her winning performance at the national event, both because it had brought her success and because it will save her money and effort. She may, for example, wear the same 'creative wear' or 'evening wear' outfit when competing at the national competition that she had worn at home, with the assumption that the vast majority of the audience will not know that she has already worn that outfit. In one stunning instance, a regional winner showed up at the national event wearing the homemade, brightly colored butterfly outfit, replete with wings and antennae, that was locally interpreted as creative and well crafted, and that certainly helped in her win back home in Mwanza (Figure 4.2). But because pageant-savvy contestants from Dar es Salaam commission fashion-forward outfits by renowned designers, the audience at the Miss Tanzania competition just a few weeks later viewed her creation as girlish, inappropriately theatrical and unsophisticated, and erupted into derisive hoots and shouts of *Toka!* ('Leave!') upon her entrance on stage. Having been nearly laughed off stage, this contestant had no chance of winning.

Perhaps more than clothing, hairstyle selection is dictated by regional and class preferences more than by access to material resources. Young women across the country put great stock in getting their hair done and choose styles based on current fashion, occasion, cost and practicality. Within

MSHIRIKI Miss Tanzania 2003, Manka Mushi, akipita na vazi la ubunifu.

Figure 4.2 Homemade creative wear outfit (from *Lete Raha*, 7–13 September 2003)

pageants across the country, hair is virtually always chemically relaxed, and is often extra given length and volume with weaves or hairpieces. Hair color is usually natural or sometimes subtly enhanced, but is almost never a boldly artificial color. Braids are nearly nonexistent at these events. For special occasions, Tanzanian women often choose styles that may last only a couple of days, their very ephemerality contributing to their allure (see Weiss, 2002, for the contrast between women's short-lived hairstyles and men's seemingly perduring and effortless cuts). Such coiffures are also favored by many contestants. One of these special-occasion styles popular in and out of pageants is the *bomba* ('pipe'), an up-do that involves relaxing the hair, curling it, then teasing and positioning the upper portion of the hair on the top of the head into a bulbous swoosh. The swoosh extends up above the crown of the head before being attached lower at the back, thus creating impressive height and volume. Sometimes, the massive curl is shaped instead into a vertically positioned roll or cylinder, with the top of the roll also extending above the crown. Other contestants choose to wear their hair long and straight, or in a simple bun, or, on occasion, in an elaborately sculpted design stacked high on top of the head.

Yet a marked divergence is apparent between the hairstyles chosen by contestants in the provinces and those from Dar. In Dar, it is unusual to see the *bomba* and extremely rare to see an intricately molded vertical sculpture. Instead, contestants from Dar overwhelming prefer to wear their hair long, past their shoulders, and either completely straight or with soft, flowing curls. Some wear their hair partially up, with tendrils falling down, or in tight buns, perhaps with a hairpiece for volume at the back. On the whole, the styles from Dar are more subtle and ostensibly simpler, and more in keeping with international, Western (even white), fashions in hair design. Similarly, internationally popular hair styles not generally worn locally find their way into Dar es Salaam pageants; in a recent year, the winner of another, competing national competition had a shaved head,[6] a style that is worn across the country by schoolgirls but not by most stylish young women. It is associated with innocence and frugality, as it costs little in time or money to execute or maintain, and it is not considered to be alluring to men (see discussion in Taylor, 2008). Yet this hairstyle, familiar in the international fashion world for being worn by very successful models of African origin such as Sudan's Alek Wek, has come to be seen by some in Dar es Salaam as globally stylish. Nonetheless, on the street in Arusha, I once heard two fashionable young women in a café ponder sardonically whether the stylish young woman with a shorn head standing close to them had forgotten her wig at home.[7] While trend-setting in Dar, this hairstyle's allure has not caught on across the country.

Like clothing, provincial contestants' hairstyles are also often immediate indices to Dar audiences of their lack of sophistication. In one striking case at the Miss Tanzania competition, a popular provincial runner-up wore her hair styled in an almost foot-high architectural design, extraordinarily rigid and shiny with carefully scaffolded swirls and loops, similar to but even more elaborate than the one she wore at her home pageant. During the group opening dance, giggles could be heard among certain members of the audience. Then when this contestant took the stage by herself for her self-introduction, the snickers became louder, and several spectators offered berating comments, including, 'This is not the bush' and 'Does she keep her toothpicks in there?'[8] Both of these statements point to the inappropriateness and lack of refinement of the hairdo from the point of view of this audience. Not actually a hairstyle one would typically see in 'the bush', the critiques highlight the common view among Dar es Salaam natives that anywhere else in the country is nowhere (Higgins, 2007). Although people in Dar es Salaam might also wear such a coiffure, the audience was aware of the international standards of the event; such a hairstyle would not travel well, so to speak, and furthermore is not one that would typically be worn by an educated Dar es Salaam elite.

Young women who reach the pageant pinnacle from their regional pageants arrive in Dar es Salaam proud of their achievements. Yet with at least two weeks of group training before the competition, living and establishing relationships with fellow contestants in a 'camp' hotel, many provincial contestants learn quickly the inadequacies of their style and dress, not to mention their language. Soon they realize they are seen as *washamba* ('country bumpkins'), their all-important confidence dashed. Without confidence, they are already at a great disadvantage, in addition to whatever linguistic or fashion non-congruencies they may exhibit in competition.

Yet, with clothing as well as with hairstyles, it is not the case that provincial contestants simply fail in trying to replicate a Dar es Salaam-based standard, or that Dar-based contestants put forth a better version of what is seen at lower-level competitions. Rather, in many cases, what wins in Dar es Salaam, and especially at the national event, is different in kind from that in the hinterland. While the general ways in which a winning contestant is described remain static from the regional events to the capital, and in large part derive from international pageant standards, the instantiation of the metasemiotic scheme differs between these two scales. Rather than purely parallel, the two modes of interpretation are, ultimately, hierarchical, because a contestant from outside of Dar, bringing with her a provincial habitus, has little chance of the life-changing success which fuels her desire to participant in the pageants to begin with.

'I am Very Good at Expressing Myself, Especially in English': The Humiliation of a Linguistic Phony

As discussed above, the hierarchies evident in the pageant circuit are not, however, just spatial, but also reflect class differences that characterize access to signs of elite upbringing and cosmopolitan orientation. While such signs are concentrated in Dar es Salaam, it is of course not the case that everyone in Dar has equal access to such resources. The final set of examples depicts a dramatic event that took place during the Q&A segment of the 2003 Miss Tanzania competition in Dar es Salaam. They illustrate the stratified nature of language use and evaluation, the high value placed on English and the lengths to which speakers will go to present themselves as English speakers. They also bring home the idea that language use is critical in these pageants, even surpassing a contestant's physical beauty in importance.

The incident is centered around Nargis Mohammed,[9] a top-five contestant who was already well known for starring in a popular music video.[10] She had earlier in the season been crowned Miss Ilala 2003, a Dar es Salaam title bearing the highest profile of all the sub-national competitions. She was loved by Tanzanians and was widely believed to be the contest's front-runner. Many attributed the fact that, in the end, she did not secure the crown to her failure to perform well linguistically. From the beginning of the exclusive event, Nargis was the picture of pageant success. Cheers erupted from the audience each time she appeared on stage with her striking confidence and warm smile. After being named in the top five, Nargis was called on stage for her Q&A. Dressed in a sparkling, spaghetti-strapped, midnight-blue evening gown, hair pulled into a loose bun garnished stylishly with a giant blue flower, she sat in the designated chair and bantered with the interviewer, in Swahili, with an ease unmatched by her competitors. It seemed to many a foregone conclusion that Nargis Mohammed would become Miss Tanzania later that night.

Following her announcement, met with cheers, that she would answer her question in English, the interviewer, a former Miss Tanzania herself, asked Nargis, 'In the recent budget, Tanzania has embarked on campaign [sic] to remove poverty. Tell us, in your view, what should be done to remove the poverty'.[11] In the following passage, one can see the contestant's repeated and ultimately unsuccessful attempts to establish and regain a verbal foothold in what was clearly a memorized speech, given in a language with which she was deeply uncomfortable. Asterisks indicate each time the contestant restarts her answer. C, contestant; A, audience; M, master of ceremonies:

```
1   C:   Thank you for the question// Good evening ladies and gentlemen/
2        First of all .. it has to be clear to the mind of people ... that ...
3        poverty is not just about not having money/ but it's all about ..
4        lack of food, shelter, social isolation =
5   A:                                      =xxxxxx
6   C:                                              ==to the
7        access- social isolation, to the access of- =
8   A:                                      =xxxxx
9   C:                                              ==to the access
10       of health services and security, powerlessness, and
11       hopelessness//
12       If we empower our people with capital services, soc- eh social
13       s- social services, human services, we have no doubt to fight/
14       we have no- .. sorry/ sorry/ sorry/=
```

```
15 A:                              =HHHHHHHHHHHHHHHHH
16    HHHHHHHHHHHHHHHHH=HHHHHHHHHHHHHHHHHHHHH
17 M:                              =It's OK/ We need your silence/
18        =We need your silence//=
19 A:  == =HHHHHHHHHHHHH=HHHHHHHHHhhhhhhhhhhhhhh
20*C:  First of all … first of all .. the people has to know that .. poverty
21     is not all about not having money/=
22 A:                              =HHHHHHHHHHhhhhhhhhhh
23 C:  ==but it's all about lack of food, shelter um social isolation,
24     access to health services … um=
25 A:                          =HHHHHHHHHHHHHHHHHHH
26    HHHHHHHH=HHHHHHHHHHHHHHHHHHH=HHHHHHHH
27 M:                    = Samahani tunaomba utulivu wenu/=
                         'Sorry we ask for your calm'
28 A:  ==HHHHHHHHHHHHHHHHHH=HHHHHHHHHHHHHHHHHH
29     = [music comes in to cue ending] =
30 M:  = Tunaomba utulivu wenu ili mshiriki aweze kujibu swali lake /
         'We need your calm so the contestant can answer her question'
31 A:  ==hhhhhhhhhhhhhhhhhhhhh=hhhhhhhhhh
32 M:                          =Nargis, can you go on?
33*C:  <3> First of all =
34 A:                  =HHHHHHHHHHHHHHHHHHHHHHHHHHHHHH
35 C:              =it has to be clear to the mind of people that
36     poverty is not all about not having money/ but it's all about
37     lack of food, shelter, clothing, and .. lack of social isolation,
38     access … to soc- to health services/ Thank you//
39 A:  ==HHHHHHHHHHHHHHHHHHHHHHHHHHHHHHHHHHHHHHH
40     [music cued, contestant stands up and is escorted off stage]
```

In this passage, Nargis struggles from the start to deliver her prepared answer. While she manages to get the farthest in her first attempt, she shows signs of confusion as early as line 2, where she pauses markedly after *people* and then again after the next word, *that*. In line 3, she pauses again following *about* but then is received by a wave of approving applause (line 5), based on the politically chic content of her response. It is this positive reaction, though, that distracts her and triggers her first significant trouble (line 7), in what turns out to be *to the access of health services…* (lines 9–10). Nargis continues briefly on track, but then in line 14 she breaks the frame of the Q&A by acknowledging her confusion with *Sorry, sorry, sorry*.

This gaffe triggers several seconds of unbridled cacophony, during which the former Miss Tanzania in charge of the session calms down the audience.

Nargis resumes the Q&A frame and starts speaking again, this time with her trademark smile and confidence gone. By the end of the second line of the contestant's reprise (line 21), the audience realizes that Nargis has simply restarted, virtually word for word, the answer she began in her first attempt. The contestant struggles through the noise and humiliation, but by the time Nargis reaches line 24, the screams of laughter and rolls of applause are deafening, and the contestant stops once again.

Eventually, the former Miss Tanzania tries yet again to calm the audience down (line 27). Her use of Swahili rather than the agreed-upon English of the Q&A frame emphasizes the severity of the circumstances; she must speak Swahili to ensure comprehension and to assert authority. Although the music is cued to end the segment (line 29), the former Miss Tanzania nonetheless offers Nargis another shot at completing her answer (line 32: *Nargis, can you go on?*), highlighting a disparity between the producers' and the former Miss Tanzania's appraisals of what should happen next.

Following a significant pause that seems to indicate her uncertainty about continuing, Nargis resumes her response again (line 33). As in the second attempt, Nargis reproduces her speech virtually word for word from the beginning, even repeating a mistake: *access to health services* (line 38), a phrase she struggled with in her first attempt as well (line 7), and the same phrase at which she abandoned her second attempt (line 24). Finally, with the crowd out of control, Nargis gives up with a closing *Thank you*, clearly not having finished (compare with lines 10–13) and she swiftly leaves the stage. The MCs then briefly address the fiasco: *That was a very hard round*, and *Most of the people – if you were up here–. That's competition, and that's the way things go*. Following several entertainment segments and special awards, Nargis received third place in the competition.

In the days following the event, the media covered the incident extensively and ferociously. Newspaper reports commented that while Nargis had been the front-runner, it was her failure to speak well that cost her first place:

Nargis aliyekuwa anapewa nafasi kubwa ya kushinda, aliangushwa na uwezo mdogo wa kujibu maswali kwa ufasaha. Mara nyingi, alionekana mwenye wasiwasi mkubwa, akishikwa na kigugumizi na pengine akitumia muda mwingi kufikiria namna ya kujibu. (*Dimba*, 7–13 September 2003)
[Nargis, who was given a strong chance of winning, was knocked down by her limited ability to answer the questions eloquently (*kwa ufasaha*). Many times she seemed very nervous, stammering and sometimes using too much time to arrive at a kind of answer.]

In the following passage, a journalist reports Nargis's own perception of 'why she failed to answer the question':

Akizungumzia kushindwa kwake kujibu swali katika mashindano ya Miss Tanzania, mrembo huyo anaeleza kuwa hata yeye mwenyewe anashindwa kuelezwa ni kitu gani hasa kilichomfanya ashindwe. 'Kwa kweli mpaka sasa siamini kama kweli nilishindwa kujieleza kiasi kile. Mimi ni mzuri sana katika kujieleza hasa kwa Kiingereza, lakini sijui ni kwa nini nilishindwa,' anaeleza msanii huyo. Anapinga maoni ya baadhi ya watu kwamba alikuwa amekariri jibu la swali lile na ndiyo sababu hata aliporudia mara tatu, bado hakuweza kufika mwisho wa sentensi yake. 'Sikuwa nimekariri, hivi wewe unaweza kukariri maswali sita?...' (*Mwanamke*, 18–24 September 2003)
[When talking about her failure to answer the question in the Miss Tanzania competition, the beauty explains that even she herself does not understand the reason that made her fail. 'I still cannot believe it is true that I failed to express myself that much. I am very good at expressing myself, especially in English, but I really don't know why I failed,' explains the artist. She disagrees with some people's opinions that she was reciting the answer and that that was the reason why even when she repeated it three times she still was not able to reach the end of her sentence. 'I was not reciting it, can you recite six questions?']

In this report, Nargis inadvertently confirms both the significance of English in these competitions and the likelihood that it was due to her inexperience with English that she did not succeed in delivering her answer: 'Mimi ni mzuri katika kujieleza hasa kwa Kiingereza...' 'I am very good at expressing myself, especially in English...'. Her insistence that it was not due to her insufficient English skills unfortunately implicates just that as the culprit. Furthermore, Nargis offers the rhetorical question 'hivi wewe unaweza kukariri maswali sita' ('Can you recite six questions?') as support for her claim that she did not memorize the answers, but this challenge backfires; she clearly was not able to memorize six questions and answers, a fact that nonetheless did not keep her from trying. Indeed, to the audience, Nargis looked very foolish, not only for having memorized her answer in advance and for having been twice unable to resume the answer at the point where she stopped in the first attempt, but in addition for having made these failures *in English*. Nargis was found out as a linguistic phony, an instance of indexical non-congruence made all the more delightful to the audience because of her celebrity.

PILSNER Ice Miss Tanzania 2003 Sylvia Bahame (katikati) akiwa na mshindi wa pili Doto Nusurupia (kushoto) na Nargis Mohammed baada ya kutangazwa washindi katika ukumbi wa Diamond Jubilee jijini Dar es Salaam jana.

Figure 4.3 Miss Tanzania 2003, Sylvia Bahame, and runners-up (from *Lete Raha*, 7–13 September 2003)

Now let us compare Nargis's response with another, delivered by contestant Sylvia Bahame (Figure 4.3), just minutes before Nargis's speech. At that time, Sylvia was a law student at the University of Dar es Salaam, had the previous month been chosen as Miss Temeke (Dar es Salaam) and by the end of the evening would be crowned the national champion. She was asked, 'Is woman's role different from man's? Explain.' Sylvia, who spent a portion of her education attending English-language international schools in the Middle East, delivered her response in a startlingly fluent, non-Tanzanian variety of English. C, contestant; A, audience.

1   **C**:   Thank you very much/
2   Good evening ladies and gentlemen, judges/
3   I would say that indeed a woman's role in the society is very
4   different from that of a man's role/

5   First of all women are predisposed to bearing children/=
6   **A:**   =xxxxxxx
7   **C:**   Therefore this means that automatically they have certain rights
8   and responsibilities that are different from those of men//
9   Secondly, I would say that women that work have a higher work-
10   load than that of men, because first of all, there's a certain mis-
11   misconception in most societies that women's role is to simply
12   work, cook, and tend to the family, and if this is so, then
13   women who work have their workload doubled//=
14   **A:**   =xxxxxxxxxx
15   **C:**   Therefore at the end of the day they are not fully appreciated/
16   Thank you//

In addition to certain non-local phonological features, such as the American postvocalic[r], Sylvia also used a refined vocabulary, including *predisposed* and *bearing* (line 5) and *misconception* (lines 10–11). She employed with ease expressions such as *if this is so* (line 12), *have their workload doubled* (line 13), and *at the end of the day* (line 15), as well as several syntactically difficult constructions, including *those/that of a man's role/men* (lines 4 and 8). By all accounts, Sylvia spoke a register of English that, in addition to being pure and standard, was also stylishly globalized (and hence highly exportable). It is no coincidence that she won the national crown and would advance to the Miss World competition in China. Her competitor Nargis received, in addition to third place, a local modeling contract.

The events of the Miss Tanzania 2003 pageant gain even more significance when seen in light of the contestants' physical characteristics. Nargis was widely considered by many to be exceptionally attractive, not particularly tall but trim and shapely with a sweet face, whereas Sylvia's appearance included a slightly stocky build and prominent front teeth. One well known pageant organizer described Sylvia to me as 'a bit chunky for Miss Tanzania'. Similarly, newspaper reportage rarely if ever commented on Sylvia's overall attractiveness but instead issued euphemistic descriptions such as 'Her stride, her smile and the gap between her teeth really made her shine' (Dimba, 2003).[12] Sylvia's greatest asset as Miss Tanzania, then, was not her physical attributes but rather her linguistic ones.

Conclusion

The story told here of class and regional hierarchies is not distinct to Tanzania, even if the ways in which these hierarchies are manifested are culturally specific. In her study of Miss India, Dewey describes the fact that contestants insist on their responsibility as a role model to young women across India, who may see them on stage or on television and imagine 'that could be me' (Dewey, 2008: 197). Yet for Dewey, the tensions and contradictions are clear between a 'that could be me' imaginary and the reality that those participating, and especially those selected to advance, are from a small privileged class within a largely poor, agrarian country. Most young Indian women would lack the resources, education and time necessary to compete. As one contestant admitted, 'maybe she is too busy cleaning houses and can't leave her job'; more subtly, class or rural lifestyle means, for many contestants, such women also lack the 'etiquette' and 'mentality' necessary to compete and achieve (Dewey, 2008: 198, 199). Skin color is also at issue, with lighter skin widely valued as a sign of beauty and associated with the northern part of India. Critically, in a huge country with many urban centers, it is only women from Mumbai, Delhi and (to a much lesser extent) Bangalore who were, at least in 2003, invited to participate at the Miss India contest. The symbolic capital valued at these pageants is so highly concentrated in these cities that smaller urban centers in the north, as well as large cities in the south, such as Calcutta, were not canvassed at all. It is symbolic capital that is linked with other kinds of capital inequalities, and the state helps structure this inequality, through differential distribution of infrastructure and resources that has exacerbated regional and class disparities (Pal & Ghosh, 2007).

The case of Miss India is instructive for both its similarities and differences with Miss Tanzania. In Tanzania, a broader segment of society participates than in India; contestants from across the country compete in their own city and regional pageants, with the successful ones making the journey to Dar to vie for the national crown. Even within the Dar city-level pageants, many of the competitors are not particularly elite and, on the whole, most competitors across the country are relatively average urban Tanzanians without notable privilege or wealth. In a nation built on the notion of family and equality (Chapter 3), it is an important ideal in Tanzania that *anyone* can compete and *anyone* can win. Yet the high concentration of symbolic capital in Dar es Salaam parallels that in Mumbai and Delhi, to the extent that, from the point of view of the national pageant enterprise, competitors from elsewhere, as well as those from less elite backgrounds, are likely deemed under-qualified. And as in India, it is, in part, a state-supported inequality, according to which resources for education, health and social services are allocated differentially across regions (Mkenda *et al.*, 2004).

On a local level in Tanzania, the bundled features of a Tanzanian beauty queen, among which some kind of English language ability is critical, signal the kind of urban, educated and independent women they strive to be off stage as well (see Chapter 3). Contestants' creative outfits and hairstyles, as well as their truncated use of English, work together to mark themselves as stylish, educated and cosmopolitan. This set of qualities hence represents for many contestants a positive way of engaging with the world, regardless of where the pageant circuit might or might not take them. The cosmopolitan fashion sense (though somewhat less revealing in daily life than on stage), the English language, the model walk, the confidence, the progressive positions on social issues (Chapter 3) and even the pageant know-how itself together mark a contestant as the kind of woman she hopes to be offstage, a *dada wa mjini* ('city sister') *par excellence* (see Stambach, 2000a).

But these local ways of being do not typically travel well – across horizontal or vertical social space – and their value plummets when on the move. With language, it is specific registers of English which are not only indexical of elite status but are also often necessary for achieving such status. As a set of ideologies, practices and policies, the place of English in Tanzania facilitates the reproduction of dramatic inequalities, inequalities that cut across geographic as well as social space, facilitating or constraining the success of would-be beauty queens, both within and outside pageants (cf. Besnier, 2002). What is more, many of the qualities of a beauty queen, including English, are *packaged* together, in large part because they are *accessed* together. In addition to the city itself, school is a place where students come into contact with the ideas, fashions, tastes, as well as the language, that inform their world-view and give shape to their lives. In Chapter 5, I will discuss the institution of education, which is at once seen as a cure-all but which is also responsible for differentially structuring and distributing the symbolic capital manifested in beauty pageants and reflective of disparity nationwide.

Notes

(1) Duranti, however, defines a speech community as 'the product of the communicative activities engaged in by a given group of people' (Duranti, 1997: 82). According to this formulation, a speech community, rather than pre-existent, is constituted entirely by acts of communication. This definition thus firmly rejects any notion that a speech community is rigidly defined or known a priori.

(2) Though, in a strange twist, Miss Tanzania 2012, Lisa Jensen, was raising three adopted children. Perhaps it is the fact that she did not give birth to them herself that makes her case a viable exception.

(3) Interviews were carried out primarily in Swahili, although codeswitching with English for style or clarification sometimes occurred. On occasion, a contestant would ask to conduct the interview in English for practice, a request which highlights the understanding of English as a commodity (Chapter 1).

(4) Dar es Salaam scores best of all regions in Tanzania on the Human Poverty Index (HPI) and the Human Development Index (HDI), though inequality within the city appears to be on the rise (United Republic of Tanzania, 2002).

(5) *Mitumba* literally means 'loads' or 'bundles', and refers specifically to second-hand clothing imported from Europe and the United States. The term comes from the fact that these clothes arrive at ports in large bails and then are redistributed across the country in smaller bundles. *Mitumba* clothing is appreciated by average Tanzanians for day-to-day as well as special occasion wear, as it offers the wearer a selection and at least a perceived quality not otherwise available new and locally. Second-hand clothing is likewise popular across the continent, as documented, for example, in Hansen's (2000) work on *salaula*, as imported used clothing is called in Zambia.

(6) Flaviana Matata won the first-ever Miss Universe Tanzania competition, in 2007, with a completely shaved head.

(7) See Stambach (1999) for a discussion of a very different set of indexicalities for women's hairstyles in Tanzania some 20 years ago.

(8) These insults were uttered in English by a group of several young Tanzanian women who shared an expensive, $50-a-head table at the Dar es Salaam competition. The women were dressed and groomed in keeping with Western norms for stylish young women and they kept themselves refreshed with bottles of South African red wine. Throughout their conversations they spoke primarily elite, fluent local English, with the occasional Swahili aside. The word 'bush' is particularly noteworthy here, as it can be very offensive in many African Englishes (see, for example, Jackson & Amvela, 2000; Rosati, 2010), as it was certainly intended by these supercilious, privileged young women.

(9) Unlike elsewhere in the volume, contestants' real names are used in this section, for several reasons: the Miss Tanzania event is highly publicized, the events that are described here were subject of extensive public discussion and the two contestants concerned had already or were about to achieve national celebrity.

(10) Nargis played the role of Vicky, a spoiled rich girl who refuses to be with a poor but good man who loves her, in the video of the song 'Zali la Mentali', by one of Tanzania's most renowned hip-hop musicians, Professor Jay.

(11) Note the apparent grammatical oddity of the question, stemming from the lack of an indefinite article. However, this is a common feature of Tanzanian English, and as such would be unremarkable to most spectators.

(12) Translated from the Swahili: 'huku miondoko, tabasamu na mwanya wake vikimzidishia sifa'.

5 'Education is the Key of Life': Contestants as Schoolgirls in Pursuit of an Escape

Kama mwaka jana tulikuwa tuna mrembo wetu mshindi wa tatu
alijipatia course ya hotel management ambayo atapata diploma yake
mwakani…. Kwa hiyo mrembo akijipatia na akishinda anaenda kujipatia
elimu hiyo na inamsaidia yeye kwa maisha yake ya baadaye.
[Last year, our beauty queen third-place winner got a hotel management training
course and she is going to get her diploma next year…. So if a beauty queen wins,
she will go there and get an education, which will help her in her future life.]
Master of ceremonies, city-level competition

Naamini kwamba ni masomo peke yake ndio yatakayoweza kumkomboa mtu
katika maisha yote na hakuna kitu kingine chochote. Vingine vyote vinapita tu
na vitu ambavyo vinaweza kutusaidia kwa namna moja au nyingine lakini hata
kama tukiwa warembo bado tuangaliae je maisha yetu baada urembo ni nini?
[I believe that it is indeed only school which will help a person achieve a
certain lifestyle,[1] and that there isn't anything else at all. All other things are
just passing and are things that can help us in one way or another, but even if
we are beautiful, we still have to think about our life after the beauty.]
Farewell address delivered by Angela Damas, Miss Tanzania 2002

Tanzanian beauty contests are steeped in a local *Zeitgeist* in which the quest for an education is an orienting factor of life. Discourses abound in and around pageants, according to which education is presented as the primary resource for social mobility and the most promising solution to society's and individuals' problems. Pageants are understood as opportunities for contestants to pursue their own education through scholarships, as fora for reiterating the value of education – and, in particular, women's education – as means of uplifting society and as organizations fostering education through outreach.

Education organizes these pageants in more subtle ways as well. Ideologies about the differential value of English and Swahili, as well as

124

ones regarding register purity, are modeled in schools and reappear on the pageant stage. Lessons acquired in school about modes of speaking, learning and manifesting knowledge are likewise exhibited by contestants. Even audiences' and judges' strategies for interacting with and evaluating contestants as suitable for the crown reflect the ways in which teachers and students communicate in the classroom. Indeed, it is the configuration of contestants foremost as schoolgirls that facilitates the ready transfer of school-based language and communication practices to the catwalk.

Together, these education-oriented discourses, ideologies and practices shape in explicit and implicit ways much of what occurs on and around the pageant stage. Referencing the commonly invoked trope of 'education is the key of life', this chapter discusses how contestants and other participants envision education as the most important component of a successful life, of a modern woman and of a Tanzanian beauty queen. Yet, I will demonstrate a mismatch between this social construction of education and the practical realities that schooling actually has to offer, within the context of beauty pageants and beyond. Extreme difficulties in obtaining an education and an improbability of finding work upon graduation (Al-Samarrai & Reilly, 2008; Stambach, 2000a; Vavrus, 2003) shape contestants' lives off stage and mean that they will not themselves reap the benefits of the education they extol on stage. Furthermore, as girls, contestants will have faced particular challenges in obtaining an education, which itself also constructs them as socially dangerous, a status only intensified by competing in these imported events. What is more, as discussed in Chapter 4, the mobilization of a specific set of linguistic skills – often the acquisition of which is understood in Tanzania to be the very purpose of an education – temporarily facilitates pageant success but ultimately fails contestants both on and off stage. Tying these elements together, I will highlight how school-based models of language use are attached with gendered categories of personhood that are themselves associated with modern, Western-style education. Such models circulate outside school walls and inform hierarchically ordered interpretations of contestants, and young women more generally, in variably positive and negative lights.

These regimented evaluations, based on contestants' linguistic and non-linguistic behaviors, are interpreted as stemming from the young women's backgrounds as schoolgirls. In this chapter, the analysis builds on the field of inquiry that Agha has called 'semiosis across encounters', or 'the capacity of linguistic signs to formulate links across semiotic events in ways that yield social formations' in locally recognized ways (Agha, 2005: 4). Contestants and other pageant participants easily, and largely implicitly, plug into school-based models of language use and evaluation, pointing to education, as well as to contestants' alter-identities as schoolgirls. It is a process Silverstein (2005: 9) has called 'type-sourced' interdiscursivity, in which a discursive genre (type) is understood not only to 'be like' another but, indeed, to presuppose the other as its source. Wortham has argued that:

> We cannot fully understand how language constitutes social relations unless we move beyond the lone speech event and attend to domains and trajectories. Even the most sophisticated analyses of linguistic forms, in use, with respect to ideologies, fail to capture how ways of speaking, models of language and social life, and individual identities emerge across events. (Wortham, 2008: 46)

This chapter will thus outline the mobility of educational models of language use and personhood in urban Tanzania from the classroom to the catwalk, as well as from provincial pageants to the national competition and beyond, and how, once mobile, they are also subject to reinterpretation, revision and hierarchical reorganization. In addition, it will show how the lessons learned in and around school serve to frame an understanding of contestants as gendered social actors, shaping their onstage performances as well as audiences' and judges perceptions of them. In so doing, this chapter will also emphasize practical problems in the ideologies, policies and practices of secondary education in Tanzania. At the same time, even if the concrete promises of an education do not materialize, it remains for many contestants and like-minded other young women the single critical ingredient in transforming their lives, in attitude if not in material substance. Indeed, the ideas and world-views accessible through secondary school create a new kind of feminine Tanzanian positionality, one that is largely celebrated in pageants and that these young women find to be a positive force in their lives.

Educational Access and the Dilemma of the Schoolgirl

Discourses in and around Tanzanian beauty pageants frame contestants in terms of their education, or lack thereof, a feature characteristic of many pageants globally (Banet-Weiser, 1999; Johnson, 1996). Most contestants have completed Form 4,[2] the baseline educational requirement for competing, although contestants have been known to falsify diplomas in order to compete. Many contestants have only recently left secondary school and are currently without work, or else are enrolled in one of the many, variably reputable, usually for-profit institutions which lure those who have not been able to continue with secondary school or university.[3]

A small fraction have exceeded the educational requirements and an even smaller number, mostly those competing in Dar es Salaam, are university students.

With a long-standing emphasis on the value of primary education for all (Nyerere, 1967a) and abolition of primary school fees (Vavrus, 2005), Tanzania enjoys relatively high basic literacy and primary enrolment rates, comparable to those in other countries in the region (Ministry of Education, Tanzania, 2008). In contrast, only a fraction of Tanzanians attend, let alone complete, secondary school, with only a 36% gross enrolment ratio (GER) through for the first four years, plummeting to 4% for the last two years (Ministry of Education, Tanzania, 2008). Only 2% of the population aged over 25 has completed secondary school (Al-Samarrai & Reilly, 2008). This situation is due to a variety of factors, including secondary school fees, which, while only about 20,000 Tanzanian shillings (approximately US$15) a year for government schools, are enough to keep many children home (Vavrus, 2005). Also, fewer secondary school positions exist than qualified students, a reality reflecting harsh economic circumstances but also a strategy held over from the colonial era, when it was intended to produce a manageably small cadre of educated African elite (Samoff, 1987). In addition, entry exams are challenging, especially since they are given in English rather than Swahili (Sumra & Rajani, 2006).

While educational access is a challenge for all Tanzanian children, it is even more so for Tanzanian girls. Though girls and boys enjoy near-equal access to primary education (Ministry of Education, 2008), this parity diminishes once students are eligible to enter secondary school. By the time children are old enough to enter Forms 5 and 6, boys are significantly more represented than girls (GER of 5.1 versus 2.9) (Ministry of Education, 2008). Reasons for the gender differential are multiple. Vavrus (2003), based on years of ethnographic fieldwork in the Kilimanjaro region of northern Tanzania, points out that parents are more likely to pay school fees for male children than for female children, having greater hopes for future earnings. Dropping out of school due to financial pressures is common, but boys are more likely to return than are girls. What is more, while both boys and girls seek sponsorship for their studies, for girls, sexual relations or a promise of marriage are often expected in return for such support (Vavrus, 2003; for examples from across the continent, see Bledsoe, 1990; Hansen, 1997). These sexual arrangements can ultimately backfire, due to complications such as unwanted relationships, pregnancy or HIV/AIDS. Stambach (2000a), also reporting on her ethnographic fieldwork in northern Tanzania, describes a variety of social pressures for female secondary school students that may result in lower enrolments. Pregnant girls are forced permanently out of school, either formally or by extreme social pressure. More insidiously, while many secondary schoolgirls talk about their desire for education partly in terms of its capacity to affect their increased independence from men, they at the same time face strong criticism from some members of their community for their pursuit of education, which earns them labels as 'prostitutes' for being too independent and modern. To make matters worse, schoolgirls receive warnings that no one will want to marry a woman with too much education.

It is in this context that young women participating in pageants are understood by Tanzanian society. As current or former secondary students, they have more education than the vast majority of Tanzanians and so are automatically understood as part of a rising middle class. They are also seen as independent, urban, Western-oriented women, lacking respect for traditional authority – all qualities considered to be linked with, even acquired through, their secondary education (Stambach, 2000a; see Chapters 3 and 4). Indeed, it is thought to be their education itself that has led them to compete in pageants.

The widespread understanding of contestants as *malaya* ('prostitutes'), with an *utovu wa nidhamu* ('lack of good behavior') (Chapter 3), parallel judgments made about schoolgirls in general, who are commonly believed to support not only their education but also their perceived desire for stylish clothing by unsanctioned sexual liaisons (Stambach, 2000a; Vavrus, 2005). Furthermore, like schoolgirls, contestants are required to be childless and unmarried, although with both categories of people there is a common assumption that fetuses may have been illegally aborted in order to proceed with their goals (Stambach, 2003). This belief is, for example, alluded to in the headline about a frontrunner for a regional competition,

Miss Arusha, uko wapi ule ujauzito wangu; kama uliutoa niambie, kama ulizaa nionyshe mwanangu. (*Kiu*, 1–3 August 2003)
[Miss Arusha, where is my baby you were pregnant with; if you aborted it tell me, if you gave birth then show me my child.]

Within pageants themselves, the framing of contestants as schoolgirls carries with it contradictory messages. On the one hand, contestants and winners are praised by organizers for their intellect, as in the following:

si uzuri tu na lakini pia na akili yaani *intelligence* jinsi gani wanaweza kuwa na umahiri wa kujibu maswali.
[it's not just beauty, but also intelligence, that is, *intelligence*, how skill-fully they are able to answers the questions.]

MCs and pageant organizers present contestants as shining hopes for Tanzania's future, with pageant themes such as 'Beauty with Progress' reinforcing this message. The winner is seen as someone who will be a local, national or even international goodwill ambassador, promoting pertinent social agendas during her reign, through her informed and articulate beneficence (Chapter 3).

On the other hand, MCs, whose responsibility it is not only to manage the flow of people on and off stage but also to be entertaining (Chapter 6), play with the image of the contestant who has been unable to finish school, as in the following (translated from Swahili):

> We're also sponsored by Arusha Training Institute. This college is located in the Sakina area; they offer hotel management training…. We are going to talk with these ladies and gentlemen in order to get these courses so that our beauty queen after this competition will go there to get an education, even if she is a dumb-ass [*limbwete*]. This is what we're about. So Arusha Training Institute, thank you very much.

The depiction of contestants as lacking intelligence or as failed students resonates as congruent with the audience's understanding of the young women, as they chuckle following the insult. The comment furthermore exemplifies the view that contestants are dropouts, because if they were currently enrolled in secondary school or university, they would not need a scholarship to a hotel management college.

Contestants are willing to face these criticisms, on one level, because these events allow them to engage in a cosmopolitanism that exemplifies the kind of urban, independent and outward-oriented life they seek. On another level, most contestants hope that pageants, like an education, will bring them an escape from a life without visible avenues to opportunity or mobility. They dream that their participation will lead to scholarships, cash prizes, travel or even contacts with influential or international people. Yet, but for a miniscule fraction of contestants whose dreams are realized, contestants are lucky to walk away with a bit of cash or a brief period of local renown, and their dreams of a more permanent escape are almost never secured.

Education is the Key of Life

Like pageants, education also fails to come through with its grand promises. Those who have completed secondary school express anxiety about their ability to find sustaining work and it is widely acknowledged that it is difficult for a person even with a Form 4 education to find a job (Stambach, 2000a; Vavrus, 2003). Yet parents and families make immense sacrifices to secure an education for their children, in the hope that it will improve their own lives and those of their offspring (e.g. Wedin, 2005).

Thus, while problematic, this 'education as panacea' (Vavrus, 2003: 7) or 'schools-to-the-rescue' (Stambach, 2000a: 3) model of education, which holds schooling to be a cure-all, for individuals, families and societies, remains an organizing principle for Tanzanians, as well as for state and international developmental programs working in the country. Here, I call this perspective on education, 'education is the key of life', or *elimu ni ufunguo wa maisha,* based on a commonly heard trope within and outside of pageants.

Discourses hailing 'education is the key of life' abound within the pageants, in comments by MCs, special guests, pageant organizers and, in particular, by contestants. Contestants have one or two opportunities to speak on stage, during which they often craft their statements to foreground education, as either a personal achievement or a social agenda. Educational background is often a key component of contestants' self-introduction, in which they state formulaically their name and provenance, as well as various other pertinent pieces of information (Chapters 3 and 4). Consider the following self-introduction, delivered in English at a regional-level competition in Arusha. C, contestant; A, audience.

1   **C**:   Good evening ladies and gentlemen/
2   My name is Rachel Samson,
3   I'm 20 years old,
4   I have comple- completed my Form 6 education/
5   **A**:   xxxxxxxxxxxxxx
6   **C**:   I enjoying reading and socializing/
7   You're mostly welcome//

Here, the contestant mentions her Form 6 educational background and this provincial audience acknowledges the relative rarity of her achievement through applause. Note also that the contestant delivers her remarks in English, a code which indexes and iconizes the education she has completed, and she goes on to win this regional competition. Compare this with the following self-introduction, delivered at the same event:

1   **C**:   *Habari za jioni mabibi na mabwana/*
            'Good evening ladies and gentlemen'
2   *Jina langu naitwa Pendo Nangale,*
            'My name is Pendo Nangale'

3   *Nina umri wa miaka kumi na nane,*
       'I am 18 years old'
4   *Ni mwanafunzi wa computer Chuo cha MGW/*
       'I am a computer student at MGW school'
5   *Mimi napenda kuogelea,*
       'I like to swim'
6   *na vazi langu la ubunifu nimebuni mwenyewe/*
       'and I designed my creative wear outfit myself'
7   *Karibuni//*
       'Welcome'

In this self-introduction, the contestant mentions her status as a computer student, but she does not include her level of secondary school education, an omission that hints at the probability that she had not completed education beyond Form 4. Through off-stage conversations with this contestant, I learned that she indeed had not completed even Form 3, but instead altered her sister's Form 4 certificate in order to be allowed to compete. Furthermore, the contestant's statement was delivered in Swahili, reinforcing her self-presentation as not highly educated.

In another case that illustrates the centrality of education to perceptions of competitors, a contestant made an unfortunate blunder that caught her in the middle of a lie aimed at aggrandizing her educational background:

1   **C**:   *Habari za jioni mabibi na mabwana/*
             'Good evening ladies and gentlemen'
2   *Kwa jina na itwa Beatrice David,*
             'My name is Beatrice David,'
3   *Nimeitimu kidato cha nne,*
             'I have completed Form 4'
4   *Nasubiri matokeo//*
             'I'm waiting for the results'
5   **A**:   HHHHHHHHHHHHHHHHHH
6   HHHHHHHHHHHHHHHHHHHHHHHHHHHHhhhhhhhhh <11>
7   **C**:   *Nina umri wa miaka kumi na nane,*
             'I am 18 years old'
8   *Ni Miss Manyara,*
             'I am Miss Manyara'
9   *Vazi langu limebuniwa na Gulamali/*
             'My outfit was designed by Gulamali'
10   *Karibuni//*
             'Welcome'

In this humiliating moment, the contestant made the mistake of claiming she was awaiting her results from the national Form 4 examination (line 4). But, as most of the audience knew, examination results had been made public the previous week. Had the contestant actually been awaiting such important news, she would have been well aware that the results had already been released. It was a mistake the audience found riotously funny (line 5), because it not only revealed her as a phony, but also indicated just how uneducated she really was, since she did not even follow the announcement of this widely anticipated news.

During the Q&A segment, the MC asks contestants, dressed in evening gowns, about personal and societal issues, and contestants frequently frame their responses in terms of 'education is the key to life'. Offering solutions to problems as diverse as street children, road accidents and HIV/AIDS, contestants craft their answers to emphasize education as not only a right to all, but also as the primary means of obtaining personal success as well as social equality and order. Consider the following response to the question 'What is your view about the question of education in Tanzania?' (all contestants' speeches from here on in this chapter are translated from Swahili unless otherwise indicated):

Thank you for your question. Concerning the issue of Tanzanian education, education in Tanzania has really failed concerning secondary school, because these days secondary schools are very few while primary schools are many. Therefore, for those who complete their Standard 7 studies, many get the opportunity to go to secondary but others fail to go because there are so few secondary schools. So I would ask the high-level leaders to increase for us the number of secondary schools so that we are able to get our educational level to increase, because today's education is really failing. Thank you for your question.

This contestant expresses a widespread sentiment concerning the problem of hierarchical access to secondary and tertiary education, in part due to the lack of availability of secondary schools. More often, contestants emphasize the importance of education without giving any substantive content, as in the next example, in which a contestant forces a prepared answer about education to a question aimed at garnering a more personal response: 'If you were given the chance to change one thing in your life, what would it be and why? Explain.'

Thank you MC for your good question and I will answer it as follows. If I were given the chance to change one thing I would like to change education, because education is indeed the key of life [*elimu ni ufunguo wa maisha*] for the world of today and when we go without education I don't think we will arrive. Thank you.

Here, the contestant uses the trope of 'education is the key of life', although offers no explanation of how it is the key, or what 'arrive' relates to. Rather, the content and rewards of an education appear self-evident, as a general means of uplifting society.

Sometimes, less savvy contestants miscalculate and talk about their own missed educational opportunities. In the next example, the contestant has just been asked the same question as above. Below is her response:

Thank you very much for your question and I would like to answer as follows. If I were to get a chance to change something in my life, I would ask to change my parent, that is, for my father to have a lot of money, because when I was going to school, it was very difficult and I had a lot of problems during that time because my father didn't have a lot of money to educate me.... I was getting turned away because of school fees. If my father told me, 'I don't have money', I had to wait until my father got money. So, I would like my father changed so that my other younger relatives who follow me would get to go to school without problems, not like me when I was going to school. Thank you.

While certainly a story familiar to many people in the audience, this contestant's response is not a tactical one. First, she publicly criticizes her father for not being able to care for the family, an incredibly non-congruent and insulting statement which garnered derisive laughter from the audience. Second, she highlights unnecessarily her own lack of education (emphasized even more by her not having used English). Even though the sentiment of her story was heartfelt and pertinent, it failed to construct her as suitably educated and sophisticated.

In contestants' speeches, then, education becomes a discursive tool, powerful because it touches on the way people conceptualize hope, success, opportunity and mobility. The references to education are more often than not vague, asserting that individuals, families, targeted segments of the population and Tanzania as a whole would be better off with more schooling. While sometimes pointing to real obstacles to securing an education, the speeches rarely reflect on the dead-ends that even highly educated people encounter, nor the gender-specific challenges that many of these young women undoubtedly face; education itself is never questioned as a means to an end.

UKIMWI Unaua: 'AIDS Kills', Family Life Education and Personal Self-Reliance

The contestant above who claimed to be waiting for results from the Form 4 exam failed to meet audience expectations in another way as well. An awareness of key social issues is indexical of an education and hence of a modern Tanzanian identity, and the ability to talk openly about such topics serves a contestant well in competition. When asked a personal question, a savvy contestant will link her own experiences with those of broader society. For example, in a mid-level competition in Dar es Salaam, the MC asked the contestant, 'Elezea historia ya maisha yako kwa kifupi na matarajio yako ya baadaye' ['Briefly explain the history of your life and your plans for the future'] and she answered (in English) as follows:

> Thank you very much. My name is Mary Kihaka. I'm 23 years of old. I am taking my O-level education, I was taking at Tabora Secondary School and my A-level I took it to Tabora Secondary School and now I am taking an advance diploma in business administration. For my future, I want be a counselor, that is, advise of the youth who are the coming nation of tomorrow. I would advise them because most of them are the victim of HIV/AIDS [cheers and applause], drug abuse [cheers and applause], I would advise them to join different groups, sporting games, and lastly to use condoms [loud cheers and applause] as a method to prevent AIDS. Thank you very much.

In this response, the contestant is able to shift during her answer from overviewing her personal history to addressing some of the problems facing Tanzanians today, a tactic which the audience indicates through their applause as congruent with their expectations. Her response is also in English. This contestant was selected as beauty queen. In contrast, a contestant who speaks only to her own personal circumstances may be seen as unsophisticated (as with the Form 4 exams above), while one who inserts her prepared answer without reference to the question may also be jeered as not having understood what was asked or as having memorized her response in advance without the flexibility of altering it on the spot (see the example in Chapter 4, p. 106 and pp. 115–116).

The connection between social issues and education in Tanzania has existed since the 1960s, as part of Nyerere's socialist program of 'Education for Self-Reliance' (Wedgwood, 2007). Yet, since 1997, gender issues have come to the fore with a program initiated by the Ministry of Education, according to which 'Family Life Education' has been integrated across the curriculum

(Rutagumirwa & Kamuzora, 2006). Lessons include AIDS education and condom use, gender-based violence and female circumcision, and today these topics are taught, to varying degrees and in idiosyncratic ways (ibid), in primary and secondary school as well as in teacher training colleges (Price *et al.*, 2003). Family life lessons are woven across school subjects, finding their way into home economics, biology, geography and civics classrooms (Rutagumirwa & Kamuzora, 2006). Since home economics classes are often gender-segregated (see Stambach, 2000a; Vavrus, 2002), some topics are taught exclusively or differentially to girls or boys.

Apart from the government-approved curriculum, students show their ownership of such programs by organizing after-school extracurricular clubs and activities around social themes, with, for example, HIV/AIDS clubs writing and performing skits for fellow students as afternoon entertainment (see e.g. Rutagumirwa & Kamuzora, 2006). These clubs are seen as useful not only for furthering education and personal commitment to changing social practices, but also as an appropriate means for channeling sexual frustration and energy and to stay away from vices (Rutagumirwa & Kamuzora, 2006); contestant Mary Kihaka, quoted above, makes reference to such clubs.

From top-down perspectives, the integration of 'Family Life Education' and similar programs into school curricula is at the heart of why it is important to ensure girls receive an education and indeed, the importance of educating of African women has long preoccupied planners. Missionaries' interest in educating East African girls was intimately connected with creating a new kind of African woman, who would bear the burden of changing society (e.g. Hodgson, 2005), and similar missionary goals have been observed across the continent and worldwide (e.g. Devens, 1992; Summers, 1996). Likewise, British colonial administrators in then Tanganyika stressed the importance of educating girls in order to inculcate Western ways into future generations, although no specific changes were made to policy (Vavrus, 2003). While later, during the beginning years of Tanzanian independence, the focus of *Ujamaa* (see Chapter 2) was on equality and hence no special attention was paid to the schooling of girls, by the mid-1970s, the government and its institutions began to create affirmative action strategies in order to increase the enrollment of girls in secondary school and at the university. Many of these programs, such as the University of Dar es Salaam's Gender Programme, continue today. In addition, since the early 1990s, a primary focus of development agencies and policy-makers globally, as well as of those working in Tanzania, has been on the education of girls and women as key to development and modernization, specifically in terms of its apparent positive effects on fertility rates, the spread of disease and even environmental degradation (Vavrus, 2003).

Yet some education scholars have raised criticisms against the great emphasis of governments and development groups on girls' education (Brock-Utne, 2000; Heward & Bunwaree, 1999; Vavrus, 2003), arguing, for instance, 'it is problematic, to say the least, to place the onus of national development largely on one group – women – and one institution – the school' (Vavrus, 2003: 134–135). Similarly, Brock-Utne argues:

> There are good reasons to ensure that girls are educated, and it may be necessary to target them especially, but the arguments for doing so should have to do with fairness, equity, and securing the best talents in important jobs rather than with having women give birth to fewer babies. (Brock-Utne, 2000: 14)

Girls' education should concern their ability to shape their own lives, rather than simply as a tool to 'develop' the nation and shape future generations. What is more, while powerful institutions, schools are not without limits in their ability to change society, especially since so many children are not able to attain an education, and students sometimes make sense of lessons in ways that are not the intended outcome (Stambach, 2000a).

Nonetheless, such development-oriented goals have been internalized by many Tanzanians as a key component of schooling, and awareness of and ability to speak about critical social concerns marks one as educated and forward-thinking. The young women who take to the stage and speak on these topics present themselves as gendered icons of the best aspects of the Tanzanian educational system. As discussed in Chapter 3, a contestant's ability to speak candidly about such historically taboo topics as HIV/AIDS (Setel, 1999), while avoiding the wide variety of slang terms which have emerged to refer to the disease (Reuster-Jahn & Kießling, 2006), distinguishes her from less sophisticated others who may also take on the role of educating society about the disease. Perhaps most importantly, in advocating for the issues that are, from an institutional point of view, the very point of educating females, contestants not only speak to concerns of national well-being and development; as women in their early reproductive years, they also stand as vessels for this very development.

Yet an irony exists, in that, as pageant contestants, these young women likely hope to bypass, or at least postpone, the domestic agenda that is central to their roles in shaping the modern nation. From the state's perspective, the home economics and Family Life Education curricula support the inculcation of just-so practices (not *too* modern, not *too* traditional; not *too* Western, not *too* African) that young modern women will pass on to the next generation of Tanzanians, under the authority of a husband. But, as Stambach (2000a) demonstrates and as the contestants in my study confirm, many young educated women dream of a life after finishing school as a single *dada wa mjini* ('city sister') rather than as a *mama wa nyumbani* ('stay-at-home mother'). In self-introductions, contestants profess a desire to become high-level career women – human rights lawyers, doctors, newscasters, poets. Though such goals will likely prove out of reach, an education for these young women provides the dream at least of escape, from the village, from poverty and from patriarchal authority, to live independently, to own property and to put into practice for their own sake, rather than for that of their children or society, the lessons learned about being a modern Tanzanian woman. Their desire for education, like their desire to be a beauty queen, concerns the attainment of personal rather than societal goals, a notion that puts on its head the socialist ideology of 'Education for Self-Reliance' put forth by Nyerere in the years of independence (see Chapter 2), and instead reveals an ideology of education for personal self-reliance (Stambach, 2000a).

Usiogope ('Don't Be Afraid'): *Ufasaha,* Confidence and Bodily Habitus

Of course, contestants are able to demonstrate their education not only through the content of their speeches, but also through form and delivery. In Chapter 4, I analyzed contestants' code choice in terms of how it enables or constrains pageant success: while contestants and pageant organizers alike insist in off-stage interviews that contestants' onstage use of Swahili or English is equally evaluated, pageant results indicate otherwise. Even though contestants' ability to speak standard English is often seriously constrained, and speeches are delivered in a non-fluent and stilted manner, it typically 'counts' as English. Instead of standardness, audiences and judges expect *ufasaha*, a formal register often equated with bookish eloquence (Ohly, 1987; Reuster-Jahn & Kießling, 2006) and ideologically and perceptually often distilled to one single feature – purity from codeswitching. Contestants' ability to speak pure English on stage is facilitated by the norm within pageants, regardless of language, of memorizing several possible responses in advance.

Yet audiences and judges typically are not bothered by the widespread knowledge that contestants memorize their responses, provided a contestant does not make blatantly clear through excessive stammering that she lacks confidence or is unable to think on her feet. Nor are spectators usually put off by the extremely formal and stilted quality of the English speeches. In fact, English speeches that seem impromptu or natural, with conversational intonation, discourse markers and pausing, are sometimes not considered to be suitably formal and adhering to *fasaha* norms, and may, in extreme cases, result in relentless audience ridicule (Billings, 2006). Memorization thus does not just facilitate contestants' use of English; the effects of memorization and recitation actually partially shape the *fasaha* English register itself.

In the following example from a mid-level competition in Arusha, a contestant responds to the question, 'If you were given a chance to change one thing in your life, what would it be and why? Explain.' C, contestant; A, audience/

```
1   C:   If .. I would {[ar]} be given a chance .. to change one ~thing .. in
2        my ~life,
3        I would {[ar]} ~like to ~change .. the system .. of women ..
4        circumcision /
5   A:   xxxxx=XXXXXXX  =
6   C:              =I will {[ar]}- =
7   A:                      == XXXXXXXXxx =xxxxxxxxxxxxxxxxxxx
8   C:                                  =I will like to ~change
9   A:   == =xxxxxxxxxxxxxxxxxxxxx  =
10  C:   == = this .. because .. it causes = many problems to woman life/
11       It causes death and another problem//
12       ~Thank you,
13  A:   XXXXXXXXXXXXXXxxxxxxxxxxxxxxxxxx
```

Not only does this speech exhibit non-standard grammar (e.g. lines 8, 10), it also was delivered in a stilted style (e.g. lines 1, 3, 10) and with awkward pronunciation (e.g. lines 1, 3, 6) and intonation (e.g. lines 2, 3, 8, 12), manifesting a clear lack of fluency. Furthermore, her answer lacks details and, while she attempts to make her response address a pertinent social issue, she does not do so with the skill of, for example, Mary Kihaka, above. This same strategy caused audiences to heckle in Dar es Salaam (see the example in Chapter 4) but here it does not seem to register and, indeed, the audience indicates through applause that her response is congruent with expectations in both form and content.

So although this contestant spoke non-standard English, ungracefully forced a memorized speech to fit a different question and was clearly not fluent, she spoke 'purely' and for this audience did not break the formal, *fasaha* frame of delivery. Her speech was almost completely devoid of referential content, but her very mention of an illegal but still performed practice, one that many urban Tanzanians, as well as the state, see as backward and indeed holding Tanzanians back, succeeded in marking her as educated and modern. She was not considered to be particularly beautiful, at least by those sitting at my table, but stood out in that she was among only two of 14 contestants to use English on stage, and the judges selected her as the winner.

Like their English-speaking counterparts, Swahili speakers sometimes memorize their speeches in advance rather than having to compose an impromptu response, but the results of these efforts stand in contrast to English ones in some important ways. Notably, Swahili-speaking contestants typically use a standard variety. Their responses are typically slightly longer in duration than English speakers', although length in and of itself is not prized (Billings, 2006). The following, from the same mid-level competition in Arusha, is a Swahili-language response to the question 'Are you of the opinion that hunger is the major reason for armed robbery and theft in our country? What measures would you suggest to the government to prevent the same?' The contestant answers as follows (underlining and superscripts indicating two kinds of complex grammatical constructions described below, bold indicating organizational features):

Asante sana kwa swali lako na nitalijibu **kama ifuatavyo.**[1] Kitu kinachosababisha[1] ujambazi katika nchi yetu sio njaa bali ni ajira kwa vijana, kwa sababu vijana wengi hawana ajira na ndio sababu wanafanya kazi ya ujambazi. **Pili** wanaingia katika madawa ya kulevya. **Tatu** wasichana wenzangu wanjiingiza katika biashara mbaya ya ukahaba ambayo huwasabishia[1] maradhi mabaya na hatimaye kufa. Na **mwisho kabisa** ni maoni yangu kwamba ningeomba serikali ingeruhusu vijana wajiajiri wenyewe ili mradi wasikiuke[2] masharti ya serikali. Asanteni.

[Thank you very much for your question and I will answer it **as follows.**[1] The thing that causes[1] theft in our country isn't hunger but rather the unemployment of youth, because many youths do not have employment and indeed because they do work of thievery. **Second**, they enter into drugs and drinking. **Third,** my fellow girls get involved in the bad business of prostitution which leads them to[1] bad diseases and even death. And **finally**, it is my opinion that I would ask the government to allow youth to work in the informal sector in order that they do not break[2] the law. Thank you.]

Like the English-speaking contestant in the previous example, this Swahili-speaking contestant spoke clearly, at an appropriate volume and without codeswitching, but the similarities end there. The Swahili-language response includes complex grammatical features, such as two types of relative clauses (superscript 1), negative subjunctive form (superscript 2) and a range of complex nominal agreements as well as sophisticated vocabulary. The contestant's statement is well ordered into several parts and ends with a conclusion.

Even as striking as the linguistic and compositional differences between the two answers, another distinction between the English- and Swahili-language responses concerns bodily habitus and manifestations of confidence. The overall effect of the Swahili speaker was that of a much more relaxed young woman, her posture and smile more natural and her words free-flowing, if still relatively formal and rehearsed, than the stiff and awkward English speaker. Nonetheless the Swahili speaker, like the vast majority of other contestants who speak Swahili on stage, did not win the contest, and instead came in third place.

More generally, while both Swahili and English speeches are often recited, those delivered in English are typically characterized by a halting rigidity, stiff delivery and sing-songy-ness, a product of the memorization process and even of the lack of full understanding of the composition. Even though Swahili-speaking contestants tend to deliver more grammatically standard speeches, expressing more complex ideas in a better-organized composition, and in a more apparently relaxed way, English-speaking contestants are nonetheless preferred, with their particular way of exhibiting 'confidence' fully congruent with audiences' and judges' expectations of them.

During the week or so prior to competition, former local beauty queens, choreographers and other experts instruct contestants on various aspects of their pageant performance, and while language form garners relatively little explicit attention, confidence emerges as a critical feature that pageant trainers attempt to instill in contestants (see Chapter 4). Goading them with phrases such as, '*Uwe na* confidence!' ('Be confident') and '*Usiogope!*' ('Don't be afraid!'), trainers coach the young women on manifestations of confidence, such as the 'model' walk, good posture, a wide smile and eye contact with the audience and judges. But confidence is also linked with language, and trainers remind their charges to speak at the appropriate volume, to enunciate and to wait for audiences to finish applauding before continuing to speak. They stress the importance of beginning one's response in the Q&A session with a version of the formulaic 'Thank you for your good question and I will answer as follows' and closing with 'Thank you'.[4] Sometimes, trainers also remind contestants to avoid *kuchanganya* ('mixing'). Failure to do any of these things can be understood as lack of confidence, as it signals that one's nerves have forced one to forget the lessons. Otherwise, explicit feedback and focus on language are limited, with most time spent learning dance steps, practicing on- and off-stage sequencing and instilling bodily confidence.

In contrast to the week or more of training that contestants undergo, judges often receive very little (if any) guidance on how to select a winner. Instead, they rely on previous experiences watching pageants on television or in person, which have given them at least a general understanding of what constitutes a suitable beauty queen. Pageant directors may share with judges a list of desirable traits in advance, and this list is often repeated by the MC or director during the pageant, as in the following (delivered in Swahili, with English self-translations, in quotes):

> Girls must have a pretty face, 'beauty of face', must have good shape, 'good figure', this is together with smooth skin, good teeth, good legs, eyes and everything important about a figure. Another qualification is her attractiveness and to be charming, to be able to know and to think and also to answer different questions.

Indeed, a contestant who has flawed skin or decayed teeth, or who is overweight or too thin, will not make a good contender. Contestants should be 'charming' – a term which implies a feminine confidence – but on the whole these guidelines give little specificity, and language itself is nowhere mentioned. Rather, the form that contestants' language takes and the ways in which their language use is evaluated draw primarily on knowledge about how to speak gained from outside the pageant world, in particular, from experiences in secondary school. It is a robust model that moves from the classroom to the pageant stage in large part due to the widespread understanding of contestants as, for better or worse, schoolgirls. Without much explicit training, contestants and spectators alike plug into this model for using and evaluating language on stage. And while often both English- and Swahili-speaking contestants seem to manifest 'confidence' to the satisfaction of their evaluators, the particular instantiations of such confidence are often distinct, linked with code choice, and informed by school-based language coaching and evaluation. In the next section, I will discuss the ways in which educational models for language and communication inform contestants' onstage behavior as well as audiences' and judges' evaluation of it.

School-Based Models of Language and Interaction

The contestant data presented above, which exhibit significant differences between the kinds of Swahili and English used, echo resoundingly observations made by scholars of language and education in Tanzania. Indeed, explicit and implicit lessons learned in schools about language use, language (e)valuation, and modes of learning and interaction, are reproduced and reworked on and around the pageant stage. From ideologies about the worthiness of codes broadly construed, to registers acquired and used primarily in formal educational settings, to bodily comportment while speaking, to strategies for achieving scholastic success, contestants' onstage language and communication skills emanate from educational experiences shared to varying degrees by most participants. In some cases, these communicative notions and practices are taken for granted, and in other cases they are explicitly rewarded. In still other instances, the very markers and products of education become indexical of a lack of education, as I will discuss in the next section.

Perhaps the most prominent connection between what happens in schools and pageants with regard to language is the clear hierarchical relationship there between English and Swahili. As overviewed in Chapter 2, Swahili is the medium of instruction in primary school, during which time English is taught as a subject. Abruptly upon entering secondary school, English becomes the medium of instruction, except for in civics and Swahili language classes. It is a situation that has been widely critiqued by many Tanzanian scholars (e.g. Mtesigwa, 2001; Mulokozi, 1991; Neke, 2003), yet upheld by other Tanzanians, including politicians, students and teachers who believe English to be invaluable to success and see the educational language policy as central to teaching students that language. This is a phenomenon well documented in other sub-Saharan African postcolonial educational contexts as well (Brock-Utne, 2000, 2002; Serpell, 1993; Williams, 2006). Studies have demonstrated, though, that the language policy in Tanzania does in fact curtail overall learning potential, as reflected in poor performance on the national examinations (e.g. Sumra & Rajani, 2006). Where this policy is successful, however, is in sending students a clear message of the differential use and utility of English and Swahili (Mulokozi, 1991; Neke, 2005; Roy-Campbell & Qorro, 1997; Rubagumya, 1994; Yahya-Othman, 1990).

Not only are schools a primary source of the ideology of English as superior to Swahili, they are also the source of the pure register of English that successful contestants speak on stage. As a written code, *fasaha* English is the expected mode of communication in many elite contexts; as a spoken code, it is not only acquired but is used almost exclusively within educational settings (Mushi, 1996). Yet the resulting English, whether spoken or written, is typically seriously non-standard (Criper & Dodd, 1984; Mlama & Matteru, 1978; Mohamed & Banda, 2008; Yahya-Othman, 1990). In a study of 40 secondary school students (Vuzo, 2002, reported in Brock-Utne,

2007a), students were asked to summarize a series of cartoons in English. The following is an excerpt from the most standard of these summaries, written by a Form 6 student who, in principle, should be ready to attend university:

> At a certain airport, there was a person who was seem like a passanger. This person was own two cases, the greater one and the smaller one. He looks to think where he can go or how to do at that particular time. Beside him the two person seem to discuss about the passanger. The person were two, Man and young man. These persons of cause they discus how to stole the cases of the passangar. (Brock-Utne, 2007a: 519)

This composition, the best exemplar of standard English in the corpus, is fraught with grammatical and spelling errors, and goes on to exhibit problems with coherence and sequencing. Indeed, Brock-Utne notes that English skills do not improve drastically over the course of secondary school; while Form 6 students' English abilities were better than those of Form 1 students, the difference was 'surprisingly small' (Brock-Utne, 2007a: 520). In the same study, students were asked to summarize the cartoons in Swahili, and in this exercise they consistently employed standard grammar, a diverse lexicon, creativity in their descriptions and sophisticated compositional organization, all missing from the English versions.

Although classrooms are officially English only, codeswitching is nonetheless very common (e.g. Brock-Utne, 2007b; Rubagumya, 1994). Unlike the deeply mixed codes spoken by highly educated scholars, politicians and other urban elites (Blommaert, 1992; Higgins, 2007), or the Swahili spoken by many Tanzanians, including contestants, with frequent idiosyncratic English borrowings (Chapter 4), codeswitching in schools is often functional, for communicative work such as asides and translations, used to support successful classroom interaction, hindered by the English-only policy (Rubagumya, 1994). Nonetheless, certain teachers, classes, assignments and circumstances call for the rigid adherence to the English-only prescription, and students are corrected for lapsing into Swahili (Rubagumya, 1994). It is through verbal and written correction that students learn the skill and expectation of code purity within formal teaching and learning interactional frames.

Furthermore, scholarship on language socialization in multilingual educational contexts (e.g. Meacham, 2004; Moore, 2006) has shown how students acquire language-linked habitus, the bundling of school-based codes with ways of being in particular languages. As such, *fasaha* English comes packaged with other, non-linguistic features. Brock-Utne (2007b) compares the affective stance of students and teachers in Swahili- versus English-medium classrooms. In Swahili classrooms, participants engaged spontaneously and even playfully with each other and the material, with a relaxed posture and fluent, uncensored speech. While the pedagogical style was still formalistic, teachers sometimes opened the floor to non-recited or open-ended contributions, and students felt freer to offer creative solutions to problems raised. In English classrooms, in contrast, teachers were humorless and physically rigid, given to a more teacher-centered and inflexible pedagogical style, and much more likely to treat students punitively. Students were understandably anxious and stiff, or else apathetically sunk into their seats, resigned to their inability to understand the lesson and to communicate effectively (see Stambach, 2000a, for similar findings). The use of *fasaha* English thus triggered and was bundled with a complex of behaviors and stances, characterized by formality, seriousness and emotional distance from the lesson.

The following excerpt of dialogue between a teacher (T) and a student (S), reported in Brock-Utne (2007b), is taken from a Form 1 geography class and illustrates this language-linked stance, as well as other features discussed above. It is followed by that author's field observations:

T: What type of vegetation will be found in desert area? Don't be shy. You there (points at a student who has not raised his hand).

S: Don't know.

T: You don't know what?

S: Silent.

T: Be comfortable. Relax! You there – (points at a student who has raised his hand.)

S: Kakati.

> The class laughs because the student has said the name for a cactus in Kiswahili…. No one in this class is relaxed. Not even the teacher. The students looked down on their desks and were afraid to be asked a question. They were punished by having to stand if they gave an incorrect answer. (Brock-Utne, 2007b: 496)

The brief exchange shows, first, the rigid and formal affective stance that is typical of speaking *fasaha* English, but that, from this teacher's point of view is too stiff, and he barks at the student 'Don't be shy' and 'Be comfortable' – reprimands strongly reminiscent of those issued by the pageant coaches described above. The exchange also illustrates the inculcation of the pure-register ideology, as seen in students' acknowledgement through laughter of the non-congruence of the respondent's use of Swahili within a *fasaha* English frame. Finally, it makes clear that the medium of instruction curtails the learning and teaching process, with time wasted with meta-level linguistic and conversational management, rather than being spent in active engagement with each other and the material.

Contestants' onstage speech reflects other school-based practices of communication and learning, such as their reliance on memorization to answer questions. Investigators have repeatedly pointed out the emphasis on memorization, recitation and a chorus-style instructional format in Tanzanian schools (Stambach, 1994; Sumra & Rajani, 2006; Vavrus, 2009). Such practices have been described in settings across Africa as 'safety strategies' (Arthur, 2001; Hornberger & Chick, 2001; Ndayipfukamiye, 1994; Wedin, 2010), because they allow teachers and students to save face by giving the appearance of successful teaching and learning, when in fact they are uncomfortable and often ill-equipped to communicate in the designated code or about the designated material. On the other hand, there may be other understandings of these classroom practices, including a lack of up-to-date teacher training, or challenges of class size and shortage of materials, making constructivist pedagogical styles impractical (Vavrus, 2009). An alternative interpretation, which may coexist with others, is that such practices have long had a place in traditional educational fora and hence find a natural and valued position in Western-style schools, apart from whatever face-saving or practical functions they may also serve (cf. Stambach, 2000a; Wedin, 2010; see also Moore, 2006, for discussion of Cameroon).[5] Indeed, as the expected interactional strategies in Tanzanian classroom settings, memorization, recitation and formalist pedagogy must to an extent be actively valued, and not simply a means of masking lack of linguistic or other knowledge (Vavrus, 2009).

Taken together, we see the linguistic and ideological model of *fasaha* English emerging in school and reappearing on the pageant stage. Through years of classroom experience, contestants are adept at composing, memorizing and reciting exemplars of *ufasaha*, and the fact that their onstage English, as opposed to their Swahili, is often non-standard, poorly organized and lacking content is consistent with what they have been accustomed to producing and hearing over the course of their secondary education. They are nonetheless competent at keeping Swahili and English separate, despite the fact that such purity differs from their more mixed conversational code. Furthermore, English-speaking beauty contestants not only use a stilted, non-fluent code, but also often appear rigid physically, offering an uncomfortable smile, standing extremely straight with their bodies completely aligned, rather than in a slightly more natural position.

This stance is integral to the spoken register itself, stemming from lack of ease with *ufasaha* but becoming indexically linked with the formal and ostensibly knowledge-bearing nature of the circumstances under which the register is typically used.

Finally, education not only trains contestants, it trains other pageant participants as well. Not only do pageant coaches, audiences and judges utilize these same lessons about language and learning in their evaluation of contestants, they also tap into a school-based model of interaction and comprehension. Mohamed and Banda (2008: 104; after Bourdieu & Passeron, 1994) have described, in the context of Tanzanian post-primary schools, a 'complicity in misunderstanding', or a willingness to ignore the lack of understanding, which goes on between teachers and students in English-language classrooms. The authors argue that teachers are aware that students do not understand the content, and students know that the teachers know, but both parties act as though comprehension is occurring. On the one hand, this complicity allows teachers to preserve authority, move on with the lesson plan and avoid admitting failure. On the other, it allows students to believe that they are getting something out of their education, and it furthermore keeps them out of trouble, as any challenge to the teacher would likely not end well. In the present context, contestants, audiences and judges are likewise engaged in a complicity of misunderstanding when it comes to English-language responses; everyone knows that almost everyone else does not understand fully the content of what is being said, but they go on with the exercise of using English nonetheless.

But in schools as well as in pageants, there is more than negative face-saving and authority-preserving reasons behind complicity in misunderstanding. Students and teachers actively value English as a resource and, indeed, as the very point of an education (e.g. Neke, 2003; Rubagumya, 1996; see also Williams, 2006, for more general discussion of Southern Africa). In pageants, where Swahili is officially allowed, English is clearly embraced, not just tolerated. Furthermore, the notion of complicity in misunderstanding conveys a sense that any critical stance on English language and communication is turned off, which does not account for the fact that spectators observe closely other register features such as code purity. Yet, as discussed in Chapter 4, as successful contestants advance through the pageant circuit, they find that the *fasaha* English speeches that earned them praise now earn little more than indifference, and sometimes even ridicule. The lessons they learned in school about how to be modern and educated fall short of indexing themselves as such on the national stage.

Learning to Lay Your Fork and Not Sound Like a Schoolgirl

As opposed to the one week of evening training sessions that is typical for lower-level pageants, Miss Tanzania contestants stay full-time at a pageant camp for two or more weeks in preparation for the main event. During this time, there is also a pre-judgment segment, during which each contestant meets with a subset of the judges for an interview, and a group reception or dinner with judges and contestants also occurs. Judges use this opportunity to get to know the young women in greater depth and to gauge their suitability for the crown more thoroughly than contestants' brief exposure on stage allows. From these encounters, judges formulate preliminary rankings which will inform their final decisions.

Despite contestants' lengthy training, the national pageant director offered a critique of the contestants who reach the Miss Tanzania pageant, indicating that the training they have received to date has not been adequate. In an article in a widely read English-language newspaper (*Sunday Observer*) the director's belief that contestants need to improve how they respond to questions is reported:

> [The] Miss Tanzania Coordinator ... has said in Dar es Salaam that the [training] exercise would be carried out by special experts to give the contestant a winning posture contrary to the traditional way of responding to questions like a secondary school student.... By doing so they appeared to have crammed the materials without understanding the respective subject. (Kapinga, 2008)

The director thus here critiques the very skill-set that has been applauded by audiences as congruent and has secured so many lower-level contenders with a crown. In using the phrase 'winning posture', he indicates that there is a complex of features that index a winner and that her response is critical to achieving that posture. The director explicitly links contestants' 'traditional way of responding to questions' with their training in secondary school, by likening their responses to having 'crammed the materials' for the 'subject'. Contestants who, by speaking *fasaha* English, were able to stand out from their Swahili-speaking counterparts, now blend in with other regional winners. Dar es Salaam contestants who speak the best, most standard version of *fasaha* English remain in the running, but it is those few elite contestants who speak less formal, more conversational, non-strictly school-based English who become the most attractive contenders for the Miss Tanzania crown. The director's comments transform what had been positively valued as the most prominent sign of education into the very opposite: a lack of education, sophistication and pageant promise.

But the director's critique does not stop with language. He continues by emphasizing the need for training in social graces:

> Usually this exercise is held when they are in [Miss Tanzania] training camp, but over the years, that [i.e. social graces] was not being covered and the result was that some candidates were taking soup as the last course meal instead of beginning with it…. Others could not differentiate a glass for juice, water and wine and did not know how to lay spoons and forks after meals. (Kapinga, 2008)

The director went on to highlight that contestants should be 'psychologically prepared' and have their 'health examined incorporating skin and mouth hygiene'. While many of these characteristics would not surface during the onstage part of the competition, they would become apparent during the pre-judgment segment. By linking linguistic with other skills and practices, the director articulates a metasemiotic scheme not only of a Miss Tanzania beauty queen, but also of an ideal urban Tanzanian woman, at once the recipient of a quality Western-style education, but also fully socialized as both modern and domestic in her bodily and social praxis. The director thus reconfigures the trope of 'education is the key of life' from one which emphasizes the value of a formal education, into one which includes the entire feminine being.

As schoolgirls, part of contestants' secondary education includes training in hygiene, manners and domesticity, following a long colonial tradition across the continent aimed at imbuing Africans' education with bodily and domestic regimes to create docile, productive and appropriately gendered subjects (Burke, 1996; Comaroff & Comaroff, 1992; Hunt, 1992). Yet Stambach (2000a) points to the superficiality and irrelevance of the home economics curriculum for schoolgirls living today in northern Tanzania, with a syllabus that includes, for example, food preparation lessons requiring refrigerated and convenience foods, and housekeeping lessons necessitating costly cleaning products.

The pageant director's comments thus acknowledge the importance of an education, while demeaning *their* education. He understands an education to include gendered domestic skills, yet he sees the specific education most contestants have received as deeply inadequate. Certainly, many contestants have not fully absorbed the impractical lessons presented to them in home economics classes, which likely did not even include such detail about table manners. Even more damning, their ability to answer questions is just not right at all, indexing an utter lack of understanding, sophistication and linguistic acumen. From his elite perspective, their education has done little more than produce schoolgirls, and it has been unsuccessful at creating modern and civilized Tanzanian women. The elite communicative skills he describes are necessarily bundled with elite bodily and domestic practices, more likely acquired in an upper-class Dar es Salaam household than through formal education itself; he laments that contestants do not know when to order a soup course, yet most contestants would never have had the opportunity to dine in a restaurant offering multi-course Western food.

Stambach (2000a) argues that Kilimanjaro schoolgirls' home economics education, while largely irrelevant in their daily lives, is more about envisioning how others live and how they themselves might possibly live someday. Here, I argue that students' overall education, especially with regard to the impracticality and artificiality of their language learning, likewise allows students to dream about better futures, integrally linked with language, more than actually preparing them to create one for themselves.

The Mobility of Social Models of Language and Personhood

In this chapter I have discussed how events occurring far from schools reflect, reproduce and sometimes challenge or contradict ideologies about and practices rooted in schooling and education. Wortham reminds us that 'educational institutions play central roles in authorizing and circulating ideologies of language through which "educated" and "uneducated" language use are associated with differentially valued types of people' (Wortham, 2008: 39). Certainly, students learn in Tanzanian secondary schools that English is, in terms of the opportunities it affords, superior to Swahili and they map those associations onto speakers as well. Furthermore, secondary education in Tanzania provides students with the particular variety of *fasaha* English that directly indexes their education, as it is neither acquired, nor really spoken, anywhere else (Mushi, 1996; Rubagumya, 1994). What is more, schooling inculcates students into Western-style beliefs and practices about the body, health, manners and gender relations, and in so doing constructs citizens as variably modern and traditional, based on knowledge of and comfort with these topics.

As we know, no language is monolithic, and what 'counts' as speaking a language, or speaking a language 'well', varies tremendously from context to context, and is also hierarchically arranged across spaces and domains (Blommaert *et al.*, 2005; Chapters 1 and 4). Here, the data also demonstrate the variability of what 'counts' as an education (Brock-Utne, 2007a, 2007b; Stambach & Malekela, 2006), itself linked with understandings of legitimate language use. In Tanzania, the irony is that while English itself has come to stand for education (Mohamed & Banda, 2008; Neke, 2005), the specific model of English language use acquired in school does not actually enable students to achieve the status and mobility they desire and that they have invested so heavily in (in terms of time, money and emotional commitment) to achieve.

The English that most students have access to in schools is not the English that, within social domains capable of offering an escape, will be interpreted as an education. As a first-order indexicality (Silverstein, 2003a), *fasaha* English indeed marks the speakers as having had some experience with secondary school. But this particular way of speaking English carries with it variable higher-order indexicalities. In provincial contexts, it marks its speakers as educated elites, as relatively few people have had the opportunity to advance past primary school. Audiences and judges plug into it readily as the register they themselves acquired in school; even with little educational access to the register, they are still able to recognize its salient features (cf. Agha, 2007: 131). In the nation's metropole, among the country's small elite, the very same *fasaha* register takes on a new set of higher-order indexicalities. Rather than indexing success, *fasaha* English may instead mark its speakers as deficient. In speaking *fasaha* English in these contexts, contestants reveal themselves as 'lacking', not just linguistically (not speaking fluent, colloquial English or another elite code) and educationally (not having attended university or international secondary schools), but also socially (not having the range of gendered skills and know-how that one acquires through being part of elite social circles, such as, for young women, familiarity with restaurant dining protocol, or trends in international hairstyles).

Ultimately, rather than a stunning beauty, what most pageant audiences, judges and organizers seek in a winning contestant is a certain kind of person, one who embodies features of what Mbilinyi (1972) called many years ago a New Tanzanian Woman, a modern citizen whose education is visible as well as critical to her own and her nation's future. Like a *dada wa mjini*, a New Tanzanian Women is confident and self-reliant, but still thoroughly domestic and without the socially dangerous quality of independence from men and children that is the siren call of city sisters. Unlike the grassroots notion of *dada wa mjini* envisioned by young women themselves, the New Tanzanian Woman works as a top-down, relatively unthreatening way of framing the value of educating girls. Language is a key component of that education, but so are other, often gendered, skills, practices and preferences in theory acquirable through schooling. Students are exposed to language and non-language lessons together, bundled in implicit and explicit ways and often along gendered lines. To the extent that contestants have absorbed these lessons, they become viable contenders for the crown. But at a certain point, mastery of the lessons is no longer sufficient, as, from an elite perspective, this education no longer counts for much; instead, what becomes critical is that one be from an elite household. While, certainly, such a contestant is likely to have achieved a high level of education, the upbringing itself will have provided her with access to the super-elite qualities – the 'education' writ-large – desired for Miss Tanzania.

The young women who compete in pageants have typically spent their lives banking on 'education is the key of life', working to attain a level of education higher than the vast majority of the population. Yet, like most who have just left secondary school, the majority of contestants find themselves unemployed, underemployed or resorting to the informal sector (cf. Al-Samarrai & Reilly, 2008). In addition to the scarcity of good jobs, many coveted jobs require fluent English, a skill that even Form 6 leavers usually have not acquired (Brock-Utne, 2007a). In their private lives, these young women expressed their desperation to continue their education, either in secondary school or, more often and more feasibly, in a for-profit training institute. Contestants explicitly link their desire to further their education with a need to improve their command of English. Unlike the national pageant director, most do not understand their education to have failed them. Rather, it is just that they have not received enough of it. Since most of the young women say that they are not ready to marry and have children, they consider finding sustaining employment key to their independence. In particular, they construe strong English skills as the primary qualification for acquiring a coveted entry-level job in tourism, banking or business. With few other possibilities, pageants offer the hope of winning enough shillings, or scholarships, to enroll in a private college offering courses in English, computers or hotel management. Such courses give these young women hope for white-collar wage labor that would allow them to live in the city and pursue a version of the life they have, through their schooling, come to see as attainable.

It is quite a conundrum. On the one hand, Tanzanians are desperate for an education, believing it to be the only way out of poverty, the only pathway to modernity and mobility. Indeed, an upper secondary or especially university education offers the recipient far more options than those without such credentials. For girls and young women in particular, a secondary education – not unlike beauty pageants – also allows them the opportunity to imagine for themselves a new set of possibilities in which their own self-reliance, their own knowledge and their own voices can help construct new kinds of independent lives. Yet, on the other hand, viewing education as 'the key to life' poses many challenges for individuals and society. Securing an education and then acquiring waged employment are tremendous obstacles. In particular, many of the jobs that do exist require expertise not gained in school, especially a knowledge of fluent English, as well as other higher-order or technology-linked skills. And for most young women, the education they have fought hard to acquire not only leaves them unemployed and under-qualified, but it also stigmatizes them as schoolgirls – promiscuous, ill-behaved and ignorant – wedging them between where they come from and where they want to go.

Notes

(1) The Swahili verb here, *kukomboa*, literally means, 'to liberate', but it is often used in the context of poverty alleviation, as Angela Damas seems to be using it here.

(2) The secondary school system in Tanzania begins with Form 1 and culminates with Form 6. Primary education comprises Standard 1 through Standard 7.

(3) Such institutions, specializing in computer skills, English language, tourism and more, abound in urban areas, functioning primarily as an opportunity for students who were not able to complete secondary school, or to attend university, to continue their training. In my fieldwork encounters, however, I witnessed repeatedly students enrolling on these courses and either not being able to finish them because of lack of money, or else, coming away without the promised, especially English, skills. In many cases, these schools are more businesses than educational institutions, churning out graduates with little competence in what they are meant to have studied. Nonetheless, Al-Samarrai and Reilly (2008) find a slight increase in wage potential for students completing such programs.

(4) In Swahili, 'Asante sana kwa swali lako zuri na nitajibu kama ifuatavyo' and 'Asanteni', respectively.

(5) Moore (2008) offers a critique of studies aimed at reforming schools in non-Western settings. Such studies, she argues, typically import Western models of pedagogy as the standard against which other approaches are judged, without an anthropologic- ally informed position of how such practices might be valued locally.

6 'Which is Your Favourite Color?' Race and Ethnicity in a Color-Blind Tanzania

> *Our country is one of those in Africa that is highly praised for its unity. We have no tribalism, no religions quarrelling, no colour discrimination, and we oppose discrimination and oppression on grounds of tribe, religion, or colour, wherever it exists.*
> Julius Nyerere, President of Tanzania, 1961–85 (Nyerere, 1973: 74)

One bright Sunday morning, I was returning from the populated hills surrounding Arusha following a Swahili-language service at my friend Sarah's Lutheran church. Sarah was in her early 20s, a former pageant contestant and a lifelong resident of Arusha. As we were walking back down the substantial hill towards Sarah's home, we overtook two elderly Meru women who had been among the almost exclusively Meru congregation in attendance that morning. As we passed, they called out a greeting in the Meru language, for they recognized Sarah, as the granddaughter of their friend. Sarah reciprocated by performing a greeting in their language (she herself is ethnically Meru), which encouraged the elderly women to continue the conversation. She, however, had to stop them after a few sentences to let them know, in Swahili and with a grin, that she did not actually know the language very well and did not understand what they were saying to her. Finding her lack of linguistic capabilities amusing, the old women slapped her on the back and said something in their language before continuing on their way, laughing for some time down the narrow path. Sarah then explained to me that she was not sure what they had said, but she believed they were jokes at her expense. Rather than particularly troubling or offensive, Sarah's inability to speak Meru appeared comical to these women, and it did not seem to bother Sarah at all. Instead, it seems to be a fact of life in Tanzania today that the younger generations, especially those living in urban areas, are often not fluent speakers of their heritage languages. At the same time, Sarah clearly self-identified as ethnically Meru, given her choice of churches, as well as other aspects of her home life, such as cuisine and certain, albeit truncated, initiation practices.

Tanzania has a long history of self-reflective discourses on ethnicity, emphasizing in particular a color-blind ethos as stated by Nyerere many years ago and repeated in the epigraph above. Rather than embracing difference, discourses and policies have, often implicitly, sought to erase or suppress ethnic affiliation (Blommaert, 1999a; Schneider, 2006). For example, the *Ujamaa* project was in large part an effort to bring social services and hence equality more efficiently to a dispersed and diverse population who themselves would pool their expertise and labor in communal, democratic and self-sufficient farms (e.g. Feierman, 1990; Mwansasu & Pratt, 1979). In addition, this policy also supported the use of the Swahili language as a lingua franca (Abdulaziz-Mkilifi, 1973), the rise of a national consciousness and the sidelining of ethnic identity in favor of a Tanzanian one (Blommaert, 1999a). Since then, official policy and discourse have been primarily to *ignore* ethnicity, while on occasion outright sanctioning outward signs of it in public, especially urban, spaces (Ivaska, 2002; Schneider, 2006). Today, and unlike in neighboring countries like Kenya, politics are officially non-ethnic; since the beginning of multi-party politics in the 1990s, political parties are required to have a 'national character', meaning they must have support from across the country (Nyang'oro, 2004). Even the national census ignores ethnicity completely. Nyang'oro paraphrases a statement delivered by Nyerere in 1995 at a political rally: 'ethnicity in Tanzania is only good for ritualistic purposes, beyond that, is [*sic*] a moribund concept with no place in modern Tanzania' (Nyang'oro, 2004: 10). Indeed, Nyang'oro concludes that the message of Nyerere's speech – which can still be heard in public spaces such as long-distances buses – has been internalized by most mainland Tanzanians, to the extent that asking people their ethnic affiliation is considered impolite.

In this chapter, I will begin with a discussion of contestants' understanding of the limited role of ethnic languages in beauty pageants and in their lives more generally. Based on these data, I will draw some tentative conclusions about the fate of these languages in urban spaces. Yet even as contestants do not speak ethnic languages in pageants, it is not the case that ethnicity has no place in urban Tanzanian society, and this will be the topic of the second part of the chapter. Self-conscious indicators of ethnicity surface in multiple ways throughout beauty pageants. Indeed, enregistered emblems of ethnicity appear to be up for the taking for all kinds of purposes: comedic and other entertainment effects, signs of rural authenticity, and even as symbols of urban *Tanzanian* identity, often characterized simply as 'Swahili'. In these cases, it seems immaterial that one actually claims a personal affiliation with the ethnicity, and often even preferential that one does not. Instead, recognized signs of ethnicity are in wide circulation and are accessible to urban Tanzanians for many artistic purposes.

But this color-blind ethos, according to which ethnicity in the city often takes on the quality of a sheer creative endeavor, may not extend to non-black minorities, especially the prominent South Asian community. The place of South Asians in Tanzania, as at once relatively well-off and also socially isolated, complicates discourses of a unified and color-blind society, and disputes have surfaced for decades over the place of Tanzanian South Asians in the national imaginary. In the final part of the chapter, I will discuss the recent crowning of a Miss Tanzania of Indian origin, which brought to the surface debates about what counts as Tanzanian, and the extent to which color-blindness should actually encompass *all* colors.

What is more, the formulation of nation = woman discussed in Chapter 3 is complicated further when race and ethnicity are considered. Banet-Weiser has argued that:

> When we take into account these facets of the specific cultural work that is performed and actualized within beauty pageants, we automatically disrupt the simple equation of women = nation. Once the category of citizen is broadened to include multiple ethnic and racial categories, the equation no longer balances in quite the same way. (Banet-Weiser, 1999: 8)

The selection of a particular woman to represent the nation is made thornier by the overlapping of race and ethnicity, especially as what counts as Tanzanian continues to be under scrutiny and subject to debate.

'There *Won't* Be Your Mother Tongue': The Public Invisibility of Local Ethnic Languages

In Chapter 2, I overviewed the linguistic landscape in Tanzania and the entrenchment of Swahili since before independence as a lingua franca, for variably pragmatic, political and symbolic purposes. The flip side of this Swahili dominance is that, for at least three decades, scholars have pointed to the imminent demise of many local ethnic languages in Tanzania (e.g. Mekacha, 1993; Mochiwa, 1979; Ndezi, 1979; Rubagumya, 1989: 109; Rubanza, 1979) and Legère (2002) claims that 39 languages are in direct danger of disappearing. According to these studies, the threat is not English – very frequently considered the force behind language shift in many parts of the world (Nettle & Romaine, 2000; Skuttnab-Kangas, 2000) – but rather Swahili.[1] For example, Mekacha describes codeswitching practices among speakers of Swahili and Ekinata, a Bantu language spoken by about 50,000 people in the northern part of Tanzania (Mekacha, 1993: 56). Ultimately, the directionality and functionality of switches, which place Swahili in a position of power and status, indicate the gradual shifting of perceived value of these two languages, in turn leading to a community-wide shift away from regular use of Ekinata. So while English is certainly coveted throughout Tanzania, Swahili is accessible, practical and the medium of instruction in primary school.[2] Relative to local ethnic languages, Swahili is a prestigious language signaling primary education and membership in the modern nation-state, and facilitating participation in civic, public life in Tanzania.

Nonetheless, despite the Tanzanian government's great efforts and successes over the years to spread Swahili throughout the country, and citizens' embracing of the ideal of a Swahili-unified nation, Tanzania remains very linguistically diverse (Gordon, 2005; see also discussions in Blommaert, 1999a, 2005). Official inattention to local ethnic languages does not equal their wholesale disappearance and, while language shift is certainly a fact of life for some communities, a visit to many rural parts of the country will readily reveal that many ethnic languages thrive. Wedin (2010), for example, documents that in the Karagwe district of north-west Tanzania, many primary school students are not even acquiring Swahili fluently for many years because of the deep local reliance across domains on their local ethnic language. From another perspective, Yoneda (2010) argues that rather than shifting away from their local languages, many rural speakers are instead hybridizing their ethnic tongues, infusing them with more and more Swahili linguistic material. More generally, several scholars have noted the slower rate of language shift in Africa than in other parts of the world, with factors such as colonization styles (Mufwene, 2004) and norms of multilingualism (Laitin, 1992) coming into play.

Yet in urban Tanzania, ethnic languages do not hold a visible place, and at pageants – a form of urban entertainment orienting towards cosmopolitan (English-linked) identities and nationalist (Swahili-linked) agendas – it is perhaps expected that markers of ethnicity, and especially ethnic languages, should not play a prominent role. In fact, ethnic languages were nearly absent from my data; the long-standing policies and public discourses aimed at making ethnicity invisible thus were highly successful in the context of these events.

Supporting the evidence gathered at pageants themselves for the inappropriateness of ethnic languages at pageants, contestants repeatedly and emphatically expressed in interviews and conversations with me that local ethnic languages did not belong in Tanzanian beauty contests. For example, Esther, a Miss Northern Zone contestant, when asked whether a contestant in this competition or others like it would be able to use her local ethnic language, replied: 'No no no no no! Only Kiswahili or English.... There *won't* be your mother tongue!' As an explanation, contestants consistently pointed to the pragmatic problem of mutual unintelligibility arising from the tremendous linguistic diversity in the country. According to Mwajuma, another contestant in the same pageant:

> ... kwa hiyo utakavyosema uongee lugha yako kwa mfano mimi ni mtu wa Kigoma *from Kigoma* kwa hiyo ukisema niongee *mother tongue* yangu wengine labda Wachaga, Wapare, Meru au Maasai hawataelewa....
> [So when you speak your own language, for example, I am *from Kigoma*, 'from Kigoma', and so if I were to speak my *mother tongue*, others, who are maybe Chagga, Pare, Meru, or Maasai, wouldn't understand.]

Grace forcefully offers a similar opinion:

> Haiwezekani sana sana. Watu wanakuwa lugha tofauti ... wataokuelewa ni wachache.
> [It is really, really not possible [to speak your local ethnic language]. People have different languages ... only a few people will understand you.]

And Hawa:

> Haiwezekani kwa sababu pale hakuna mtu mkalimani wa kutafsiri, kwa hiyo itakuwa hawaelewi.
> [It is impossible, because there [at the pageant] there is no translator to translate, therefore they wouldn't understand [you].]

Since even smaller cities in Tanzania are ethnically diverse, serving as hubs for regional commerce as well as for those who have relocated from rural areas or other urban centers in a quest to find a better life, contestants' insistence that they would not be understood in their own local ethnic languages is well founded. In fact, the ethnic diversity within cities is mirrored among contestants themselves. Take, for example, the Miss Northern Zone 2003 competition: of the 12 contestants, two self-identified as Chagga, two as Maasai and two as Nyakyusa. One each self-identified as Sukuma, Bena and Nyaturu, while the remaining three claimed not to have an ethnic affiliation (this probably meant that they were ethnically Swahili). In terms of the languages associated with these ethnic groups, five are in the Bantu family, while one, Maa, is a Nilotic language, and they are all considered mutually unintelligible. Furthermore, several of these ethnic groups are not indigenous to the area. Among the six ethnic groups represented by contestants in this event, only Chagga is local, whereas Sukuma is from the western part of the country, Nyaturu is from the north-central portion, just south of Singida, and Bena and Nyakyusa are from far to the south, in the Southern Highlands area around Mbeya. The Maasai, while traditionally a group associated with the steppe of the north-central portion of Tanzania surrounding the Northern Zone, are nomadic and hence do not have a homeland per se. Even at city-level pageants, ethnic diversity was still pronounced. For example, in offstage interviews at a Miss Arusha competition, 6 of 11 competitors claimed two different local ethnic affiliations, while the remaining 5 identified with groups from elsewhere.

The ethnic diversity of the contestants highlights the fact that they, like many Tanzanians today, live in a place where they were not born, and which may be far from their parents' traditional home (the MEASURE Project, 2004).[3] In interviews with the 12 Northern Zone 2003 contestants, only four said that they have always lived in a single region, with three of these from Arusha or Moshi and one from the area around Lake Manyara. The remaining eight contestants said that they moved around the country while growing up, for boarding school or because of parents transferring or looking for work. Six of the young women had lived in Dar es Salaam at one point or another, and one had lived in Nairobi for several years. Given their diverse backgrounds and frequent relocating, it is clear that among contestants there would not be a commonly held local ethnic language in which to communicate.

But beyond the frequently cited concern for mutual intelligibility, there is another reason why local ethnic languages are not spoken in these beauty pageants. Most contestants with whom I spoke said, when pressed, that they do not in fact know their local ethnic language well, if at all. Hawa's description below of how it came to be that she does not speak the Chagga language very well is representative of other contestants' stories:

Wazazi wangu mimi walizoea kunisemea English na Kiswahili. Hiyo lugha nyingine labda niende kwa bibi na babu ndio wanisemea. Kwa sababu muda wa kukaa na kuongea na watu wa mitaani ulikuwa mchache, kwa sababu nikitoka shule naenda tuition nilikuwa nasoma days, sio boarding. Naenda shule nikitoka shule, saa sita mchana naenda tution mpaka saa 12 jioni kwa hiyo nilikuwa sina muda wa na watu wa mitaani nilikuwa sina kwa hiyo ndio sababu nilikuwa siongei. Kwa hiyo naongea kidogo sana. Kuna maneno mengine sielewi…. Wanajua. Wote wanajua. Wenyewe wanajua kwa sababu kuna dada zangu walisoma mpaka Darasa la saba ile kuanzia Form 1 mpaka Form 4. Baba alikuwa amesafiri kwa hiyo wakabaki na bibi. Kwa hiyo bibi akawa anawasemesha ile lugha, kwa hiyo ndio wakawa wanaongea ile lugha lakini wenyewe wanaelewa kabisa, hakuna neno ambalo hawalijui. Ila mimi naweza nikaongea watu wananicheka kwa sababu siwezi.

[My parents always spoke to me in English and Swahili. This other language [Chagga], maybe I would go to my grandfather and grand-mother's house and they would speak it to me. But time to stop and talk with people in the streets was always short, because I went to day school, not boarding school. And so I went to school and came home from school – I was there from noon until six in the evening – so I never had time to talk with people in the streets, therefore I never spoke in that language. Therefore I speak it only a very little. There are many words I don't understand.... They [my siblings] know it. They all know it. They know it because my sisters studied there up to Standard 7, rather from Form 1 to Form 4. My father was always traveling so they were left with my grandmother. Therefore my grandmother used to make them speak the language, so that's why they speak the language, they know it really well, there is not a word they don't know. As for me, I can try to speak it but people laugh because I can't really.]

Hawa's testimonial is revealing of the place of local ethnic languages in Tanzania. First, she expresses a direct link between the Chagga language and older generations. She indicates that while she would use Chagga from time to time when visiting her grandparents, she grew up speaking only English and Swahili with her parents. Her sisters know Chagga well ('there is not a word they don't know') because, unlike Hawa, they lived with their grand-mother for a significant period of time. Furthermore, Hawa's statement shows the very limited social contexts in which local ethnic languages are used in Tanzania; she indicates that her only opportunity to use Chagga was en route between school and home but, because of her tight schedule, she says, 'I never had time to talk with people in the streets, therefore I never spoke in that language'. Hawa's comments make clear an understanding by young urbanites of ethnic languages as a critical part of certain Tanzanian lives, but not *their* lives. These codes are linked with rural spaces, slower lifestyles and, to an extent, older generations. They are relevant as heritage, not as their own identity or for day-to-day communication.

Finally, the issues of intelligibility and competence are critical in making sure that contestants do not speak ethnic languages on stage, yet, as discussed in Chapters 4 and 5, neither of these issues prevents another language, English, from being used extensively and in various forms in these contexts. Rather, beyond practical communicative concerns, there is yet another, more ideological factor at play. Through *Ujamaa*'s focus on equality and non-tribalism, preceded by the British colony's concerns with ease of administrative communication, local ethnic languages in Tanzania have been constructed as 'private' or 'home' languages (see Chapter 2). This has led to a situation in which local ethnic languages have been virtually *erased* (Irvine & Gal, 2000) from public, modern life, a status echoed in Hawa's statement above in which she associates Chagga with her grandparents' generation and with a very limited range of social contexts. The success of the erasure can be seen in the fact that in the excerpt above, Hawa did not seem to question that Chagga is not used in school. As discussed in Chapter 2, it can also be seen in the virtual nonexistence of these languages in discussions of Tanzanian language policy, in which Swahili and English are typically considered the only viable options.

Double-Voiced Ethnicity on Stage

Despite the general erasure of ethnicity from public spaces in Tanzania, enregistered emblems of ethnicity circulate and appear with relative frequency within pageants for artistic and creative purposes. In this section, I briefly discuss three examples, highlighting the ways in which ethnicity is self-consciously brought into play in beauty pageants. Rather than an earnest manifestation of an individual's ethnic identity, each case instead deploys ethnic emblems – linguistic as well as non-linguistic – in some kind of projection of the ethnic 'other'. Useful here is Bakhtin's (1981) notion of *double-voicing*, a single utterance that contains a deliberate reference to someone else's words or speech, in interaction with the voice of the originator. Bakhtin's classic example of double-voicing is parody, when a speaker pits one voice, the parodist, against another, the kind of person characterized by those features being parodied. For Bakhtin, parody serves to destabilize, critique or co-opt the genre it imitates. And while parody is often comedic in nature, it need not be. In his Bakhtin-inspired study, Morson notes that:

> Parody recontextualizes its object so as to make it serve tasks contrary to its original tasks.... The direction and tone of the parody will depend on the nature of the parodist's disagreement with or disapproval of the original and the point of view from which he disagrees or disapproves. (Morson, 1989: 69)

Here, I will describe three cases in which pageant participants double-voice ethnicity for varying effects, both comedic and at least somewhat laudatory. But all three examples serve ultimately to *support*, rather than undermine, the historic construction of ethnicity-free urban life in Tanzania.

'Yes, that dress really shines!' A double-voiced ethnic joke (with a sexist *double-entendre*)

Masters of ceremony (MCs) are common figures in many kinds of events in Tanzania, including weddings and musical performances, as well as in pageants. In pageants, MCs' responsibilities include managing the flow of contestants on and off stage, informing audiences about details of the pageants and the evening's events, and interacting on stage with judges, special guests and organizers with a professional flair. Critically, MCs should also be entertaining and funny, with stereotypes of gender and ethnicity making common fodder for jokes (see description in Gahnström, 2012).

The first example of the appearance of ethnicity in pageants occurred during the evening gown segment of a Miss Arusha competition. During this portion of the pageant, each contestant takes the stage individually, walks the catwalk, then leaves the stage to make room for the next contestant. She does not speak, as she has already introduced herself earlier and will respond to a question later if selected to be in the top five. At this pageant, the MC was a middle-aged, well-dressed man in dress shirt and tie, who was occupied with announcing each contestant's name and provenance, and providing her with cues to signal that it was time to turn around and exit the stage. In this example, the MC briefly adopts three different comedic personae over the course of a particular contestant's final seconds

Figure 6.1 Master of ceremonies making an ethnic joke about a contestant (video-still)

before leaving the stage (Figure 6.1). For the MC's first persona, he speaks in a falsetto voice in imitation of contestants' self-introductions, just as the contestant begins her walk back towards the MC. M, master of ceremonies; A, audience.

1   **M**:   *Mnaniona?*
        'You see me?'
2   *Ndio mwenyewe bwana,*
        'Yes you sir,'
3   *Sophia Urio mimi.*
        'I'm Sophia Urio'
4   *Miaka yangu 19 tu*
        'Just 19 years old.'
5   *Majaji mnaniambiaje, majaji hapo?*
        'Judges, judges are you there?'
6   **A**:   HHHhhhhhhhhhhhhhhhh

Coyly tilting his head to the side and batting his eyelashes, his imitation included very informal Swahili, a register that no contestant would actually use onstage (see Chapters 4 and 5). Rather than mocking this particular young woman who did not stand out in any way, he was imitating young, female contestants in general, attention-hungry, under-educated and eager to please men. The audience reacts briefly with chuckles.

As the contestant finishes her return down the platform, the man resumes his 'true' MC persona, saying, in standard Swahili,

7   **M**:   *Hii sio mchezo hii. Heh heh heh.*
        'This here is not a joke. Ha ha ha.'

With this comment he becomes again the responsible MC, reining in his comedic side in order to continue the more serious business at hand. Yet he follows this statement with a chuckle, indicating that, indeed, it *is* all a joke to him.

Then, in his final persona, the MC shifts into a strongly accented variety of Swahili, characterized primarily by the neutralization of the l/r distinction. The MC says:

8   **M**:   *Harafu rinangaa hiro vazi.*
        [*Halafu, linangaa hilo vazi.*]
        'Yes, that dress really shines!'
9   **A**:   HHHhxhxhxhxhxhxhxhx

While this flattening is common in many dialects of Swahili, it is frequently used in mocking Haya ways of speaking. The Haya are a large ethnic group from north-west Tanzania – hundreds of miles from the location of this pageant – and they are also subject to many stereotypes (Gahnström, 2012). I conducted two focus groups and several interviews on this particular incident, and there were two dominant interpretations of the MC's parody. While the Haya are often stereotyped as advantaged in education and employment, and also as haughty and ostentatious, their homeland is the poor, rural, culturally peripheral (from an eastern Tanzanian perspective) region of Kagera. Therefore, in the context of this pageant in Arusha – a relatively wealthy and international city in the north-eastern part of the country – several viewers interpreted the comment as a parody of an unsophisticated ethnic Haya persona, one who is dazzled by the evening gown and the glitz and glamour of the event: 'that dress really shines'. But others focused on another, very widespread ethnic stereotype – of the female Haya prostitute. Haya women were historically involved in the urban sex trade (White, 1990) and, in conjunction with this profession, Haya women are still commonly understood to desire money and material possessions, necessary for their trade and purchased through their sex-earned wages (Weiss, 1993). The MC's reference to the contestant's shiny dress, in a Haya accent and in the context of a beauty pageant, was, for many who viewed the clip, an undeniable reference to Haya prostitution.

Yet no one to whom I showed the footage seemed concerned whether the contestant herself was Haya; indeed, her name did not indicate such ethnic heritage, nor did she have a dark complexion, a common Haya stereotype. Furthermore, no one had trouble with the MC – also not Haya – drawing on ethnicity to make jokes. Unlike cases discussed by scholars in which comedians elsewhere have license to make ethnic jokes because of some claim to that ethnicity themselves (Chun, 2004; Labrador, 2004), the opposite is true here. It is the geographic distance from the Haya homeland, as well as the urban setting of the event, that makes the double-voiced parody legitimate and fully in keeping with an MC's professional charge. Through his dress, comportment and standard Swahili, the MC himself is the embodiment of an urban African man whose ethnicity is, as it should be, concealed (see Thompson, 2006). In parody, he pushes ethnicity into the realm of the 'other', that of a rural, unsophisticated persona dazzled by urban clothing and unable to speak standard Swahili. What is more, though explicitly taking aim at a gendered ethnic stereotype based in a distant region, he does so in reference to a specific young woman on stage without marked ethnicity. Hence, he is able, indirectly, to express the conception of *all* contestants – urban, independent and Western-oriented – as amoral and materialistic prostitutes, a typecast which resonates even with many pageant fans.

Ultimately, while the first reading of the joke points to the unsuitability of ethnicity in urban spaces, the second reading suggests the corruptibility of not just Haya, but all, young women in the city. It is a double-voiced *double-entendre*, one which, according to some with whom I consulted, might have been intended for a Haya friend of the MC's in the audience, as such in-jokes are part of a good MC's skill-set. This joke works in Arusha and would likely work in Dar es Salaam as well. It likely would not work, however, in Kagera; it is the social and geographic distance that licenses the ethnic joke as double-voicing ethnicity, even as its sexist, possibly non-ethnic reading is able to stick.

'Performative primitive': Parodying the ethnic other through dance

Dance troupes are a common form of urban entertainment in Tanzania, and while some troupes perform *ngoma* 'traditional' dances,[4] affiliated with particular ethnicities, others perform contemporary genres such as *dansi* ('urban jazz'). In pageants, dance troupes frequently figure among the evening's entertainment. Most often, these are *dansi* troupes, outfitted in stylish and form-fitting urban dance attire. In the following case, however, a dance troupe at a Miss Arusha pageant performed a 'traditional' dance rife with recognized emblems of ethnicity. Rather than derived from a single ethnic heritage, however, their performance was a double-voiced caricature that served to index the rural 'other', all the while it reified the urban, sophisticated and decidedly non-ethnic identities of the audience, contestants and even the troupe's front man himself.

The performance began after the contestants' self-introductions, with a man wearing an animal-pelt skirt, black face paint, ankle rattles and a backpack made of an entire animal skin running onto stage and jumping around frenetically. Ululating and gesticulating wildly, he was joined by two voluptuous women dressed in leopard-print outfits, swaying their hips in a slow, sexual movement. Soon, another grass-skirted man appeared on stage (he would reappear in a later routine) to hand a large snake to the charismatic front man. The front man then spent the next several minutes wrapping the snake round his body, pulling it in a sexually suggestive way back and forth between his legs, and even inserting its head in and out of his mouth. The snake was then removed from the stage, at which point the front man pulled out medicine-man paraphernalia from his backpack. He intermittently shook his curative rattles around the dancing women. At one point, a female dancer lay down and feigned grave illness while the

Figure 6.2 Performative primitive (video-stills; clockwise from top left): Face paint and pelt outfits; medicine man and backpack; snake in mouth; and facial expressions and snake handling

man draped her body with a hide. Following his energetic and sexualized healing, the woman enacted a slow regaining of consciousness and began again her sensual swaying. The entire time, the front man made wild faces and frequently let out body-shaking shrieks, and he intermittently mouthed words to the Swahili-language song playing in the background (Figure 6.2).

Scholars of Tanzanian music and dance (e.g. Askew, 2002; Edmonson, 2007) have noted that in *ngoma* performances, dancers need not share the purported ethnic origins of the dance itself. Instead, students of dance learn a dance canon, and in sanctioned, urban performance or competitive contexts they may dance a routine from that canon regardless of their own ethnic affiliation. While sometimes – when poorly rehearsed – such performances garner critiques of inauthenticity, they may likewise be well received. Here, it was the pastiche of ethnic elements combined with the front man's over-the-top vocalizations and facial expressions that made this an example of what Edmonson (2007: 75) calls, following MacCannell (1992: 26), 'performative primitive'. The dance included an amalgam of recognized ethnic emblems from several heritages: characteristic of the *mbuji* dance from the Tanga region were the eponymous ankle rattles, while snake charming is known as a Sukuma tradition from the west; the black face paint and animal backpack are most typical of the *limbondo* dance, whereas *mganga*, or medicine man, elements occur in many *ngoma* performances.

MacCannell (1992: 26) originally coined the term, 'performative primitive' to refer to genres in the Western tourism industry in which there is an adoption, exaggeration and commodification of elements of non-Western and non-industrial performance or ritual. In the Tanzanian case, Edmonson (2007) argues that 'performative primitive' is more likely used for popular *Tanzanian* rather than international audiences; the state does not approve of such performances, especially for foreigners, and such dances may strike visitors as inauthentic. For many urban Tanzanians, however, the double-voiced, parodic expression of ethnicity in 'performative primitive' serves to distance themselves from the stereotype of rural, unsophisticated, even pre-modern Tanzanians. Rather than referencing any particular ethnicity, these emblems together conjure up the bush, a world far from the city – rural, base, primitive and purely African – which stands as a foil to the evening's main event. On the other hand, Edmonson (2007) points to the class distinctions in enjoyment of 'performative primitive' and, indeed, several people in the audience with whom I spoke found the particular performance inappropriate for what they perceived as a sophisticated event, an attitude perhaps reflected in the stoic politeness of some of the spectators during the routine.

As in the previous example of parody, it did not matter that the dancers were likely not affiliated with any of the ethnicities they were performing; no one seemed to have any concern whatsoever about issues of legitimacy. Everyone assumed the front man was a trained, urban performer and, as such, had license to co-opt whatever components of life in the bush were entertaining. Indeed, it was through his very use of this exaggerated, impossible combination of enregistered emblems that the performer makes his own, off-stage, 'real' Swahili identity known. This recalls an anecdote told by Edmonson (2007), in which the country's only female snake handler wanted it to be clear to audiences that she was *not* a member of the Sukuma snake-handling ethnic group and had *not* come by these skills 'naturally', but that, instead, she studied and learned the performance over time. As such, she wished to cast herself in the realm of urban performance artist rather than as traditional ethnic woman.

Finally, the intersection of ethnicity and gender emerges here again. In general, the hyperactive man and hypersexual and passive women seen in this example are characteristic of many *ngoma* dances (Edmonson, 2007). Yet unlike the frontman, with his extreme facial expressions and hybrid ethnic orientation, the women in this example were not caricatured; their dress, movements and demeanor were very similar if not identical to what occurs in other, non-parodic *ngoma*. The message seems to be, echoing Nyerere's Arusha Declaration sentiment discussed in Chapter 3, that the rural man is comical and out of place, while the rural woman is natural and productive. Furthermore, the silent, undulating and round female dancers stand in distinct contrast with the contestants on stage, hence perhaps offering a similar but more pointed meaning: that urban men are at home, while urban women are threatening and deviant. Edmonson remarks that

> the oscillating tension between gender and ethnicity [serves] as a reminder of the threat that 'tribalism' and female identity pose to the nation. It seems that one cultural 'sore zone' (Herzfeld 1997: 27) could be safely challenged without censure, but never the two shall meet through the performance of *ngoma*. (Edmonson, 2007: 83)

On the one hand, the fusion of ethnic markers in the parodied dance upholds the state's position against tribalism by mixing ethnic emblems into a non-threatening amalgam, especially as the front man's onstage language – the most potent symbol of all – remained Swahili. On the other hand, the wild-eyed, volatile man embracing ethnicity (even if not his own) stands in contrast to an understanding of masculine modernity put forward by Nyerere, in which even rural men work the land and suppress their ethnic affiliations. Adding a parodic feminine type would be too overtly political for this, and probably most any, public performance, especially when the contestants on stage already pose, to some, a threat to Tanzanian national identity.

Double-voicing Maasai ethnicity

The last of these examples involves an incident at a Miss Northern Zone competition in the city of Arusha, in which, unlike the earlier examples, a participant employs a double-voiced emblem of ethnicity that is parodic, as defined above, but not comedic or caricatured. As discussed in Chapter 3, the Maasai are a very visible ethnic minority in Tanzania who have long been the focus of the state's attempts to shape national culture and to encourage 'development' by suppressing outward manifestations of ethnic affiliation in the city, especially in relation to the Maasai and their distinctive *shuka* dress (Ivaska, 2002; Schneider, 2006). The Maasai have perennially been in tension with the state, which has taken issue with their continued adherence to a nomadic lifestyle, their regular crossing of national boundaries and their lack of cooperation with conservation efforts and delivery of social services (see e.g. Askew, 2002; Hodgson, 1999, 2011). While the Maasai themselves often embrace the stereotype that they are fierce, traditional warriors, many today live in urban areas and to varying degrees enjoy the benefits of sedentary, modern lives (Hughes, 2006). Some Maasai who have become city dwellers have left behind outward signs of ethnicity, while others are visible on busses and city streets wearing their brightly colored *shukas*, handmade sandals and colorful beads. They are often occupied, among other endeavors, as guards and promoting ecotourism (men), and selling their bead-work (women). The Northern Zone is the region where most ethnically Maasai Tanzanians live, whether in rural areas or in cities like Arusha.

This example took place during the creative wear part of the pageant, during which each contestant dons an original design while delivering her self-introduction. As described in Chapter 3, creative wear outfits range from sophisticated gowns befitting international fashion shows to whimsical creations with limited appeal beyond the very local context, to casual and revealing designs crafted from the quintessentially Tanzanian fabrics *kanga* and *kitenge*. At this event, a contestant took to the stage, instead, in a version of a female Maasai *shuka*. This outfit was knee-length and included uncharacteristically voluminous arm drapes, but otherwise the rather modest shift was similar to a more authentic version and was accompanied with beaded ear, forehead and neck jewelry. Unlike traditional Maasai women, however, this contestant wore full face makeup and softly curled hair pinned in a glamorous up-do. Furthermore, she did not seem ethnically Maasai in name or physical bearing – she was petite with rounded features, as opposed to the stereotyped tall and aquiline Maasai phenotype (Figure 6.3). While originally from the Kilimanjaro region, the contestant declared that she resided in Dar es Salaam and was pursuing a career in the airline industry. Notable here is that, while participants insist there is no place for ethnic *languages* in pageants, this contestant's wearing of ethnic dress was fully appropriate and even unremarkable to the audience.

How are we to interpret this choice of outfits? Over the course of my research, I witnessed two examples (including this one) of Maasai-inspired creative wear, in Arusha and Mwanza, and Higgins (2009) likewise has noted these outfits in Dar es Salaam pageants. Never, however, did I witness other ethnic-inspired outfits worn by contestants, and I argue that there are several reasons for this. First, as Maasai are one of the few groups in Tanzania to wear ethnic dress on a day-to-day basis, dressing up as a Maasai indexes a real-life way of being Tanzanian. Second, due to their mobility and presence in cities, there is broad familiarity with Maasai dress. Third, and importantly, Maasai are ethnically and linguistically distinct from the

Figure 6.3 Contestant wearing a version of Maasai ethnic dress (video-stills)

majority Bantu population in Tanzania, so wearing Maasai dress means, for most Tanzanians, adopting something quite different from their own heritage. While wearing ethnic dress associated with one's own background might be interpreted as tribalism and could index one's own connections with the bush, the double-voiced ethnicity displayed by this contestant wearing Maasai clothing allowed her to draw a clear distinction between herself and the persona she was imitating.

In performance contexts, Tanzanian men also have license to dress up as Maasai. For example, young men dressed as Maasai warriors escorted contestants on and off stage at one mid-level Northern Zone competition, and I also attended a wedding in Dar es Salaam at which the MC was dressed up as a Maasai warrior, and none of these people was likely of Maasai heritage. While Maasai men are widely stereotyped in Tanzania as dirty, backwards and ignorant (Thompson, 2006), they are nonetheless admired for their masculinity and, in these cases, a man dressing up as a Maasai signals traditional virility and fierceness, a persona that is up-for-the-taking by Tanzanian men within creative realms.

But for beauty contestants, dressing up as a Maasai woman has a distinct set of meanings. For their part, Maasai women are often understood by urban

Tanzanians as obedient and downtrodden workhorses, subjected to abusive initiations and deprived of an education, the very antithesis of a beauty queen. Yet in the context of beauty pageants, a contestant adorning herself as Maasai takes on a completely different significance. Contestants, having viewed international pageants for training and entertainment purposes, are familiar with the custom of each representative wearing a 'national costume' and, for the reasons discussed above, Maasai ethnic costume is the most viable. For Tanzanian beauty contestants, wearing these outfits marks them as familiar with international pageantry, a sign that they are sophisticated enough to be sent to Miss World. Furthermore, for these contestants, like the national representatives at Miss World and Miss Universe, every other aspect of their being – hair, makeup, gait and even presence in a pageant – distances themselves from the indigeneity of their dress. Instead, such attire becomes a double-voiced fashion statement, one that has the potential to appeal to an international crowd for its simultaneously exotic and trend-setting qualities but that also does not fully have to do with the 'real' woman behind the outfit. Contestants thus may participate in the 'happy face' of cosmopolitanism (Hannerz, 2004), showing an appreciation of difference and awareness of global expectations that may set them apart from their more provincially oriented competitors.

From another angle, donning these outfits can become a non-verbal participation in cosmopolitics, or cosmopolitanism with a 'worried face' (Hannerz, 2004: 71; Hannerz, 2005). In recent years, the Maasai have, probably more than any other group in Tanzania, become involved in international indigenous rights movements (Hodgson, 2011). Maasai leaders visibly interact, as ethnic citizens, with globally linked people, organizations and politics, both at home and abroad. These engagements make local newspaper headlines and have become part of an understanding of Maasai that stands alongside their other, negative stereotypes. For contestants wearing Maasai attire draws on the local and international visibility of Maasai in creating a cosmopolitan fashion statement. Through their attire, contestants may reference a trendy awareness of the Maasai as part of an international consciousness of ethnic struggles.

It is indeed ironic, given the history of state-level efforts to curtail manifestations of Maasai ethnicity, that Maasai dress should become, in this context, a version of national dress, as somehow representative of the nation as a whole. Hodgson (2011) points to the fact that the Maasai have long been used by Tanzanian authorities to support international tourism, even despite the state's antipathy to Maasai ways. In the form of a glossy government-approved brochure or postcard, such traditionalism at once appears authentically Tanzanian but also not true of *all* Tanzanians (such as those who created the brochures, etc.). In such publicity as well as in the examples above, it is the double-voicing of ethnicity that sanctions its presence. Furthermore, as in the cases above, gender and ethnicity work together to give shape to interpretations, and in the following section I discuss the local racial category of Asian as it intersects gendered understandings of Tanzanianness and femininity in the context of beauty pageants.

Mhindi Mhindi Tu ('An Indian Is an Indian'): Race, National Identity and the Crowning of a South Asian as Miss Tanzania

On 1 September 2007, Richa Adhia was a top-five finalist in the Miss Tanzania competition. For her question, Richa was asked her favorite color, a common but loaded pageant question elsewhere as well (Banet-Weiser, 1999). To this question, the contestant responded 'white', because for her it symbolized peace and purity. She went on to suggest that the Tanzanian flag be amended to include white for that symbolism. Like most national title-holders, Richa was tall, slim, light-skinned and spoke cosmopolitan elite English. But when the chief judge, former Miss Nigeria and Miss World 2001 Agbani Darego, later took to the stage and announced Richa as the winner, the audience erupted in equal parts elation and furor. What was at issue was that Richa was of Indian heritage, and her crowning sparked a renewed wave of debate over the centrality of race and ethnicity in constituting Tanzanian nationality (Figure 6.4).

While most Tanzanians embrace the ideal of a society that is blind to local *ethnic* differences, the place of race is not clear. In particular, where exactly the visible South Asian community stands in Tanzanian national identity has long been contentious ground. While several thousand South Asians already lived in Tanganyika during the mid to late 19th century, a result of the long history of trade throughout the Indian Ocean, it was during the British colonial era in East Africa that their numbers grew rapidly (Nagar, 1996). Recruited from India for manual labor in building the East African railway, many South Asians remained in East Africa after the completion of their contracts and began successful livelihoods as merchants and artisans. Following World War I, large numbers of South Asians emigrated from India to East Africa due to economic hardship in their homeland. Their numbers continued to increase until the end of the British colonial rule, as South Asians were sought for mid-level positions in the East African civil service (Nagar, 1996). Many Tanzanians understood Indians to be responsible, through their success in commerce and preferential treatment by colonists,

Figure 6.4 Miss Tanzania 2007, Richa Adhia, and runners-up
Credit: Issa Michuzi

for impeding 'African self-improvement' (Brennan, 2006: 404). Africans came in regular contact with Indians in offices, markets and stores, and they hence were a more visible target of frustration than the fewer and less visible white Europeans. In reaction to Africans' ire, Indians responded by ridiculing Africans for their laziness, incompetence and inability eventually to rule themselves (Brennan, 2006; Nagar, 1996).

Once the era of independence was ushered in, the romanticized ideal of indigenous African socialism, called *Ujamaa*, or familyhood,[5] that framed socialist politics and thought Tanzania during that era took hold. *Ujamaa* was to be an 'attitude of mind', according to which, in the extended family of Tanzanians, no individual or group would exploit another (Brennan, 2006). But the ideals of *Ujamaa*, once disseminated, took on a life of their own, and public discourse began to focus on qualifications for citizenship and who should be excluded from the extended family. Groups such as *wahuni* ('hooligans') as well as practitioners of witchcraft targeted for their *unyonyaji*, or 'sucking', were seen as not pulling their own weight and being a burden on the 'family' (Brennan, 2006).

In this context, discussion of citizenship also oriented around the relative wealth and segregation of the local Asian minority (Brennan, 2006). Africans resented that South Asians maintained comfortable, segregated lives in coveted urban neighborhoods. Furthermore, and in contrast to the *Ujamaa* focus on rural life and well-being, South Asians typically did not take to the land, and neither did they participate much in nationalist *Ujamaa* activities such as marches and rallies (Brennan, 2006). In Parliament, debates about citizenship – reflecting those occurring on street corners and in the popular press – frequently pointed to a perceived lack of loyalty among Asians, who 'have one leg in Tanganyika and one in Bombay' (quoted in Nagar, 1996: 66). Some voices, in keeping with the Nyerere ideal, conveyed opposition to 'marrying citizenship to colour', while others expressed the 'strong feeling ... that assimilation cannot take place and that the minority communities will remain as separate and distinct people with separate and distinct economic interests' (Nagar, 1996: 66). Indeed, families were (and still are) known to diversify citizenship within the family, with passports from the UK, India and elsewhere, should the need or opportunity to emigrate arise (Nagar, 1996).

While many Asians fled Tanzania during the early postcolonial period because of uncertainty around their future legal status, means of making a living and even safety in that country, some stayed behind and often prospered (Nagar, 1996). Economic liberalization brought further opportunity to Asian traders and merchants, whose ability to increase their wealth continued to rise, along with resentment among Africans of Asians' seemingly privileged place in society (Nagar, 1996). In the early 1990s, an 'indigenization debate' resumed the question over citizenship, race and inequality, with attention paid to Asians' prosperity, social isolation and resistance to speaking Swahili. Part of the solution put forth by many black Tanzanians was intermarriage with indigenous Africans (Nagar, 2000). Today, while a significant number of Asians in Tanzania are middle- and working-class people living in mixed neighborhoods, the perception among many black Tanzanians is that South Asians remain as a self-segregating, elitist and wealthy group of outsiders, too self-interested to commit fully to being Tanzanian.

It is in this context that pageant spectators interpreted the success of Richa Adhia. For some, her crowning signaled the realization of Tanzania's quest for a color-blind society; for others, it reinforced the conception of Asians as sucking up all of the country's wealth and opportunity. Immediately upon her being named Miss Tanzania, the Tanzanian blogosphere exploded in renewed controversy. Following the announcement of Richa's winning on the popular blog 'Issa Michuzi' (http://issamichuzi. blogspot.com/), an anonymous reader posted the following comment on 2 September 2007:

I'm speechless. Kwanza swali alilopewa kujiba kuwania taji la miss TZ, aliulizwa 'which is your favourite color', akajibu WHITE! Na akaendelea kuisifu rangi nyeupe na jinsi gani anavyoipenda, kuwa ni pure.... Automatically inaonyesha jinsi gani anavyoona rangi nyeupe ni bora kuliko zote. Anatamani na bendera yetu ingekuwa na weupe kudhihirisha sisi ni nchi yenye amani. Rangi nyeusi in many generations BC and AD imekuwa ikifananishwa na giza, misikba, mashetani na kila kitu kisichokuwa bora. Na imejengeka katika fikra zetu kuwa mtu mweupe ni bora kuliko mwenye ngozi nyeusi. Na mastereo type wanaendeleza hiyo fikra, kuwa mtu mweupe ni mzuri kuliko mabinti zetu wenye ngozi nyeusi. I'm so %*#@?^!!$.

[I am speechless. First, the question that she was given to answer to compete for the crown of Miss Tanzania, she was asked, 'which is your favorite color', then she answered WHITE! And then she went on to praise the color white and in what ways she likes it, that it is pure.... Automatically it shows how she sees the color white as better than all the others. She believes that our flag should have white to show that we are a country of peace. The color black in many generations BC and AD has been compared with darkness, disasters, demons and every thing that is not good. And it has gotten built on the idea that white people are better than those with black skin. And the stereotypes continue this idea, that a white person is better than our girls with black skin. I'm so %*#@?^!!$.]

Here, the issue is distilled to race and, in particular, the skin color of women. The writer is angry, calling upon discourses with long histories based on colonial exploitation and postcolonial structural inequalities that have fallen along racial lines. The writer draws the obvious parallel between Richa's love for the color white and her own light skin, and concludes that the pageant should support 'our girls with black skin'.

Many other online contributors focused on language as a signal of Richa's outsider status. While, like most Miss Tanzania winners, Richa used English during her question-and-answer session, her use of English was taken by many as a rejection or ignorance of Swahili. Richa in fact spoke Swahili in a pre-recorded self-introduction aired during the pageant, and her Swahili was standard, with only a trace of an Asian accent. Some viewers may have missed this segment, because many blog readers who submitted comments asserted that she did not know how to speak the national language. Others may have interpreted her Swahili as a memorized performance. On the Bongo Celebrity blog (bongocelebrity.com),[6] a reader named Linda posted the following on 2 September 2007:

Kemcho richa? hivi huyo miss anaongea kiswahili kweli?
[Hello [in Gujarati] Richa. Does this beauty queen really speak Swahili?]

Here, the blogger foregrounds language and identity in two ways. First, the commonly known Gujarati greeting 'Kemcho' is used sardonically to emphasize the beauty queen's outsider and Asian background. Secondly, the writer openly questions Richa's ability to speak Swahili, as an index of that outsider status. In another comment on Bongo Celebrity (posted 6 November 2007), a writer (A.E. i o u) emphasizes the critical nature of using Swahili as a symbol of national unity or 'integrity':

Hello Richa Adhia, you are a representative of Tanzania. At least, see to it that you speak the language of Tanzanians. Familiarise yourself with Swahili and make statements in Kiswahili as well…. Do not betray our integrity as a nation.

In retort to a plethora of negative postings, others called upon Nyerere's message of unity and color-blindness, emphasizing non-racial markers of Tanzanian national identity, including Richa's use of Swahili in the opening segment:

Why are there so many racist comments posted for such a beautiful contest. Come on mate! Even Richa possesses a green passport. Even she speaks kiswahili. Even she likes Muhogo. And besides she answered the best out of all the other contestants. All of us should be proud of the Tanzanian Culture, which blends in itself so many tribes, cultures and races…. Come on, build the country together…. My dear fellow Tanzanians, lets live up to Mwalimu Nyerere's legacy of brother hood and keep aside hate and difference…. (Posted by Rio on Bongo Celebrity, 10 September 2007)

For this writer, Richa's ability to speak Swahili, her Tanzanian passport and her embracing of East African cuisine is enough to make her Tanzanian. The writer characterizes Tanzanian culture as a singular amalgam of 'so many tribes, cultures and races' without drawing a distinction between indigenous and non-indigenous ones, and calls upon Nyerere's message of unity in building a color-blind and egalitarian society.

But as above, gender intersects understandings of race and ethnicity, and on the Issa Michuzi message board, another contributor questions why the existence of Asian and Arab politicians in Tanzania is relatively unproblematic, while an Asian Miss Tanzania is:

Hivi mbona hatulalamiki kuwa na wabunge wahindi na waarabu???
Mohamed Daewji, Rostam na Arfi wa Mpanda ni wabunge
waliochaguliwa na wananchi kwa kuwaona wanafaa. Baba wa taifa
Mwalimu Nyerere aliwachagua Jamal, Derek Bryson na Alnoor Kassam.
Hao ni wahidni [sic] na mzungu waliokuwa kwenye baraza la mawaziri.
Bryson alikuwa kipenzi cha watu wa kinondoni na watu hawakuangalia
rangi yake. Leo hii tumeanza kuwabagua ndugu zetu kwa kusema ni
wahindi au wazungu. La msingi ni kwamba mtu akiwa mtanzania ana
haki zote bila kujali rangi yake.Leo tukianza na wandi [wahindi] kesho
tutabaguana kwamba wewe ni mkurya au msukuma au mhaya....
[Why don't we complain about Members of Parliament of Indian and
Arab origins??? Mohamed Dewji, Rostam and Arfi from Mpanda, are
parliamentarians who were elected by citizens as being fit to lead. The
Father of the Nation, Mwalimu Nyerere, chose Jamal, Dereck Byceson
and Al Noor Kassam. Those are Indians and a European who served in
the cabinet.... Now we have started to discriminate against our brethren,
saying, that person is Indian, that person is white. What matters is that
if a person is a Tanzanian, he/she has all the rights regardless of his color.
If we start with Asians today, tomorrow we will start discrimination
against ourselves, that you are a Kurya, a Sukuma or Haya....]

The comparison of the election of racially and ethnically diverse political
representatives with an Asian Miss Tanzania beauty queen brings to light
the fact that what is at issue in the pageants is not just race or ethnicity, but
a gendered racial identity (Banet-Weiser, 1999). The pageants themselves are
sometimes publicly critiqued for being businesses operated by Asian men,
reinforcing the understanding of Asian masculinity in terms of successful
business ownership. In contrast, the issue with Richa is that she is a young
Asian woman, and that has its own set of indexicalities, in particular ones
having to do with the common perception of Asian women as not inter-
marrying with African men, as in the following post from the Issa Michuzi
blog on 2 September 2007:

Tusidanganyane jamani mhindi mhindi tu mbona basi hawakubali
kuolewa na waswahili na wakifanya hivyo wanatengwa, mbona
hatuwaoni wakijichanganya na waswahili...?
[Let's stop lying to ourselves, an Indian is an Indian, why don't they
[female Indians] agree to marry[7] Waswahili [black Tanzanians], and
if they do, then they get separated, and why don't we see them even
mingling with Waswahili...?[8]]

Skin color, gender and self-isolation are folded in together here in a sentiment that reflects the idea that, in postcolonial Tanzania, South Asians have constructed rigid community boundaries through the policing of female sexual purity, in particular, by preventing 'contamination' from outside the community (Nagar, 1998: 133). While Asian men have conjugal and non-conjugal sexual relations with black African woman with relative impunity, to the extent that black women may be wholly accepted into extended Asian families as one of their own, Asian women who are involved sexually with or marry African men face ostracization for defiling not only themselves but their community as well (Nagar, 2000). In the Asian social hierarchy, African men are at the bottom, in that they are unmarriable to Asian woman, or, according to one Goan man, 'to us a black man is a worker, a house boy' (quoted in Nagar, 1998: 134). As the wearer of the Miss Tanzania crown represents, among other things, an object of desire, the selection of an Asian seemed especially offensive to the writer of the blog post above because it emphasized the unattainability and isolation of not just the Asian community, but of Asian women in particular, who stand as an icon of that isolation.

A third-generation Tanzanian of Indian heritage, Richa was born in Dar es Salaam, spent much of her childhood in the western city of Mwanza, before relocating back to Dar with her family. In a blog interview upon her crowning as Miss Kinondoni, prior to winning the Miss Tanzania competition, Richa was asked whether she felt 'offended by the race issues raised', to which she responded:

> Not really, it doesn't offend me but it does surprise me. Our father of the Nation the late Julius Kambarage Nyerere himself said once that we should stop discriminating each other because we are all brothers and sisters. I totally agree with his words. Racial discrimination has long past its phrase [sic] and is considered history, so it's high time Tanzanians bury the past. (Bongo Celebrity, 12 July 2007)

The events of September 2007 indicate that, while not alone in her sentiment, Richa expresses a view that is widely contested. The ability to speak Swahili is certainly a critical symbol of the nation and a key ingredient of citizenship still today, but even Swahili-speaking Asians in Tanzania serve as a reminder to many of the vast inequalities characteristic of Africans' lives and visible in many cases right outside their front doors. While Asian men, as merchants and traders, represent financial privilege and mobility, Asian women signify, even if implicitly, the social isolation that typifies Asian communities for many black Tanzanians today.

Conclusion

Nyerere's ideal of a color-blind society has been internalized by Tanzanians, but what exactly that means is still up for debate. Often, his vision means *not* the acceptance of difference but instead its virtual erasure. Today, ethnic dress, languages and politics have very little place in public urban space in Tanzania. On the other hand, dichotomies of rural versus urban, and ethnic versus Tanzanian, remain strong, and urbanites' ability to play with emblematized indices of ethnicity allows them to draw upon certain features of that ethnicity, for variable effects, at the same time that they distance themselves from it.

Typically referencing indigenous ethnicity, color-blindness may also reference other minority populations, such as the South Asian community in Tanzania. In the case of the Miss Tanzania of South Asian heritage, her crowning brought to the surface concerns over Indians' self-segregation and relative wealth. Simultaneously, it was a source of pride for some Tanzanians as a fulfillment of Nyerere's vision many decades ago. In pageants, as state-monitored events that rely on public interest and support, the selection of Richa Adhia reflects a sentiment among many Tanzanian that South Asians are in fact *real* Tanzanians, and that embracing *all* diversity is in the spirit of the national ethos of color-blindness. But as pageants are operated by businesses whose greatest goal is to produce successful Miss World contestants (see Chapter 7), the selection of Richa Adhia as Miss World also successfully casts Tanzania, to local and especially international followers, as a cosmopolitan, globalized nation-state, inhabited by cosmopolitan, globalized, not to mention racially diverse, citizens.

In all of this, gender structures and shapes how ethnicity and race are interpreted. An ethnic slur takes on layers of meaning when one considers gender stereotypes in relation to ethnic ones. A double-voiced ethnic dance parodies rural, ethnic masculine identity while legitimizing a feminine one. And playing dress-up in Maasai clothing can either signal primitive virility and strength, or invite the viewer to consider its wearer as a stylish cosmopolite. In the cases of the ethnic slur and the ethnic dance, the notion that women's place is in the bush is repeated, but when a contestant dresses like a Maasai, the place of ethnicity within urban, cosmopolitan imaginings is brought to the fore.

Finally, even as the search for Tanzanian identity continues, and is often defined in terms of negatives (Blommaert, 1999a), the Swahili language continues to be significant. While for most contestants, speaking Swahili onstage signals a lack of education, for someone such as Richa Adhia, whose identity as Tanzanian is on the line, the ability to speak the national language is critical, for both supporters and detractors, in constituting her belonging. Swahili remains, then, the symbolic unifier of the Tanzanian people, who, in all of their diversity, still seek, in variable ways, the unity heralded by their first, most famous President.

Notes

(1) In another pattern of language shift, Winter's (1979) research focused on the shift from one local ethnic language to another in East Africa. He outlines the 100-year decline and eventual extinction of Aasáx, a Cushitic language that was spoken in northern Tanzania until 1976, when the last speaker died. During this time, speakers shifted to Maa, the language of the much more dominant Maasai.

(2) But see Wedin (2010) for a discussion of the limits of entrenchment even of Swahili in certain rural areas, where students' grasp of the language in primary school is not strong.

(3) Publications on public health (in particular AIDS and refugee issues) in Tanzania make frequent reference to the high mobility of the populace, but actual data are difficult to come by. One study (the MEASURE Project, 2004) shows that 37% of urban women and 31% of urban men aged 20–24 in Tanzania report having lived at their current residence for less than five years.

(4) Edmonson (2007) discusses the fact that even though conceived of as 'traditional', *ngoma* dances undergo constant reworking and reinterpretation, making them anything but static.

(5) The metaphor of familyhood was common in postcolonial discourse across the continent (Schatzberg, 2001).

(6) *Bongo*, meaning 'brains', is slang for Tanzania's cultural capital, Dar es Salaam.

(7) Here, it is the use of the passive verb *–olewa* that makes clear the otherwise gender-neutral subject is referring to women. In Swahili, the active verb *–oa* is used for a man marrying a woman, while the passive verb *–olewa* refers to a woman marrying a man.

(8) While technically referring to ethnically Swahili people, the term *Waswahili* has come to refer to Tanzanians in general, or even anyone of African origin in the region (Lewinson, 1999; Thompson, 2006).

7 *Kutafuta Maisha*: 'Looking for a Life' from the Edge of the Globe

Kutafuta Maisha

In his work on barbershops in Arusha, Brad Weiss (2009) discusses the effects of the boom then bust following the opening up of the Tanzanian economy in the 1990s:

> Tanzanian society was simultaneously opened to media, goods, and ideologies never before available, while the decline of state services and subsidies led ... to the collapse of a host of employment opportunities. This sudden crash on the heels of unprecedented and exhilarating possi-bilities – unrealized by the vast majority of Tanzanians as anything *but* possibilities – made it possible for a broad swath of people to desire the signs and styles of a global order while finding ever narrower means by which to satisfy them. (Weiss, 2009: 9)

The result of this disconnect between reality and desire is, according to Weiss, that the majority of Tanzanians are 'convinced that life is better elsewhere, and that the grind of struggle and poverty, of *kutafuta maisha* (looking for a life), is immeasurably eased anywhere but here' (Weiss, 2009: 72). Indeed, in a place where sustaining wage labor is hard to come by, even for the most educated segments of society, opportunity is understandably thought to be located elsewhere. One need only ask a Tanzanian cab driver his background or whether he is from that city and he is likely to tell you he came from a smaller place in order to *kutafuta maisha* (see Moyer, 2003; Setel, 1999; Weiss, 2009). In Tanzania, the trope of *kutafuta maisha* frames fantasies, plans and life stories in which movement, money and ambition are defining elements. In its essence, though, *kutafuta maisha* typically concerns finding any kind of modest livelihood, typically away from home. People move in order to seek a better life, relocating from the village to a nearby city, or from a regional capital to a big city, with Dar es Salaam being the peak of perceived opportunity within Tanzania. What is more, many Tanzanians dream of pursuing educational, work and business opportunities around the globe, with Nairobi and South Africa figuring frequently in discussions of a better life. They dream about prosperity out of Africa as well, referencing the lives of family, friends or people they have only heard about, living in Dubai, England or the United States.

Strategies for looking for life are diverse, though foremost of them is the pursuit of an education. Education – and the acquisition of English skills through education – is prominent in this quest for a better life, as captured in the phrase *elimu ni ufunguo wa maisha* (Chapter 5). Securing an education means continuing secondary and, ideally, post-secondary schooling; in addition, for-profit language, technical and trade institutes also offer hope for many. But even as both men and women seek an education for a better life, for young women the dream of an education offers the additional lure of autonomy, much sought-after even with the moralizing stigma often attached to single women in the city. For young women, the promise of education is the promise of independence made possible through gainful employment. Young men, aware of their female counterparts' common desire for independence and their, albeit equally tenuous, place in the labor market, are sometimes resentful of these women, a fact that fuels inter-pretations of them as ill-behaved, untrustworthy and promiscuous (Ivaska, 2002; Stambach, 2000b; Weiss, 2009).

Yet for most young Tanzanians, finances and other impediments have limited their ability to achieve an education and to acquire English, and therefore they engage in a wide variety of other ways of *kutafuta maisha*. Very often, these strategies are gendered and unfold in the informal economy. While typically producing an extremely slim living, such ways of occupying oneself are often seen as a route to something better. Weiss (2009) discusses *vinyozi* ('barber shops') in the northern city of Arusha, where barbers are often young men with some secondary schooling but with, at present, few other opportunities. Orienting their shops, attitudes, as well as hair and clothing fashions towards American hip-hop culture, these men's pro-fessional world takes place at the intersection of fantasy and reality. With English names such as 'Brooklyn Haircut' and 'Boyz II Men Haircutting', the barbershops reference far-away places and identities seen to represent more prosperous lives. They reflect the cosmopolitan aspirations of the barbers and their customers, serving, through their names, their services and their communal space, as an opportunity to interact with and interpret – without simple mimicry – globally sourced trends in masculine grooming and ways of being. But the life of a barber is typically not prosperous. Such young men might alternatively seek their fortune in the dangerous tanzanite mines, as did Justina's brother in Chapter 1. While this work is physically dangerous and more likely to secure a serious injury than a large stone, young men nonetheless hope for the mother lode. Weiss describes such hope in the seemingly impossible, seen likewise in hip-hop imaginings, as stemming from their grim economic circumstances and coupled with their awareness of other, more prosperous, lives: 'In a world where tomorrow is only a dim prospect, striking it rich is hardly more fantastical than scraping by' (Weiss, 2009: 95).

Young women also participate in street-level activities, such as vegetable and used-clothes vending or selling *maandazi* ('doughnuts') to passing day laborers. But for other young women, a cosmopolitan imaginary drives their efforts to find a better life, and their strategies for getting by are designed to facilitate their participation in a particular kind of urban lifestyle. 'Sugar-daddy' relationships (see Chapter 3; Nyanzi & Nyanzi-Wakholi, 2004) offer a possibility for providing the material comforts befitting their sensibilities. For still others, these arrangements are not appealing and do not offer the independence they desire; indeed, many young women expressed the belief that African men are abusive and untrustworthy, and they are better off without them (see e.g. Stambach, 2000a).[1]

Beauty pageants are another, cosmopolitan strategy for looking for life. Like Weiss's (2009) barber shops, pageants sit at the intersection of a global imaginary and a local reality. Even as a one-time endeavor, beauty pageants allow contestants to enjoy the clothing, hairstyles and glamour that links them with like-minded women worldwide. Furthermore, it allows them to fantasize, like pageant hopefuls everywhere, that 'that could be me' (Dewey, 2008: 197). For many contestants, this fantasy is not only, or even primarily, about securing adoration and fame; indeed, contestants are very aware of the vulnerable place participating puts them within their families and Tanzanian society more broadly. Rather, participating is often about the tangible rewards that even lower-level pageants offer. One success-ful contestant described the tension with her father between reputation and reward:

… kwa baba, kwa waafrika, utakuta tamaduni zetu inakuwa ngumu sana kwa baba kukubali kuwa mtoto wake aende kufanya mashindano kama hayo. Kwa sababu wana ile imani kuwa ni uhuni; mtoto wako akienda kushiriki anakuwa hayuko kwenye ile tamadani ambayo tumelelewa. Kwa hiyo mwanzani ilikuwa ngumu lakini baadaye nikamuelewesha nikamwambia, baba, ni fani kama fani nyingine yoyote na pia sio kwamba nafanya tu. Pamoja na kuwa napenda kuna kitu ambacho ninapata kutokana na kushiriki kwenye mashindano, kwa sababu nitalipwa na nitaweza kuendelea shule, na pia nitapata jina, nitafahamika, na mimi nitaweza kuwa karibu na jamii yangu na kuwasaidia.

[… for my father, for Africans, you will find that in our cultures it is very difficult for a father to agree to his child going to do contests like these. Because they have the belief that it is prostitution; if your child goes to participate she is outside of the cultures in which we have been raised. Therefore, the first time it was difficult but later I made him understand and I told him, father, it is an interest of mine like any other and also it is not just that I participate. I also like that there is something I get from participating in the contests, because I will be paid and I will be able to continue with schooling, and also I will get a title, everyone will know me, and I will be able to be near to my society and to help them.]

This contestant mentions the money and scholarships that make her participation potentially lucrative. The modest funds awarded to winners offer them a practical, if circumscribed, answer to their problems, while the small electronics and showy sofa sets that are often part of a winner's booty allow contestants to participate, even if temporarily, in a commodity-indexed prosperity that otherwise is largely out of reach. But the lure of beauty pageants extends well beyond these transient rewards, with many contestants mentioning the successes of past beauty queens, and especially their mobility, as evidence of what is possible for their future lives. In the world of pageants, contestants are acutely aware of the success stories of former Tanzanian beauty queens such as Happiness 'Millen' Magese (Chapter 1) and, for these young women, engaging in beauty pageants is an entertaining and creative way of participating in global trends and discourses, at the same time that it offers a dream that it will provide them with a similar escape.

Yet while the images, products and ideas of the wider world are often deeply felt by urban Tanzanians to enrich their lives, in terms of life prospects, these are rather limited ways of participating in the promise of the global order and serve as daily reminders to Tanzanians of the fact that globalization has not treated them as well as it has people elsewhere. Urban Tanzanians engage in local cosmopolitanisms that allow them to take part in and remake global trends, and draw certain affinities with observable lives elsewhere, at the same time that they are deeply aware of the inequalities that characterize their lives *as Tanzanians*. The circumstances that have produced the characteristic flows of globalization (Chapter 1), flows that allow for playful engagement with hip-hop, pageantry, not to mention language, have simultaneously produced a sense of what is possible, on the human scale, for others, even if not for themselves. For Weiss (2009: 72), it is 'an awareness of Tanzania as a place within this nexus of places. For most of the residents of Arusha, this is a profoundly troubling scene.'

Miss Tanzania to Miss World and Back Again

The pleasure, promise and disappointment of global fantasies are epitomized by Miss Tanzanias' pursuit of the Miss World crown. While contestants from regional peripheries point to Arusha, Mwanza or, especially, Dar es Salaam, as the place where Miss Tanzania winners come from (Chapter 4), the pyramid of real and imagined opportunity does not peak there. Contestants, beauty queens and Tanzanians more generally understand that national crown holders from other countries hold a much greater chance for success at Miss World than does Miss Tanzania. Indeed, many Tanzanians obsess about Miss Tanzania's perennial under-performance at Miss World and engage in frequent speculation about why she cannot seem to do better.

When Miss Tanzania, the best contestant the nation has to offer, arrives at the Miss World competition in a far-away city like London, Johannesburg or Sanya, China, she typically feels her value plummet, just as it had for provincial contestants arriving in Dar es Salaam. One of the first women to be crowned Miss Tanzania described to me several years after her reign the humiliation and loneliness she felt while at the Miss World camp. Her first time out of the country and on an airplane, she was forced to go without a female companion, due to the pageant committee's financial constraints. During the month of training and preliminary rounds for the world event, she felt very isolated; most contestants around her seemed to speak English far better than she did, and so she was frequently embarrassed to speak. She described the humiliation of having only three nice outfits to wear, while her competitors appeared to change clothes several times each day. Many of them brought along stylists to dress and groom them, but she had to manage these preparations by herself. In addition to being personally trying, these circumstances left her at a distinct material disadvantage on the Miss World stage, a reality only exacerbated by her extreme lack of confidence that such disadvantage generated in her.

More recently, the Tanzanian organizing committee has improved the situation, paying for Miss Tanzania to bring a guest and providing an allowance with which she may buy suitable clothing for her journey and for the competition. In addition, the organization now invests in the representative's grooming and physique, employing advisers and specialists to prepare her for the big event. While certainly mitigating the personal hardships for the national crown-holder, these efforts have not proved sufficient to secure victory. Miss Tanzania has never come close to winning the Miss World competition; the winning of the regional sub-event, 'Miss World Africa', by Miss Tanzania 2005, Nancy Sumari, has been the highest victory achieved.

The regularly disappointing performance of Miss Tanzania at Miss World garners much attention and speculation, both publicly and among pageant participants, and is frequently addressed in newspaper coverage surrounding the events. Conjecture about the national representative's perennial losses takes several strands. National pageant organizers and directors, who, as business people, have an interest in encouraging pageant enthusiasm among sponsors, would-be contestants and fans alike, typically frame past failures and future prospects at Miss World in the optimistic terms of lessons learned, experience gained and hard work ahead. While the national director was once quoted as saying Tanzania's losses were an issue of 'gene pull [*sic*] ... Tanzanian girls have either been short [or] too African' (Toroka, 2002), usually explanations for poor performance focus on logistical and practical issues. Timing is frequently mentioned, with the fact that Miss Tanzania is crowned so close in time to the Miss World competition that there is little opportunity for in-depth preparations. In contrast, people frequently cite the fact that India – considered to operate a highly successful pageant enterprise – holds its national event in March or April, allowing plenty of time before the December world event.[2] Differences in competitive segments between the local and world events are also often noted. Historically, the Miss World competition has included competitive segments – in particular, talent and sports – not represented at the Miss Tanzania competition, so that Tanzanian delegates have had to compete in areas that they have never competed in before and which did not figure in the criteria determining their win.

Like organizers, contestants take an optimistic perspective, stressing practical differences in the pageants and the hard work that will prepare them for success.[3] One segment – the swimsuit competition – has been a particular focus of contestants, not to mention the public at large. As discussed in Chapter 3, Tanzanian pageants include a 'beach wear' competition, in which, by Tanzanian law, contestants may wear a swimsuit but must cover the upper thighs with a sarong or shorts. This practice leaves contestants, so they argue, at a disadvantage at the Miss World competition, because they do not have *uzoefu* ('experience') or confidence modeling such outfits. What is more, many contestants have realized that at Miss Tanzania they are not judged on muscle tone and fitness minutiae in the same way as at the international pageant, which also makes them less qualified than other competitors and leaves them in need of time and resources for body-toning activities.

In an effort to correct for some of these perceived practical disadvantages, the Miss Tanzania organizing committee instituted in 2011 several pre-competition competitive events, including Miss Talent and Miss Sports, which mirror similar events at Miss World. At both the national and international pageant, these segments, which occur prior to the main event, are called 'fast track' competitions, because they afford their winners an automatic place in the semi-finals. In the following newspaper interview, a contestant justifies the importance of the Miss Tanzania 'Sports Day' because of sport's prominence in the world competition and because of the fact that many of the Miss World sports are outside Tanzanian women's athletic repertoire:

> One of the contestants, Glory Lory, said the day was extremely important to all models considering that they have learnt several sports that were completely new to them. She said apart from keeping themselves in good shape, they have expanded their knowledge on sports, given that sports are among the categories that Miss World contestants must participate in. (*Daily News*, 2011a)

In contrast to the positive tone of contestants and organizers, a far more critical perspective is common among those not directly involved in pageants in explaining contestants' failings on the world stage; many point to corruption as a primary reason. Judges, they argue, are swayed into selecting unsuitable contestants as winners for personal – financial or sexual – gain. In one newspaper editorial, the writer links the substantial prize package – a new Jeep and 8 million Tanzanian shillings (about US$5000) – with the increased likelihood that participants and even their families will attempt to corrupt the judges. Contestants themselves are understood to be, or to become through the process of competing, morally corrupt (Chapter 3) and according to critics their *utovu wa nidhamu* (lack of good behavior) makes them the driving forces in the corrupt choices judges make.

The pessimistic view of Miss Tanzania's prospects for global domination is often conveyed in newspapers with words like 'shame' and 'failure', as seen in an editorial entitled, 'Miss World: Are we sending the right material?':

> Year in year out, Tanzania has been sending its 'most beautiful' girl to represent the country in the annual Miss World beauty pageant. The sad thing, however, is that year in year out, the girls have failed to get any

tangible results for the country. The only time our contestant did well in the international event is in 2005 when Nancy Sumari won the Miss Africa World at the Miss World beauty pageant in China. From then on, it has been the same old story of failure ... failure ... failure.... (*Daily News*, 2010)

Tanzanians often understand this 'failure' as an issue of national pride, and as characteristic of Tanzanians' lack of success relative to other countries in other competitive realms as well:

Like everything else, TZ seem to be playing second (if not last) fiddle to others. Take track and field for example. We have talents that is [*sic*] never developed. Teams sent out for competitions are composed of more officials than athletes. We all come out as a laughing stock. I am sure miss TZ [Miss Tanzania] competitions are no exceptions. (*Daily News*, 2010 [readers' comments])

Until and unless Tanzanians agree to get out of this limbo by electing committed leaders who through leadership and visionary skills will provide the platform for real change and quality development leading to national pride, we should expect a continuation of this. Not only in beauty pageants but in EVERYTHING. We should agree that we have got a problem and then we should be ready to painstakingly agree to tackle the problem.... (*Daily News*, 2010 [readers' comments])

... one day Tanzania will be as popular in every beauty pagent [*sic*] in the world as Venezuala [*sic*] and India are. (Posted by Rio to Bongo Celebrity, 10 September 2007)

For Tanzanians, part of the issue is a quest against other countries in a spirit of nationalist competition like that fostered by international sporting events (e.g. Vidacs, 2011). Dewey makes similar observations in the case of India, where newspapers report that Indian beauty pageants help put India 'on the map' and 'on par' with more 'developed' countries (Dewey, 2008: 201). Through the hard work of pageant training, contestants will have access to the wealth, success and fame available – perhaps more easily – to those from other countries, especially those in the global north. Such language serves to put all Indians in the same figurative boat, as underdogs in the global order, creating a collective mission in showing the world that they are good enough to compete in, and even win, international competitions. This underdog mentality is particularly of note in the case of India, given its successes on the global pageant stage; with five wins, Miss India is the second most successful representative, after Miss Venezuela, to compete at Miss World. Miss India has also won Miss Universe twice, thereby tying with several other countries for fifth most successful representative. But such victories stand in stark contrast to Tanzania's lackluster track record and, indeed, serve as beacons for Tanzanians' competitive aspirations.

Yet nowhere in the talk of Tanzanian competitive strategy and disadvantage in the global pageant arena is language mentioned; indeed, English is rarely an issue because of the high place of English in the local selection criteria. Even globally, there is a widespread belief that English is a critical component of winning Miss World. For example, Miss Italy 2009 remarked that:

> I'm preparing to [sic] Miss World going to the gym and taking care of my body and my skin. Then, I'm playing the piano everyday and, obviously, I'm speaking English whenever I can. (http://staging.missworld.com. php5-13.dfw1-2.websitetestlink.com/contestant/showcontestant/italy)

Yet numerically, many Miss World winners are not English-speaking. In the 10 years between 2003 and 2012, five winners spoke a language other than English in competition (Miss China 2012, Miss Venezuela 2011, Miss Russia 2008, Miss China 2007 and Miss Peru 2004). While speaking English certainly provides some advantages for a contestant – the ability to communicate more widely and to avoid the use of an onstage translator – not speaking English certainly does not preclude winning the crown.

In Tanzania, though, the significance of English is that it serves as an index of all of the other features – poise, intelligence, confidence, Western knowledge, cosmopolitanism – that are deemed necessary for a crownholder. What is more, it is acquired in conjunction – whether in school or in an elite household – with these other desirable qualities (see Chapter 5). While largely unquestioned, the value placed on English for Miss Tanzania was cast into doubt by one blogger immediately following the crowning of Miss World 2011, a non-English speaker from Venezuela:

> ... kigezo anachotumia lundenga kwenye miss Tanzania lazima miss ajue english,mbona miss world wa sasa kutoka Venezuela ajui english, je tz tunakosea kutumia kigezo cha english tu? (jamiiforums blogspot, 8 November 2011)
> [... the yardstick that lundenga [the national pageant director] uses in miss Tanzania is that the beauty queen must know english, but why does the current miss world from Venezuela not know english? So why tz [Tanzania] do we make the mistake of using just the yardstick of english?]

The blogger's question, of course, speaks to similar questions about English as the yardstick of education and of personal worth, as embedded in institutionally supported policies and practices. It is painfully ironic here, however, that seeking a speaker of standard English – rather than someone who meets the largely physical standards put forth by the Miss World committee, in which a model's height, weight and muscle tone are critical components – likely sabotages Tanzania's success on the world stage.

But there are other issues as well that account for Tanzania's performance, which concern the fact that Tanzania is a poor country in the global south, sending competitors to the international contest with distinct disadvantages. In June 2012, Tanzania crowned Lisa Jensen as the national winner. Due to date changes in the Miss World competition, in which the preliminaries would be in July rather than in November, Tanzania was not able to uphold its typical schedule and instead threw together a back-room competition made of hand-selected former contestants.[4] Lisa Jensen had been second runner-up in Miss Tanzania 2006, and since then had worked locally as a model and actor. Upon her return from her unremarkable performance at the Miss World 2012 competition, Lisa gave a newspaper interview in which she explained many of the hardships she faced at the competition:

'The preparations were insufficient, as we all know the finals took place in June less than a month to my departure to China,' she says. It naturally meant that there was no room for her to carry out any projects which would qualify her in the category of 'Beauty with a Purpose';[5] she had to resort to work that she had done five years ago [for the Miss Tanzania 2006 competition]....

'... I was told that I had to take a sculpture which represents some of our cultural heritage and that is why I was given a Maasai sculpture,' she says... 'Other contestants had come with very expensive gifts such as diamond necklaces and it was at that point that I wondered why I had not thought of carrying our unique tanzanite,' says Lisa.

Even the choice of talent activity that was chosen for her, also became a cryptic puzzle as she was required to dance, something that she says she has never been good at.... On that night at the auditions as her turn was about to arrive she walked over to the judges and choreographers and told them she wasn't ready to dance. '...I was there to represent my country and I wasn't about to disgrace it with a certain form of dance that I had not practiced,' she says....

... Lisa believes she represented her country to the best of her knowledge and ability. 'I tried as much as possible to make my country known. I distributed a couple of books on Tanzania and by the time we left the camp I wasn't called Tanzania, many referred to me by my first name,' she says.

Though there hasn't been any recognition Lisa admits that winning the crown was a dream come true. (Owere, 2012)

Lisa, tall, very light-skinned (with European and African heritage) and a fluent speaker of a standard, internationalized variety of English as well as Swahili, felt herself at an extreme disadvantage due to organizational, cultural, as well as monetary issues she faced at Miss World. As she moved across competitive scales, a reworking of orders of indexicality took place, reconfiguring her skills, assets and overall value. Her skin color and language abilities that served as critical components of her success in the Miss Tanzania competition were commonplace at Miss World. Rather, her un-preparedness, inability to perform a talent and shortcomings as a national ambassador (in which capacity she only 'distributed a couple of books' and provided what she came to see as mundane tchotchke as her nation's gift), if nothing else, doomed her to the ranks of the crownless. Even so, and simul-taneously orienting towards different centers of value-granting authority, she mitigated the shame of her international experience with her pride as national winner, saying that being Miss Tanzania was 'a dream come true'.

Here, I argue that Miss Tanzania has become an icon of Tanzanian womanhood in the new millennium, embodying the qualities of education, mobility and independence so coveted in a *dada wa mjini*. Engagement in pageants allows young women to feel themselves part of the cosmopolitan world order, through readily available language, commodities and practices. For pageant participants, like Weiss's (2009) barbers and other young urban Tanzanians, the orientation towards the global, as at once pleasurable, potentially profitable and life-changing, gives real shape to their lives. But it is also an orientation that puts into high relief the inequalities that are nearly inescapable strictures of their lives on the global periphery.

Justina, Part Two

In closing, I would like to revisit briefly the life of Justina, the young Tanzanian women whom I profiled in Chapter 1, who participated in pageants as one thread of her attempts to *kutafuta maisha* ('look for a life'). In Chapter 1 her story stopped at a point several years ago, when Justina was attempting to secure an English education in Nairobi, Kenya, in order to gain the linguistic skills necessary to pursue her dream of working in the tourism industry. Here, I will offer a kind of postscript that takes us to life after beauty pageants, a glimpse of life-seeking strategies for a *dada wa mjini* who has aged out of pageantry. Justina's story illustrates the feeling of prosperity just out of grasp, as physically located elsewhere and in others' hands. It highlights her awareness of the global hierarchies of scale that shape her own opportunity and desire, and it exemplifies the reordering of normativity that places her repeatedly at a disadvantage. As she moves through her 20s, she continues to seek a particular kind of cosmopolitan life, perhaps just reachable with the right combination of luck, planning and imagination.

Believing Kenya to be a locus of better English than Tanzania, Justina was able to finance her tuition at an English school in Nairobi with help from her brother's mining earnings. She also secured a free room with a relative living there, but soon her lodging situation became abusive. Having nowhere else to go, she abruptly returned to Arusha. In the next few months, she found work again as a hotel maid at a mid-range tourist hotel around Mount Kilimanjaro. Though acknowledging the job was not a good one – long hours, poor pay, physically exhausting and low respect – Justina insisted that the job's main benefit was that it would gain her access to an *mzungu* ('European/white' man; *wazungu* [pl]) as a way to a better life.[6] Yet, working as a maid, she had very little contact with *wazungu* clientele and even when she did, her limited English skills (and the hotel guests' likely extremely limited Swahili skills) made communication with them very difficult. Still not giving up her hopes, she explained to me in an email why an *mzungu* was so important to her:

> *About* mzungu sabrina ni kwamba nimewachoka sana wanaume wa uku ni waongo sana, ninavyojua mimi wazungu wengi ni wakweli na wachache ndio waongo, tofauti na wanaume wa uku wengi sana ni waongo … ninaomba unitafutie tu mwaume wa kizungu sabrina.
>
> [About the *mzungu* sabrina it is because I am very tired of the men from around here, they are really liars, and as I know, many *wazungu* are truthful and only a few are liars, different from the men here, many [of whom] are really liars … I ask you to find me an *mzungu* man sabrina.]

Rather than about romance, her quest for an *mzungu* was about survival and escape, as seen in another email excerpt:

> Naomba unitafutie kazi kama utaweza nchi yoyote ata katika *industries* uko, au ninaomba ata unipatie ela ya kufanya biashara ya kuuza *cement* au *cooking oil, pls* sasa hivi ninaitaji kitu cha kunisaidia katika maisha yangu, *pls* ata kama ni kukopa nirudishe kidogo kidogo nitafurai na

ukija utaona iyo biashara,na utaona chumba nilichopangisha, naomba unitafutie basi na *boyfriend* najua unaweza, *life is so hard to me.* [I ask you to find me work if you are able, in any country, even in industries there, or I ask even that you give me money for a business selling cement or cooking oil, pls right now I need something to help me in my life, pls even if it is borrowing I would give it back little by little I will be happy, and if you come you will see the business, and you will see the room that I rent, so I ask that you find me a boyfriend, I know you are able to, life is so hard to me.]

Here, Justina implores me for a job, for start-up money and, finally, for help finding an *mzungu* boyfriend, all avenues for an escape.[7] For her, an *mzungu* boyfriend not only would treat her well but would also likely take her far away from her poverty to a land of opportunity and equality. Later, she posted a MySpace profile and initially felt very excited by several responses. Yet she needed help deciphering these responses, as they were all in English and she had trouble knowing their origins or true intentions. In the end, every potential suitor turned out, with a small amount of sleuthing, to be a fellow African. She then put her hopes on hold and instead married a significantly older local man with whom she became pregnant; she moved from the city to his village some distance away. Though married and caring for her small child, a recent email indicated to me her desire to continue looking for an escape and that an *mzungu* remained to her the most realistic avenue, at this point in her life.

Over the course of several years, Justina's attempts at sustenance, fulfillment and escape ranged from the practical to the ambitious to the rather fantastical, usually reflecting an at once cosmopolitan and distinctly feminine orientation to life. In engaging in pageants, Justina envisioned the likelihood of short-term financial gains, the opportunity to participate first hand in a global imaginary and the dream of reaping the many rewards of a big-time beauty queen. In enrolling in school, she actively sought an education which would, in theory, qualify her for satisfying work that would allow her to live an independent, modern and even transnational life. In seeking a foreign partner – an arrangement that is sometimes visible in her cosmopolitan hometown of Arusha – she sought a physical removal from her circumstances, a passport or a green card that would get her out. It is not that Justina's life now is without joy or fulfillment. She expresses her love for her child and her nearby family, she is very involved in her church and she deeply enjoys Tanzanian and American music and music videos. She enjoys fashion – both vicariously as well as through her own assemblages of second-hand pieces. At the same time, her continued quest for an *mzungu* makes clear that her life is not the one she had imagined as a schoolgirl and as a beauty queen, and that she sees her channels for fashioning a future to be rapidly dwindling.

Every step of the way, Justina felt the limits of her education. In particular, her quest for English, as perhaps her most practical means of escape, was in some ways also the most fantastical strategy of all. Her secondary schooling left her with some textbook knowledge of the grammatical and lexical nuts and bolts of English but an extremely limited ability to speak it. The language schools in which she later enrolled were fly-by-night institutions that issued diplomas after only a few months. While some English in Tanzania is indeed local, the empowering, fluent and standard English she sought is almost completely out of reach, as much the provenance of the well-to-do as is wearing the crown of Miss Tanzania. Thus, in her quest for English, in her pursuit of a pageant crown and in her faith in an *mzungu*, Justina is like many young urban Tanzanians whose lives take place at the precarious crossroads of hard work, creative planning and fantastical visions of a future life elsewhere.

Notes

(1) I also frequently heard young Tanzanian men describe Tanzanian women as untrustworthy.
(2) In 2012, the Miss World organization, in what it reported to be a permanent change, shifted the Miss World contest and its related events to July and August (see note 4 below).
(3) A notable exception was Miss Tanzania 2006, Wema Sepetu, who accused Miss World of racism in failing to select her. This accusation was largely dismissed by the Tanzanian public because of Wema's already poor reputation, based in no small part on her short-term jail sentence for assault.
(4) These date changes were announced the previous September, allowing many countries enough time to rework their typical pageant schedule.
(5) 'Beauty with Purpose' is the theme of the world as well as national pageants and is also a competitive segment at Miss World. It is judged in large part by a video submitted by the contestant to the committee in advance.
(6) See Cole (2010) for a fascinating analysis of similar aspirations of young Malagasy women.
(7) Of course, these difficult-to-read passages also illustrate the conflation of our roles as researchers and human beings and the complications of being a relatively wealthy person from the West relying on the kindness, patience and assistance of people much less well off. These and related issues of subjectivity in fieldwork have been explored by many an anthropologist (e.g. De Soto, 2000; Kulick & Willson, 1995).

Appendix

Transcription Conventions

General transcription conventions were adapted from Gumperz and Berenz (1993). Laughter and applause transcription conventions were adapted from Clayman (1992).

..	pause of less than 0.5 s
...	pause of greater than 0.5 s (unless precisely timed)
<2>	pause, precise unit of time (2 s pause)
,	slight rise, as in listing intonation (more is expected)
/	slight fall
//	final fall
?	rising intonation
~	fluctuating pitch over a single word
=	overlap
==	latching of utterance to speaker's previous one
-	truncation (self-interruption)
{[ ]}	non-lexical phenomena that overlay the lexical stretch
[ ]	transcription notes
( )	unintelligible
hhhh	quiet audience laughter
HHHH	loud audience laughter
xxxx	quiet audience applause
XXXX	loud audience applause
hoo	audience hoots, often rhythmic, and used in critique of the person on stage

References

Abdulalziz, M.H. (1971) Tanzania's national language policy and the rise of Swahili political culture. In W.H. Whiteley (ed.) *Language Use and Social Change* (pp. 160–178). London: Oxford University Press.

Abdulaziz-Mkilifi, M. (1973) Triglossia and Swahili–English bilingualism in Tanzania. *Language in Society* 1 (2), 197–213.

A.E. i o u (2007) *Bongo Celebrity* blog post, 6 November 2007. See www.bongocelebrity.com/2007/09/01/miss-tanzania-2007-ni-richa-adhia (accessed September 2012).

Agha, A. (2005) Introduction: Semiosis across encounters. *Journal of Linguistic Anthropology* 15 (1), 1–5.

Agha, A. (2007) *Language and Social Relations*. Cambridge: Cambridge University Press.

Al-Samarrai, S. and Reilly, B. (2008) Education, employment and earnings of secondary school and university leavers in Tanzania: Evidence from a tracer study. *Journal of Development Studies* 44 (2), 258–288.

Álvarez-Cáccamo, C. (1993) The pigeon house, the octopus, and the people: The ideologization of linguistic practices in Galiza. *Plurilinguismes* 6, 1–26.

Anderson, B. (1983) *Imagined Communities: Reflections on the Origin and Spread of Nationalism*. London: Verso.

Anonymous (2007) *Issa Michuzi*, blog post, 2 September 2007. See http://issamichuzi.blogspot.com/2007/09/breking-nyuuuuuuzzzzzz.html (accessed September 2012).

Antoine, P. and Nanitelamio, J. (1991) More single women in African cities: Pikine, Abidjan and Brazzaville. *Population: An English Selection* 3, 149–169.

Appadurai, A. (1996) *Modernity At Large: Cultural Dimensions of Globalization*. Minneapolis: University of Minnesota Press.

Arthur, J. (2001) Perspectives on educational policy and its implementation in African classrooms: A comparative study of Botswana and Tanzania. *Compare* 31 (3), 347–362.

Askew, K. (2002) *Performing the Nation: Swahili Music and Cultural Politics in Tanzania*. Chicago: University of Chicago Press.

Baars, J., Dannefer, D., Phillipson, C. and Walker, A. (2006) *Aging, Globalization and Inequality: The New Critical Gerontology*. Baywood, Amityville, NY.

Bakhtin, M. (1981) Discourse in the novel. In M. Holquist (ed.) *The Dialogic Imagination: Four Essays* (pp. 259–422). Austin, TX: University of Texas Press.

Ballerino Cohen, C., Wilk, R. and Stoeltje, B. (eds) (1996a) *Beauty Queens on the Global Stage: Gender, Contests, and Power*. New York: Routledge.

Ballerino Cohen, C., Wilk, R. and Stoeltje, B. (1996b) Introduction. In C. Ballerino Cohen, R. Wilk and B. Stoeltje (eds) *Beauty Queens on the Global Stage: Gender, Contests, and Power* (pp. 1–11). New York: Routledge.

Banet-Weiser, S. (1999) *The Most Beautiful Girl in the World: Beauty Pageants and National Identity*. Berkeley, CA: University of California Press.

Banner, L. (1983) *American Beauty*. Chicago, IL: University of Chicago Press.

Barber, K. (1997) Preliminary notes on audiences in Africa. *Africa* 67, 347–362.

Barnes, N.B. (1994) Face of the nation: Race, nationalisms, and identities in Jamaican beauty pageants. *Massachusetts Review* 35 (3–5), 471–492.

Beardsley, R.B. and Eastman, C. (1971) Markers, pauses and code switching in bilingual Tanzanian speech. *General Linguistics* 11, 17–27.

Besnier, N. (2002) Transgenderism, locality, and the Miss Galaxy beauty pageant in Tonga. *American Ethnologist* 29 (3), 534–566.

Besnier, N. (2004) Consumption and cosmopolitanism: Practicing modernity at the second-hand marketplace in Nuku'alofa, Tonga. *Anthropological Quarterly* 77, 7–45.

Besnier, N. (2007) Language and gender research at the intersection of the global and the local. *Gender and Language* 1, 65–76.

Bhabha, H. (1996) Unsatisfied: Notes on vernacular cosmopolitanism. In L. Garcia-Morena and P.C. Pfeifer (eds) *Text and Nation: Cross-Disciplinary Essays on Cultural and National Identities* (pp. 191–207). Columbia, SC: Camden House.

Billig, M. (1995) *Banal Nationalism*. London: Sage.

Billings, S. (2006) Speaking beauties: Language use and linguistic ideologies in Tanzanian beauty pageants. PhD dissertation, University of Chicago.

Billings, S. (2009) Speaking beauties: Linguistic posturing, language inequality, and the construction of a Tanzanian beauty queen. *Language in Society* 38, 581–606.

Billings, S. (2011a) Education is the key of life: Language, schooling, and gender in Tanzanian beauty pageants. *Language and Communication* 31, 295–309.

Billings, S. (2011b) And the winner is…. Hierarchies of language competence and fashion sense in Tanzanian beauty pageants. *Crossroads of Language, Interaction, and Culture* 8 (1), 1–32.

Bledsoe, C. (1990) School fees and the marriage process for Mende girls in Sierra Leone. In P.R. Sanday and R.G. Goodenough (eds) *Beyond the Second Sex: New Directions in the Anthropology of Gender* (pp. 284–309). Philadelphia PA: University of Pennsylvania Press.

Blommaert, J. (1992) Codeswitching and the exclusivity of social identities: Some data from Campus Kiswahili. In C. Eastman (ed.) *Codeswitching* (pp. 57–70). Clevedon: Multilingual Matters.

Blommaert, J. (1996) Language planning as a discourse on language and society: The linguistic ideology of a scholarly tradition. *Language Problems and Language Planning* 20 (3), 199–222.

Blommaert, J. (1999a) *State Ideology and Language in Tanzania*. Cologne: Rüdiger Köppe Verlag.

Blommaert, J. (ed.) (1999b) *Language Ideological Debates*. Berlin: Mouton de Gruyter.

Blommaert, J. (2005) Situating language rights: English and Swahili in Tanzania revisited. *Journal of Sociolinguistics* 9 (3), 390–417.

Blommaert, J. (2009) Language, asylum and the national order. *Current Anthropology* 50 (4), 415–441.

Blommaert, J. (2010) *The Sociolinguistics of Globalization*. Cambridge: Cambridge University Press.

Blommaert, J. (2013) Enregistering the globalized nation in Tanzania. Tilburg Papers in Culture Studies 68. (Draft of Chapter 6 of J. Blommaert, *State Ideology and Language in Tanzania*, 2nd revised edition. Edinburgh: Edinburgh University Press, to appear 2014.) See www.tilburguniversity.edu/upload/cf99d679-edb0-4926-88df-195238f100da_TPCS_68_Blommaert.pdf (accessed August 2013).

Blommaert, J. and Verschueren, J. (1998) *Debating Diversity: Analysing the Discourse of Tolerance*. London: Routledge.

Blommaert, J., Collins, J. and Slembrouck, S. (2005) Spaces of multilingualism. *Language and Communication* 25, 197–216.

Bloomfield, L. (1935) *Language*. London: Allen & Unwin.

Boddy, J. (2007) *Civilizing Women: British Crusades in Colonial Sudan*. Princeton, MA: Princeton University Press.

Bongo Celebrity (2007) I am proudly Tanzanian – Miss Kinondoni 07. Blog interview, 12 July. See www.bongocelebrity.com/2007/07/12/i-am-proudly-tanzanian-miss-kinondoni-07/#axzz2AQuUm3XU (accessed October 2011).

Borland, K. (1996) The India Bonita of Monimbó: The politics of ethnic identity in the new Nicaragua. In C. Ballerino Cohen, R. Wilk and B. Stoeltje (eds) *Beauty Queens on the Global Stage: Gender, Contests, and Power* (pp. 75–88). New York: Routledge.

Bourdieu, P. and Passeron, J.C. (1994) Language and relationship to language in the teaching situation. In P. Bourdieu, J.C. Passeron and M.S. Martin (eds) *Academic Discourse: Linguistic Misunderstanding and Professorial Power* (pp. 1–34). The Hague: Polity Press.

Breed, A. (2008) Performing the nation: Theatre in post-genocide Rwanda. *TDR: The Drama Review* 52 (1), 32–50.

Brennan, J. (2006) Blood enemies: Exploitation and urban citizenship in the nationalist political thought in Tanzania, 1958–75. *Journal of African History* 47, 389–413.

Briggs, C. (1996) Conflict, language ideologies, and privileged arenas of discursive authority in Warao dispute mediation. In C. Briggs (ed.) *Disorderly Discourse: Narrative, Conflict, and Inequality* (pp. 204–242). New York: Oxford University Press.

Brock-Utne, B. (2000) *Whose Education For All? The Recolonization of the African Mind*. New York: Routledge.

Brock-Utne, B. (2002) *Language, Democracy, and Education in Africa*. Uppsala: Nordiska Afrikainstitutet.

Brock-Utne, B. (2007a) Language of instruction and student performance: New insights from Tanzania and South Africa. *International Review of Education* 53, 509–530.

Brock-Utne, B. (2007b) Learning through a familiar language versus learning through a foreign language: A look into some secondary school classrooms in Tanzania. *International Journal of Educational Development* 27, 487–498.

Bruner, E.M. and Kirschenblatt-Gimblett, B. (1994) Maasai on the lawn: Tourism realism in East Africa. *Cultural Anthropology* 9 (4), 435–470.

Bucholtz, M. (1995) From Mulatta to Mestiza: Passing and the reshaping of ethnic identity. In K. Hall and M. Bucholtz (eds) *Gender Articulated: Language and the Socially Constructed Self* (pp. 351–374). New York: Routledge.

Bucholtz, M. (1999) You da Man: Narrating the racial other in the linguistic production of white masculinity. *Journal of Sociolinguistics* 3 (4), 443–460.

Bucholtz, M. (2006) Word up: Social meanings of slang in California youth culture. In J. Goodman and L. Monaghan (eds) *Interpersonal Communication: An Ethnographic Approach* (pp. 243–267). New York: Blackwell.

Bucholtz, M. (2009) From stance to style: Gender, interaction, and indexicality in

Mexican immigrant youth slang. In A. Jaffe (ed.) *Stance: Sociolinguistic Perspectives* (pp. 146–170). New York: Oxford University Press.

Bucholtz, M. and Hall, K. (2004) Theorizing identity in language and sexuality research. *Language in Society* 33, 469–515.

Bucholtz, M. and Trechter, S. (eds) (2001) Discourses of whiteness. *Journal of Linguistic Anthropology* 11 (1), 3–150.

Burgess, T. (2002) Cinema, bell bottoms, and miniskirts: Struggles over youth and citizenship in revolutionary Zanzibar. *International Journal of African Historical Studies* 35 (2–3), 287–313.

Burke, T. (1996) *Lifebuoy Men, Lux Women: Commodification, Consumption, and Cleanliness in Modern Zimbabwe*. Durham, NC: Duke University Press.

Bwenge, C.M. (2002) Codeswitching in political discourse in Tanzania: A case study of parliamentary proceedings. PhD dissertation, University of Virginia.

Cameron, D. (2001). *Good to Talk?* London: Sage.

Campbell, J. (1999) Nationalism, ethnicity and religion: Fundamental conflicts and the politics of identity in Tanzania. *Nations and Nationalism* 5 (1), 105–125.

Canagarajah, A. (1999) *Resisting Linguistic Imperialism in English Teaching*. Oxford: Oxford University Press.

Castells, M. (1996) *The Information Age: Economy, Society and Culture. Vol. 1: The Rise of the Network Society*. Cambridge, MA: Blackwell.

Chimhundu, H. (1992) Early missionaries and the ethno-linguistic factor during the invention of tribalism in Zimbabwe. *Journal of African History* 33, 255–264.

Chun, E.W. (2004) Ideologies of legitimate mockery: Margaret Cho's revoicings of mock Asian. *Pragmatics* 14 (2/3), 263–289.

Clayman, S. (1992) Caveat orator: Audience disaffiliation in the 1988 presidential debates. *Quarterly Journal of Speech* 78, 33–60.

CNN Online (2002) Miss World leaves Nigeria, 22 November. See www.cnn.com/2002/world/africa/11/22/nigeria.missworld/index.html (accessed September 2012).

Cole, J. (2004) Fresh contact in Tamatave, Madagascar: Sex, money and intergenerational transformation. *American Ethnologist* 31(4), 571–586.

Cole, J. (2010) *Sex and Salvation: Imagining the Future in Madagascar*. Chicago, IL: University of Chicago Press.

Collins, J. (1998) Our ideologies and theirs. In B. Schieffelin, K. Woolard and P. Kroskrity (eds) *Language Ideologies: Practice and Theory* (pp. 256–270). New York: Oxford University Press.

Comaroff, John and Comaroff, Jean (1992) Homemade hegemony. In K. Hansen (ed.) *Ethnography and the Historical Imagination* (pp. 265–295). Boulder, CO: Westview Press.

Comaroff, Jean and Comaroff, John (1993) *Modernity and Its Malcontents: Ritual and Power in Postcolonial Africa*. Chicago, IL: University of Chicago Press.

Corcoran, C. (2004) A critical examination of the use of language analysis interviews in asylum proceedings: A case study of a West African seeking asylum in the Netherlands. *International Journal of Speech, Language and the Law* 11 (2), 200–221.

Coupland, N. (2007) *Style: Language Variation and Identity*. Cambridge: Cambridge University Press.

Coupland, N. (2010) Introduction: Sociolinguistics in the global era. In N. Coupland (ed.) *The Handbook of Language and Globalization* (pp.1–27). Malden, MA: Wiley-Blackwell.

Cowie, C. (2007) The accents of outsourcing: the meanings of 'neutral' in the Indian call centre industry. *World Englishes* 26 (3), 316–330.

Crawford, M., Kerwin, G., Gurung, A., Khati, D. Jha, P. and Regmi, A.C. (2008) Globalizing beauty: Attitudes toward beauty pageants among Nepali women. *Feminism and Psychology* 18 (1), 61–86.

Creighton, C. and Omari, C.K. (2000) Introduction: Family and gender relations in Tanzania – inequality, control and resistance. In C. Colin and C.K. Omari (eds) *Gender, Family, and Work in Tanzania* (pp. 1–16). Aldershot: Ashgate.

Criper, C. and Dodd, W. (1984) *Report on the Teaching of English and Its Use As a Medium of Instruction.* London: ODA/British Council.

Cutler, C. (1999) Yorkville crossing: White teens, hip hop and African American English. *Journal of Sociolinguistics* 3 (4), 428–442.

Daily News (2010) Miss World: Are we sending the right material?, 4 November. See http://dailynews.co.tz/home/?n=14261 (accessed October 2011)

Daily News (2011a) Miss Tanzania contestants take part in sports day, 27 August. See http://allafrica.com/stories/201108290051.html (accessed August 2012).

Daily News (2011b) TAZARA hosts Miss Tanzania for train ride, 16 September. See www.dailynews.co.tz/home/?n=23734 (accessed August 2012).

Daily Times (2003) Zanzibar bans beauty contests, 13 April. See www.dailytimes.com.pk/default.asp?page=story_13-4-2003_pg9_9 (accessed August 2013).

Davis, P.J. (2000) On the sexuality of town women in Kampala. *Africa Today* 47 (3–4), 28–62.

Deford, F. (1971) *There She Is: The Life and Times of Miss America.* New York: Viking.

De Soto, H.G. (ed.) (2000) *Fieldwork Dilemmas: Anthropologists in Postsocialist States.* Madison, WI: University of Wisconsin Press.

Devens, C. (1992) 'If we get the girls, we get the race': Missionary education of native American girls. *Journal of World History* 3 (2), 219–237.

Dewey, S. (2008) *Making Miss India Miss World.* Syracuse, NY: Syracuse University Press.

Dimba (2003) Miss Tanzania 2003, 7–13 September.

Dorian, N. (1982) Defining the speech community to include its working margins. In S. Romaine (ed.) *Sociolinguistic Variation in Speech Communities* (pp. 25–33). London: Arnold.

Duranti, A. (1997) *Linguistic Anthropology.* New York: Cambridge University Press.

Duranti, A. and Brenneis, D. (1986) The audience as co-author. Special issue of *Text* 6 (3), 239–347.

Dyers, C. (2009) From ibharu to amajoin: Translocation and language in a new South African township. *Language and Intercultural Communication* 9 (4), 256–270.

Eckert, P. (1989) *Jocks and Burnouts: Social Categories and Identity in the High School.* New York: Teachers College Press.

Edmonson, L. (2007) *Performance and Politics in Tanzania: The Nation on Stage.* Bloomington, IN: Indiana University Press.

Eisenlohr, P. (2006) *Little India: Diaspora, Time, and Ethnolinguistic Belonging in Hindu Mauritius.* Berkeley, CA: University of California.

Ekström, Y. (2010) City sisters navigating the glocal mediascapes in Dar es Salaam. *Global Times: The Communication for Development Web Magazine* 15 (December). See http://wpmu.mah.se/glocaltimes/?p=101 (accessed May 2012).

Errington, J.J. (2000) Indonesian('s) authority. In P.V. Kroskrity (ed.) *Regimes of Language* (pp. 205–27). Santa Fe, NM: School of American Research Press.

Errington, J.J. (2007) *Linguistics in a Colonial World: A Story of Language, Meaning and Power.* New York: Blackwell.

Fabian, J. (1986) *Language and Colonial Power: The Appropriation of Swahili in the Former Belgian Congo 1880–1938.* Berkeley, CA: University of California Press.

Fardon, R. and Furniss, G. (1994) Introduction. Frontiers and boundaries – African languages as political environment. In R. Fardon and G. Furniss (eds) *African Languages, Development, and the State* (pp. 1–29). New York: Routledge.

Feierman, S. (1990) *Peasant Intellectuals: Anthropology and History in Tanzania.* Madison, WI: University of Wisconsin Press.

Ferguson, J. (1999) *Expectations of Modernity: Myths and Meanings of Urban Life on the Zambian Copperbelt.* Berkeley, CA: University of California Press.

Finnegan, R. (2007) *The Oral and Beyond: Doing Things with Words in Africa.* Chicago, IL: University of Chicago Press.

Freeman, C. (2000) *High Tech and High Heels in the Global Economy: Women, Work and Pink-Collar Identities in the Caribbean.* Durham, NC: Duke University Press.

Freeman, C. (2001) Is local:global as feminine:masculine? Rethinking the gender of globalization. *Signs: Journal of Women, Culture and Society* (special issue *Gender and Globalization*) 26 (4), 1007–1037.

Gahnström, C.S.L. (2012) Ethnicity, religion and politics in Tanzania: The 2012 general elections and Mwanza region. Unpublished master's thesis, University of Helsinki.

Gal, S. (1998) Multiplicity and contention among language ideologies: A commentary. In B. Schieffelin, K. Woolard and P. Kroskrity (eds) *Language Ideologies: Practice and Theory* (pp. 317–331). New York: Oxford University Press.

Gal, S. and Irvine, J.T. (1995) The boundaries of languages and disciplines: How ideologies construct difference. *Social Research* 62, 967–1001.

Geiger, S. (1987) Women in nationalist struggle: TANU activists in Dar es Salaam. *International Journal of African Historical Studies* 20 (1), 1–26.

Goffman, E. (1959) *The Presentation of Self in Everyday Life.* New York: Anchor Books.

Goodwin, C. (1986) Audience diversity, participation, and interpretation. *Text* 6, 283–316.

Gordon, R.G. Jr (ed.) (2005) *Ethnologue: Languages of the World* (15th edn). Dallas, TX: SIL International. See www.ethnologue.com (accessed July 2013).

Guardian (2003) Zanzibar bans beauty contests, 13 April.

Guardian (2010) Vodacom Miss Tanzania aspirants in Arusha tourist destinations. 25 August. See www.ippmedia.com/frontend/index.php?l=20240 (accessed August 2012).

Gumperz, J. and Berenz, N. (1993) Transcribing conversational exchanges. In J.A. Edwards and M.D. Lampert (eds) *Talking Data: Transcription and Coding in Discourse Research* (pp. 91–121). Hillsdale, NJ: Lawrence Erlbaum.

Haney, P.C. (2003) Bilingual humor, verbal hygiene, and gendered contradictions of cultural citizenship in early Mexican American comedy. *Journal of Linguistic Anthropology* 13, 163–188.

Hannerz, U. (1996) *Transnational Connections: Culture, People, Places.* London: Taylor and Francis.

Hannerz, U. (2004) Cosmopolitanism. In D. Nugent and J. Vincent (eds) *A Companion to the Anthropology of Politics* (pp. 69–85). Malden, MA: Wiley-Blackwell.

Hannerz, U. (2005) Two faces of cosmopolitanism: Culture and politics. *Statsvetenskaplig Tidskrift* 107(3), 199–213.

Hansen, K.T. (1997) *Keeping House in Lusaka.* New York: Columbia University Press.

Hansen, K.T. (2000) *Salaula: The World of Second-Hand Clothing and Zambia.* Chicago, IL: University of Chicago Press.

Haram, L. (2004) Prostitutes or modern women: Negotiating respectability in northern Tanzania. In S. Arnfred (ed.) *Re-Thinking Sexualities in Africa* (pp. 211–232). Uppsala: Nordic Africa Institute.

Harries, L. (1968) Swahili in modern East Africa. In J. Fishman, C. Ferguson and J.D. Gupta (eds) *Language Problems of Developing Nations* (pp. 415–429). New York: Wiley.

Harries, L. (1969) Language policy in Tanzania. *Africa* 39 (3), 275–280.

Harvey, D. (1989) *The Condition of Postmodernity: An Enquiry into the Origins of Cultural Change.* New York: Wiley.

Hattery, A.J., Embrick, D.G. and Smith, E. (eds) (2008) *Globalization and America: Race, Human Rights, and Inequality.* Lanham, MD: Rowman & Littlefield.

Haviland, J. (2003) Ideologies of language: Reflections on language and US law. *American Anthropologist* 105, 764–774.

Heller, M. (2010a) Commodification of language. *Annual Review of Anthropology* 39, 101–114.

Heller, M. (2010b) Language as resource in the globalized new economy. In N. Coupland (ed.) *The Handbook of Language and Globalization* (pp. 350–365). Oxford: Wiley-Blackwell.

Herzfeld, M. (1997) *Portrait of a Greek Imagination: An Ethnographic Biography of Andreas Nenedakis;* Chicago, IL: University of Chicago Press.

Heward, C. and Bunwaree, S. (eds) (1999) *Gender, Education and Development: Beyond Access to Empowerment.* London: Zed Books.

Higgins, C. (2007) Shifting tactics in intersubjectivity to align indexicalities: A case of joking around in Swahinglish. *Language in Society* 36, 1–24.

Higgins, C. (2009) *English as a Local Language: Postcolonial Identities and Multilingual Practices.* Bristol: Multilingual Matters.

Hill, J. (1998) 'Today there is no respect': Nostalgia, 'respect' and oppositional discourse in Mexicano (Nahuatl) language ideology. In B. Schieffelin, K. Woolard and P. Kroskrity (eds) *Language Ideologies: Practice and Theory* (pp. 68–86). New York: Oxford University Press.

Hirsch, S.F. (1998) *Pronouncing and Persevering: Gender and the Discourses of Disputing in an African Islamic Court.* Chicago, IL: University of Chicago Press.

Hobsbawm, E. (1990) *Echoes of the Marseillaise: Two Centuries Look Back on the French Revolution.* London: Verso.

Hobsbawm, E. (2007) *Globalization, Democracy and Terrorism.* London: Little, Brown.

Hodgson, D.L. (1999) Once intrepid warriors: Modernity and the production of Maasai masculinities. *Ethnology* 38 (2), 121–150.

Hodgson, D.L. (2005) *The Church of Women: Gendered Encounters between Maasai and Missionaries.* Bloomington, IN: University of Indiana Press.

Hodgson, D.L. (2011) *Being Maasai, Becoming Indigenous: Postcolonial Politics in a Neoliberal World.* Bloomington, IN: Indiana University Press.

Hoffman, K.E. (2006) Berber language ideologies, maintenance, and contraction: Gendered variation in the indigenous margins of Morocco. *Language & Communication* 26, 144–167.

Hornberger, N. and Chick, K. (2001) Co-constructing school safetime: Safetalk practices in Peruvian and South African classrooms. In M. Martin-Jones and M. Heller (eds) *Voices of Authority: Education and Linguistic Difference* (pp. 31–55). Westport, CT: Ablex.

Hughes, L. (2006) 'Beautiful beasts' and brave warriors: The longevity of a Maasai stereotype. In L. Romanucci-Ross, G.A. De Vos and T. Tsuda (eds) *Ethnic Identity: Problems and Prospects for the Twenty-First Century* (pp. 264–294). Lanham, MD: AltaMira Press.

Hunt, N.R. (1992) Colonial fairy tales and the knife and fork doctrine in the heart of Africa. In K.T. Hansen (ed.) *African Encounters with Domesticity* (pp. 143–171). New Brunswick, NJ: Rutgers University Press.

Hunt, N.R. (2005 [1991]) Noise over camouflaged polygamy, colonial morality taxation, and a woman-naming crisis in Belgian Africa. In A. Cornwall (ed.) *Readings in Gender in Africa* (pp. 53–64) Indianapolis, IN: University of Indiana Press.

Hunter, M. (2002) The materiality of everyday sex: Thinking beyond prostitution. *African Studies* 61 (1), 99–120.

Hunter, M. (2009) Providing love: Sex and exchange in twentieth-century South Africa. In L. Thomas and J. Cole (eds) *Love in Africa* (pp. 135–156). Chicago, IL: University of Chicago Press.

Hutcheon, L. (1985) *A Theory of Parody: The Teachings of Twentieth-Century Art Forms.* London: Methuen.

Hymes, D. (1964) Introduction: Toward ethnographies of communication. *American Anthropologist* 66 (6), 1–34.

Hymes, D. (1975) Breakthrough into performance. In D. Ben-Amos and K.S. Goldstein (eds) *Folklore: Performance and Communication* (pp. 11–74). The Hague: Mouton.

Hymes, D. (1996) *Ethnography, Linguistics, Narrative Inequality: Toward an Understanding of Voice.* London: Taylor and Francis.

Inoue, M. (2006) *Vicarious Language: Gender and Linguistic Modernity in Japan.* Berkeley, CA: University of California Press.

Irvine, J. (1989) When talk isn't cheap: Language and political economy. *American Ethnologist* 16 (2), 248–267.

Irvine, J. and Gal, S. (2000) Language ideology and linguistic differentiation. In P.V. Kroskrity (ed.) *Regimes of Language* (pp. 35–83). Santa Fe, NM: School of American Research Press.

Ivaska, A. (2002) 'Anti-mini militants meet modern misses': Urban style, gender, and the politics of 'national culture' in 1960s Dar es Salaam, Tanzania. *Gender and History* 14 (3), 584–607.

Jackson, H. and Amvela, E.Z. (2000) *Words, Meaning, and Vocabulary: An Introduction to Modern English Lexicology.* London: Continuum.

Jacquemet, M. (2005) Transidiomatic practices: Language and power in the age of globalization. *Language & Communication* 25, 257–277.

Jaspers, J. (2005) Linguistic sabotage in a context of monolingualism and standardization. *Language & Communication* 25 (3), 279–297.

Joel, L. (2011) Manyanya thirst for mother of all beauty pageants. *Tanzania Daily News*, 28 July. See http://allafrica.com/stories/201107290586.html (accessed August 2013).

Johnson, M. (1996) Negotiating style and mediating beauty: Transvestite (gay/bantut) beauty contests in the southern Philippines. In C. Ballerino Cohen, R. Wilk and B. Stoeltje (eds) *Beauty Queens on the Global Stage: Gender, Contests, and Power* (pp. 89–104). New York: Routledge.

Jørgensen, J.N. (2008) Introduction: Polylingual languaging around and among children and adolescents. *International Journal of Multilingualism* 5 (3), 161–176.

Jørgensen, J.N., Karrebæk, M.S., Madsen, L.M. and Møller, J.S. (2011) Polylanguaging in superdiversity. *Diversities* 13 (2), 32–54.

Kalokola, S. (2011) Where are all the English speaking Tanzanians? *The Citizen*, 20 June. See www.thecitizen.co.tz/magazines/33-success/12115-where-are-the-english-speaking-tanzanians.html (accessed August 2012).

Kapinga, O. (2008) Miss Tanzania 2008 for special training. *Sunday Observer*, 14 September.

Kearney, M. (1995) The local and the global: The anthropology of globalization and transnationalism. *Annual Review of Anthropology* 24, 547–565.

Kellner, D. (1989) *Critical Theory, Marxism and Modernity.* Cambridge, UK, and Baltimore, MA: Polity Press and Johns Hopkins University Press.

Kelly-Holmes, H. (2005) *Advertising as Multilingual Communication.* London: Palgrave Macmillan.

Kerber, L.K. (1980) *Women of the Republic: Intellect and Ideology in Revolutionary America.* Chapel Hill, NC: University of North Carolina Press.

Kimati, B. (2010) Tanzania opens doors to English teachers. *Daily News Online,* 15 December. See www.dailynews.co.tz/home/?n=15468 (accessed September 2012).

Kishe, A.J. (1995) The Englishization of Tanzanian Kiswahili: A study in language contact and convergence. PhD dissertation, University of Illinois at Urbana-Champaign.

Kroskrity, P. (1998) Arizona Tewa kiva speech as a manifestation of a dominant language ideology. In B. Schieffelin, K. Woolard and P. Kroskrity (eds) *Language Ideologies: Practice and Theory* (pp. 103–122). New York: Oxford University Press.

Kroskrity, P. (2000) Regimenting languages: Linguistic ideological perspectives. In P. Kroskrity (ed.) *Regimes of Language* (pp. 1–34). Santa Fe, NM: School of American Research Press.

Kulick, D. and Willson, M. (eds) (1995) *Taboo: Sex, Identity, and Erotic Subjectivity in Anthropological Fieldwork.* London: Routledge.

Labov, W. (1966) *The Social Stratification of English in New York City.* Washington, DC: Center for Applied Linguistics.

Labov, W. (1972) *Sociolinguistic Patterns.* Philadelphia, PA: University of Pennsylvania Press.

Labrador, R.L. (2004) 'We can laugh at ourselves': Hawai'i ethnic humor, local identity, and the myth of multiculturalism. *Pragmatics* 14 (2/3), 291–316.

Laitin, D. (1992) *Language Repertoires and State Construction in Africa.* Cambridge: Cambridge University Press.

Lawuo, Z.E. (1984) *Education and Social Change in a Rural Community: A Study of Colonial Education and Local Response among the Chagga between 1920 and 1945.* Dar es Salaam: University of Dar es Salaam Press.

Lee, E. and Norton, B. (2009) The English language, multilingualism, and the politics of location. *International Journal of Bilingual Education and Bilingualism* 12 (3), 277–290.

Legère, K. (2002) The 'Languages of Tanzania' project: Background, resources, and perspectives. *Africa & Asia: Göteborg Working Papers on Asian and African Languages and Literatures* 2, 163–186.

Leseth, A. (2004) Culture of movement: Walkers, workers and fitness performers in Dar es Salaam, Tanzania. PhD dissertation, Norwegian University of Sport.

Leseth, A. (2010) Michezo: Dance, sports, and politics in Tanzania. *Anthropological Notebooks* 16 (3), 61–75.

Lewinson, A.S. (1999) Going with the times: Transforming visions of urbanism and modernity among professionals in Dar es Salaam. Unpublished PhD thesis, University of Wisconsin–Madison.

Lewinson, A.S. (2000) Renovating the modern home: Gender, marriage, and weddings among professionals in Dar es Salaam. In C. Colin and C.K. Omari (eds) *Gender, Family, and Work in Tanzania* (pp. 266–291). Aldershot: Ashgate.

Linda (2007) *Bongo Celebrity* blog post, 2 September. See www.bongocelebrity.com/2007/09/01/miss-tanzania-2007-ni-richa-adhia (accessed September 2012).

Lovegrove, K. (2002) *Pageant: The Beauty Contest.* Düsseldorf: teNeues.

MacCannell, D. (1992) Cannibalism today. In D. MacCannell (ed.) *Empty Meeting Grounds* (pp. 17–73). London: Routledge.

Makoni, S. (2003) From misinvention to disinvention of language: Multilingualism and the South African constitution. In S. Makoni, G. Smitherman, A.F. Ball and A.K. Spears (eds) *Black Linguistics: Language, Society, and Politics in Africa and the Americas* (pp. 132–153). London: Routledge.

Makoni, S. and Pennycook, A. (2007) Disinventing and reconstituting languages. In S. Makoni and A. Pennycook (eds) *Disinventing and Reconstituting Languages* (pp. 1–41). Clevedon: Multilingual Matters.

Martin, J.R. (1992) *English Text*. Amsterdam: John Benjamins.

Maryns, K. (2006) *The Asylum Speaker: Language in the Belgian Asylum Procedure*. Manchester: St Jerome.

Massamba, D. (1989) An assessment of the development and modernization of the Kiswahili language in Tanzania. In F. Coulmas (ed.) *Language Adaptation* (pp. 60–78). Cambridge: Cambridge University Press.

Masvawure, T. (2010) 'I just need to be flashy on campus': female students and transactional sex at a university in Zimbabwe. *Culture, Health and Sexuality: An International Journal for Research, Intervention and Care* 12 (8), 857–870.

Mazrui, A. and Mazrui, A. (1995) *Swahili State and Society: The Political Economy of an African Language*. London: James Curry.

Mbilinyi, M.J. (1972) The 'new woman' and traditional norms in Tanzania. *Journal of Modern African Studies* 10 (1), 57–72.

McAllister, C. (1996) Authenticity and Guatemala's Maya Queen. In C. Ballerino Cohen, R.Wilk and B. Stoeltje (eds) *Beauty Queens on the Global Stage: Gender, Contests, and Power* (pp. 105–124). New York: Routledge.

McCall Smith, A. (2002) *Morality for Beautiful Girls*. New York: Anchor Books.

McClintock, A. (1995) *Imperial Leather: Race, Gender and Sexuality in the Colonial Contest*. London: Routledge.

McLaughlin, F. (2009) Introduction to the languages of urban Africa. In F. McLaughlin (ed.) *The Languages of Urban Africa* (pp. 1–18). London: Continuum.

Meacham, S.S. (2004) Constructing agency out of language contact: Evidentiality in Japanese high school English lessons and the production of socio-cultural identity. PhD dissertation, University of California Los Angeles.

The MEASURE Project (2004) *AIDS in Africa During the Nineties. Tanzania Youth Report: A Review and Analysis of Surveys and Research Studies*. Tanzania National AIDS Control Programme and Tanzania National Bureau of Statistics. Online at http://gametlibrary.worldbank.org/FILES/293_AIDS%20in%20Africa%20during%20the%2090s%20-%20meta%20analysis%20of%20surveys-Tanzania%20youth.pdf (accessed July 2013).

Meeuwis, M. and Blommaert, J. (1998) A monolectal view of code-switching: Layered code-switching among Zairians in Belgium. In P. Auer (ed.) *Codeswitching in Conversation: Language, Interaction, and Identity* (pp. 76–99). London: Routledge.

Mekacha, R.D. (1993) *The Sociolinguistic Impact of Kiswahili on Ethnic Community Languages in Tanzania: A Case Study of Ekinata*. Bayreuth: Bayreuth African Studies.

Mendoza-Denton, N. (2008) *Homegirls: Language and Cultural Practice Among Latina Youth Gangs*. Malden, MA: Blackwell.

Mesthrie, R. (2006) Language, transformation and development: A sociolinguistic appraisal of post-apartheid South African language policy and practice. *Southern African Linguistics and Applied Language Studies* 24 (2), 151–163.

Meyer, B. and Geschiere, P. (1999) Introduction. In B. Meyer and P. Geschiere (eds) *Globalization and Identity: Dialectics of Flow and Closure* (pp. 1–16). Oxford: Blackwell.

Mills, M.B. (2003) Gender and inequality in the global labor force. *Annual Review of Anthropology* 32, 41–62.

Ministry of Education and Vocational Training (2008) Basic statistics in education 2008 – national. Dar es Salaam, Tanzania. See http://moe.go.tz/statistics.html (accessed October 2010).

Minja, C. (2011) Kasunga graces St Thomas graduation emphasizing importance of Kiswahili. *Arusha Times*, 17–23 September.

Mkenda, A.F., Luvanda, E.G., Rutasitara, L. and Naho, A. (2004) Poverty across Tanzania: Comparisons across administrative regions. An interim report. Ministry of Finance, Poverty Monitoring, United Republic of Tanzania. See www.povertymonitoring.go.tz/researchreport/poverty_comparisons_regionally_Luvanda_et_al.pdf (accessed September 2012).

Mlama, P. and Matteru, M. (1978) *Haja ya kutumia Kiswahili kufundisha katika elimu ya juu*. Dar es Salaam: BAKITA.

Mochiwa, Z.S.M. (1979) The impact of Kiswahili on ethnic languages: A case from Handeni district. Unpublished MA thesis, University of Dar es Salaam.

Mohamed, H.I. and Banda, F. (2008) Classroom discourse and discursive practices in higher education in Tanzania. *Journal of Multilingual and Multicultural Development* 29 (2), 95–109.

Monson, J. (2009) *Africa's Freedom Railway: How a Chinese Development Project Changes Lives and Livelihoods in Tanzania*. Bloomington, IN: Indiana University Press.

Moore, L. (2006) Learning by heart in Qur'anic and public schools in northern Cameroon. *Social Analysis* 50 (3), 109–126.

Moore, L. (2008) Language socialization and second/foreign language and multilingual education in non-Western settings. In P.A. Duff and N.H. Hornberger (eds) *Encyclopedia of Language and Education. Volume 8: Language Socialization* (2nd edn) (pp. 175–185). New York: Springer.

Morgan, M. (2004) Speech community. In A. Duranti (ed.) *A Companion to Linguistic Anthropology* (pp. 3–22). Malden, MA: Blackwell.

Morson, G.S. (1989) Parody, history, metaparody. In G.S. Morson and C. Emerson (eds) *Rethinking Bakhtin: Extensions and Challenges* (pp. 63–86). Evanston, IL: Northwestern University Press.

Mosse, G.L. (1985) *Nationalism and Sexuality: Respectability and Abnormal Sexuality in Modern Europe*. New York: Howard Fertig.

Moyer, E. (2003) In the shadow of the Sheraton: Imagining localities in global space in Dar es Salaam, Tanzania. PhD thesis, University of Amsterdam.

Msanjila, Y.P. (1999) The use of Kiswahili in rural areas and its implications for the future of ethnic languages in Tanzania. PhD thesis, University of Dar es Salaam.

Mtesigwa, P. (2001) Tanzania's educational language policy: The medium of instruction at the secondary level. Unpublished PdD dissertation, Columbia University.

Mufwene, S. (2004) Language birth and death. *Annual Review of Anthropology* 33, 201–222.

Mühlhäusler, P. (1995) *Linguistic Ecology: Language Change and Linguistic Imperialism in the Pacific Rim*. London: Routledge.

Mulokozi, M.M. (1991) English versus Kiswahili in Tanzania's secondary education. In J. Blommaert (ed.) *Swahili Studies: Essays in Honour of Marcel van Spaandonck* (pp. 7–16). Gent: Academie Press.

Mushi, S. (1996) Some general ideas informing second language teaching globally: Obstacles to their utilisation in Tanzania. *Language, Culture and Curriculum* 9 (2), 133–147.

Mwakyusa, A. (2011) Forum stresses mastery of English among graduates. *Tanzania Daily News*, 27 May. See http://in2eastafrica.net/forum-stresses-mastery-of-english-among-graduates (accessed September 2012).

Mwansasu, B.U. and Pratt, C. (1979) Tanzania's strategy for the transition to socialism. In B.U. Mwansasu and C. Pratt (eds) *Towards Socialism in Tanzania* (pp. 3–15). Toronto: University of Toronto Press.

Myers-Scotton, C. (1993a) *Duelling Languages: Grammatical Structure in Codeswitching*. Oxford: Clarendon Press.

Myers-Scotton, C. (1993b) *Social Motivations for Codeswitching: Evidence from Africa*. Oxford: Clarendon Press.

Nagar, R. (1996) The South Asian diaspora in Tanzania: A history retold. *Comparative Studies of South Asia, Africa, and the Middle East* 16 (2), 62–80.

Nagar, R. (1998) Communal discourses, marriage, and the politics of gendered social boundaries among South Asian immigrants in Tanzania. *Gender, Place and Culture* 5 (2), 117–139.

Nagar, R. (2000) I'd rather be rude than ruled: Gender, place and communal politics among South Asian communities in Dar es Salaam. *Women's Studies International Forum* 23 (5), 571–585.

Naidoo, K. and Misra, K. (2008) Poverty and intimacy: Reflections on sexual exchange, reproduction and AIDS in South Africa. *South African Review of Sociology* 39 (1), 1–17.

Ndayipfukamiye, L. (1994) Codeswitching in Burundi primary classrooms. In C.M. Rubagumya (ed.) *Language and Education in Africa: A Tanzanian Perspective* (pp. 79–95). Clevedon: Multilingual Matters.

Ndezi, E. (1979) The changing pattern of multilingualism in Igunga. Unpublished MA thesis, University of Dar es Salaam.

Neke, S.M. (2003) English in Tanzania: An anatomy of hegemony. PhD thesis, University of Ghent.

Neke, S.M. (2005) The medium of instruction in Tanzania: Reflections on language, education and society. *Changing English* 12 (1), 73–83.

Nelson, N. (1987) 'Selling her kiosk': Kikuyu notions of sexuality and sex for sale in Mathare Valley, Kenya. In P. Caplan (ed.) *The Cultural Construction of Sexuality* (pp. 217–239). London: Tavistock.

Nettle, D. and Romaine, S. (2000) *Vanishing Voices: The Extinction of the World's Languages*. New York: Oxford University Press.

Ngonyani, W. (2010) Miss Tanzania beauties to visit tourist attractions. *Business Times*, 20 August. See www.businesstimes.co.tz/index.php?option=com_content &view=article&id=203:miss-tanzania-beauties-to-visit-tourist-attractions& catid=39:sports-and-entertainment&Itemid=61 (accessed August 2012).

Nurse, D. and Spear, T. (1985) *The Swahili: Reconstructing the History and Language of an African Society, 800–1500*. Philadelphia, PA: University of Pennsylvania Press.

Nyairo, J. and Ogude, J. (2005) Popular music, popular politics: Unbwogable and the idioms of freedom in Kenyan popular music. *African Affairs* 104 (415), 225–249.

Nyang'oro, J. (2004) Ethnic structure, inequality and governance of the public sector in Tanzania. United Nations Research Institution for Social Development. See www.tzdpg.or.tz/uploads/media/Ethnic_Structure_Gov_PubSector_2004_01.pdf (accessed June 2012).

Nyanzi, S. and Nyanzi-Wakholi, B. (2004) 'It's more than cash!' – Debunking myths about 'sugar-daddy' relationships in Africa. *Sexual Health Exchange* 3–4, 8–9.

Nyerere, J. (1967a) Education for self-reliance. *Ecumenical Review* 19 (4), 382–403.

Nyerere, J. (1967b) *Freedom and Unity (Uhuru na Umoja): A Selection from Writings and Speeches, 1952–1965*. London: Oxford University Press.

Nyerere, J. (1968) *Ujamaa: Essays on Socialism*. Dar es Salaam: Oxford University Press.

Nyerere, J. (1973) *Freedom and Development/Uhuru na Maendeleo*. Dar es Salaam: Oxford University Press.

O'Barr, W. (1976) Language use and language policy in Tanzania: An overview. In W. O'Barr and J. O'Barr (eds) *Language and Politics* (pp. 35–48). The Hague: Mouton.

Ochs, E. (1992) Indexing gender. In A. Duranti and C. Goodwin (eds) *Rethinking Context: Language as an Interactive Phenomenon* (pp. 335–358). Cambridge: Cambridge University Press.

Odhiambo, N. (1999) Tanzania lifts 'bikini ban'. *The Express*, 18 June. See http://mg.co.za/article/1999-06-18-tanzania-lifts (accessed April 2012).

Ofcansky, T.P. and Yeager, R. (1997) *Historical Dictionary of Tanzania* (2nd edn). Lanham, MD: Scarecrow Press.

Ogot, F. (2009) Miss TZ 2009: Victory beyond wildest dreams. *Guardian on Sunday*, 4 October. See www.ippmedia.com/frontend/?l=8138 (accessed August 2012).

Ohly, R. (1987) *Swahili–English Slang Pocket-Dictionary*. Vienna: Afro-Pub.

Olatunji, S.O. and Robbin, A.A. (2011) Investigation into Nigerian undergraduates' preferred expressions for HIV/AIDS eradication campaigns. *Journal of Social Science* 26 (3), 195–201.

Owere, P. (2012) In the cold: Lisa Jensen's tale of misery. *The Citizen*, 21 September. See www.thecitizen.co.tz/magazines/26-thebeat/25902-in-the-cold-lisa-jensens-tale-of-misery.html (accessed October 2012).

Pal, P. and Ghosh, J. (2007) *Inequality in India: A Survey of Recent Trends*. DESA Working Paper No. 45. United Nations, Department of Economics and Social Affairs.

Parameswaran, R.E. (2004) Spectacles of gender and globalization: Mapping Miss World's media event space in the news. *Communication Review* 7 (4), 371–406.

Pennycook, A.D. (2001) *Critical Applied Linguistics: A Critical Introduction*. Mahwah, NJ: Erlbaum.

Pennycook, A.D. (2007) *Global Englishes and Transcultural Flows*. London: Routledge.

Perullo, A. and Fenn, J. (2003) Language ideologies, choices, and practices in Eastern African hiphop. In H.M. Berger and M.T. Carroll (eds) *Global Pop, Local Language* (pp. 19–51). Jackson, MS: University Press of Mississippi.

Pierre, J. (2008) 'I like your colour': Skin bleaching and geographies of race in urban Ghana. *Feminist Review* 90 (1), 9–29.

Pomeroy, S. (1975) *Goddesses, Whores, Wives, and Slaves: Women in Classical Antiquity*. New York: Schocken.

Price, N., Hawkins, K. and Ezekiel, M. (2003) Addressing the reproductive health needs and rights of young people since ICPD: The contribution of UNFPA and IPPF. UNFPA and IPPF Evaluation: Tanzania country report. Euro Health Group, University of Heidelberg. See www.unfpa.org/monitoring/country_evals/tanzania/tanzania_countryeval1-2.pdf (accessed August 2013).

Qorro, M. (2006) *Does Language of Instruction Affect Quality of Education?* HakiElimu Working Papers, 06.8. Dar es Salaam: HakiElimu.

Ram, K. (2008) 'A new consciousness must come': Affectivity and movement in Tamil Dalit women's activist engagement with cosmopolitan modernity. In P. Werbner (ed.) *Anthropology and the New Cosmopolitanism* (pp. 135–158). Oxford: Berg.

Rampton, B. (1995) *Crossing: Language and Ethnicity Among Adolescents*. London: Longman.

Raymos-Zaya, A.Y. (2003) *National Performances: The Politics of Class, Race, and Space in Puerto Rican Chicago.* Chicago, IL: University of Chicago Press.

Reed, S.A. (2009) *Dance and the Nation: Performance, Ritual, and Politics in Sri Lanka.* Madison, WI: University of Wisconsin Press.

Renfrow, D.G. (2004) A cartography of passing in everyday life. *Symbolic Interaction* 27 (4), 485–506.

Reuster-Jahn, U. and Kießling, R. (2006) Lugha ya mitaani in Tanzania: The poetics and sociology of a young urban style of speaking with a dictionary comprising 1100 words and phrases. In R.M. Beck, L. Diegner, C. Dittemer, G. Thomas and U. Reuster-Jahn (eds) *Swahili Forum 13.* Mainz: Universität Johannes Gutenburg.

Rio (2007) *Bongo Celebrity* blog post, 10 September. See www.bongocelebrity.com/2007/09/01/miss-tanzania-2007-ni-richa-adhia (accessed September 2012).

Robbins, B. (1998) Actually existing cosmopolitanism. In P. Chea and B. Robbins (eds) *Cosmopolitics* (pp. 1–19). Minneapolis, MI: University of Minnesota Press.

Robi, A. (2012) English 'a major obstacle' for job seekers. *Daily News Online,* 20 June. See http://www.dailynews.co.tz/index.php/local-news/6442-english-a-major-obstacle-for-job-seekers (accessed September 2012).

Romaine, S. (1982) What is a speech community? In S. Romaine (ed.) *Sociolinguistic Variation in Speech Communities* (pp. 13–24). New York: Edward Arnold.

Rosati, F. (2010) Imported words and new coinages in twenty-first century South African English. In O. Palusci (ed.) *English, But Not Quite: Locating Linguistic Diversity* (pp. 175–194). Trento: Tangram Edizioni Scientifiche Trento.

Roy-Campbell, Z.M. (2001) *Empowerment Through Language. The African Experience: Tanzania and Beyond.* Trenton, NJ, and Asmara, Eritrea: Africa World Press.

Roy-Campbell, Z.M. and Qorro, M. (1997) *Language Crisis in Tanzania: The Myth of English Versus Education.* Dar es Salaam: Mkuki na Nyota Publishers.

Rubagumya, C.M. (1989) English-medium instruction in Tanzanian secondary schools: A conflict of aspirations and achievements. *Journal of Multilingual and Multicultural Development* 11, 107–115.

Rubagumya, C.M. (1994) Language values and bilingual classroom discourse in Tanzanian secondary schools. *Language, Culture and Curriculum* 7 (1), 41–53.

Rubagumya, C.M. (1996) *What Research Tells Us About Language of Instruction.* Nairobi: International Development Research Centre.

Rubanza, Y.I. (1979) The relationship between Kiswahili and other African languages: The case of Kihaya. Unpublished MA thesis, University of Dar es Salaam.

Rutagumirwa, S.K. and Kamuzora, P. (2006) Secondary school childrens' voice in HIV/AIDS prevention interventions in Tanzania: A case study of Mbeya region. Paper produced as part of a capacity-building programme of the Regional Network on Equity in Health in east and southern Africa (EQUINET). See www.equinetafrica.org/bibl/docs/CBP1AIDSKamuzora.pdf (accessed March 2012).

Salazar, N. (2009) A troubled past, a challenging present, and a promising future: Tanzania's tourism development in perspective. *Tourism Review International* 12, 1–15.

Samoff, J. (1987) School expansion in Tanzania: Private initiatives and public policy. *Comparative Education Review* 31 (3), 333–360.

Sarkar, M. and Winer, L. (2006) Multilingual code-switching in Quebec rap: Poetry, pragmatics and performativity. *International Journal of Multilinguistics* 3 (3), 173–192.

Schatzberg, M.G. (2001) *Political Legitimacy in Middle Africa: Father, Family, Food.* Bloomington, IN: Indiana University Press.

Schieffelin, B., Woolard, K. and Kroskrity, P. (eds) (1998) *Language Ideologies: Practice and Theory.* New York: Oxford University Press.

Schneider, L. (2006) The Maasai's new clothes: A developmentalist modernity and its exclusions. *Africa Today* 53 (1), 100–131.

Schulz, D.E. (2000) Mesmerizing *missis*, nationalist musings: Beauty pageants and the public controversy over 'Malian' womanhood. *Paideuma* 46, 111–135.

Serpell, R. (1993) *The Significance of Schooling: Life-Journeys in an African Society.* Cambridge: Cambridge University Press.

Setel, P.W. (1999) *A Plague of Paradoxes: AIDS, Culture, and Demography in Northern Tanzania.* Chicago, IL: University of Chicago Press.

Silverstein, M. (1976) Shifters, linguistic categories, and cultural description. In K. Basso and H. Selby (eds) *Meaning in Anthropology* (pp. 11–55). Albuquerque, NM: University of New Mexico Press.

Silverstein, M. (1985) Language and the culture of gender: At the intersection of structure, usage and ideology. In E. Mertz and R. Parmentier (eds) *Semiotic Mediation* (pp. 219–259). Orlando, FL: Academic Press.

Silverstein, M. (1993) Metapragmatic discourse and metapragmatic function. In J. Lucy (ed.) *Reflexive Language: Reported Speech and Metapragmatics* (pp. 33–58). Cambridge: Cambridge University Press.

Silverstein, M. (1996) Monoglot 'standard' in America: Standardization and metaphors of linguistic hegemony. In D. Brenneis and R. Macauley (eds) *Matrix of Language* (pp. 284–306). Boulder, CO: Westview Press.

Silverstein, M. (1998) Contemporary transformations of local linguistic communities. *Annual Review of Anthropology* 27, 401–426.

Silverstein, M. (2003a) Indexical order and the dialectics of sociolinguistic life. *Language & Communication* 23, 193–229.

Silverstein, M. (2003b) Translation, transduction, transformation: Skating 'glossando' on thin semiotic ice. In P.G. Rubel and A. Rosman (eds) *Translating Cultures: Perspectives on Translation and Anthropology* (pp. 75–106). Oxford: Berg.

Silverstein, M. (2005) Axes of evals: Token vs. type interdisursivity. *Journal of Linguistic Anthropology* 15 (1), 6–22.

Silverstein, M. and Urban, G. (1996) The natural history of discourse. In M. Silverstein and G. Urban (eds) *Natural Histories of Discourse* (pp. 1–17). Chicago, IL: University of Chicago Press.

Skutnabb-Kangas, T. (2000) *Linguistic Genocide in Education or Worldwide Diversity and Human Rights.* Mahwah, NJ: Lawrence Erlbaum.

Spitulnik, D. (1998) Mediating unity and diversity: The production of language ideologies in Zambian broadcasting. In B. Schieffelin, K. Woolard and P. Kroskrity (eds) *Language Ideologies: Practice and Theory* (pp. 163–188). New York: Oxford University Press.

Spronk, R. (2009) Media and the therapeutic ethos of romantic love in middle-class Nairobi. In J. Cole and L.M. Thomas (eds) *Love in Africa* (pp. 181–203). Chicago, IL: University of Chicago Press.

Stambach, A. (1994) 'Here in Africa, we teach, students listen': Lessons about culture from Tanzania. *Journal of Curriculum and Supervision* 9 (4), 368–385.

Stambach, A. (1999) Curl up and dye: Civil society and the fashion-minded citizen. In J.L. Comaroff and J. Comaroff (eds) *Civil Society and the Political Imagination in Africa: Critical Perspectives* (pp. 251–266). Chicago, IL: University of Chicago Press.

Stambach, A. (2000a) *Lessons from Kilimanjaro: Schooling, Community, and Gender in East Africa.* New York: Routledge.

Stambach, A. (2000b) Evangelism and consumer culture in northern Tanzania. *Anthropological Quarterly* 73 (4), 171–179.

Stambach, A. (2003) *Kutoa mimba*: Debates about schoolgirl abortion in Machame, Tanzania. In A. Basu (ed.) *The Socio-Cultural and Political Aspects of Abortion* (pp. 79–102). Oxford: Clarendon.

Stambach, A. and Malekela, G. (2006) Education, technology, and the 'new' knowledge economy: Views from Bongoland. *Globalization, Societies and Education* 4 (3), 321–336.

Stiglitz, J.E. (2002) *Globalization and Its Discontents*. New York: W.W. Norton.

Stivens, M. (2008) Gender, rights and cosmopolitanisms. In P. Werbner (ed.) *Anthropology and the New Cosmopolitanism* (pp. 87–110). Oxford: Berg.

Stroud, C. (2001) African mother-tongue programmes and the politics of language: Linguistic citizenship versus linguistic human rights. *Journal of Multilingual and Multicultural Development* 22 (4), 339–355.

Summers, C. (1996) 'If you can educate the native woman...': Debates over the schooling and education of girls and women in Southern Rhodesia, 1900–1934. *History of Education Quarterly* 36 (4), 449–471.

Sumra, S. and Rajani, R. (2006) *Secondary Education in Tanzania: Key Policy Challenges*. Dar es Salaam: HakiElimu.

Swigart, L. (1994) Cultural creolisation and language use in post-colonial Africa: The case of Senegal. *Africa* 64 (2), 175–189.

Swilla, I.N. (2000) Voluptuous vacuous vamps: Stereotyped representation of women in Kiswahili press. *African Study Monographs* 21 (4), 159–171.

Synnott, A. (1989) Truth and goodness, mirrors and masks, part 1. *British Journal of Sociology* 40 (4), 607–636.

Tarimo, J. (2011) English not cause of mass exam failures – govt. *Guardian*, 8 April.

Taylor, A. (2008) Negotiating 'modernity': Migration, age transition, and 'development' in a training camp for female athletes in Arusha, Tanzania. Unpublished masters thesis, University of Canterbury.

Thomas, L. (2009) Love, sex, and the modern girl in 1930s Southern Africa. In J. Cole and L. Thomas (eds) *Love in Africa* (pp. 31–57). Chicago, IL: University of Chicago Press.

Thompson, K.D. (2006) The stereotype in Tanzania comics: Swahili and the ethnic other. *International Journal of Comic Art* 8 (2), 228–247.

Toroka, E. (2002) On fashion designing and beauty contests. *Business Times*, 22 March.

United Republic of Tanzania (website) National website: Education. See www.tanzania.go.tz/educationf.html (accessed November 2010).

United Republic of Tanzania (URT) (2002) *Poverty and Human Development Report 2002*. See www.tanzania.go.tz/prsp.html (accessed September 2012).

Urciuoli, B. (1998) *Exposing Prejudice: Puerto Rican Experiences of Language, Race, and Class*. Boulder, CO: Westview Press.

Van Onselen, C. (1982) Prostitutes and proletarians, 1886–1914. In C. Van Onselen (ed.) *Studies in the Social and Economic History of the Witwatersrand, Vol. I*. Harlow: Longman.

Vavrus, F. (2002) Making distinctions: Privatization and the (un)educated girl on Mount Kilimanjaro, Tanzania. *International Journal of Educational Development* 22 (5), 527–547.

Vavrus, F. (2003) *Desire and Decline: Schooling Amid Crisis in Tanzania*. New York: Peter Lang.

Vavrus, F. (2005) Adjusting inequality: Education and structural adjustment policies in Tanzania. *Harvard Educational Review* 75 (2), 174–201.

Vavrus, F. (2009) The cultural politics of constructivist pedagogies: Teacher education reform in the United Republic of Tanzania. *International Journal of Educational Development* 29, 303–311.

Vidacs, B. (2011) Banal nationalism, football, and discourse community in Africa. *Studies in Ethnicity and Nationalism* 11 (1), 25–41.
Vuzo, M.S. (2002) Pedagogical implications of using English as a language of instruction in secondary schools in Tanzania. Masters thesis, Institute for Educational Research, Oslo.
Vuzo, M.S. (2005) Using English as a medium of instruction in Tanzania secondary schools: Problems and prospects. In B. Brock-Utne, M. Desai and Z. Qorro (eds) *LOITASA Research in Progress* (pp. 55–82). Dar es Salaam: KAD Associates.
wa Kuhenga, M. (2012) New parliamentary rule wanted: No 'Kiswa-English' please! *Daily News Online*, 17 August. See www.dailynews.co.tz/index.php/columnists/columnists/makwaia-wa-kuhenga/8646-new-parliamentary-rule-wanted-no-kiswa-english-please (accessed September 2012).
Wallerstein, I. (2004) *Historical Capitalism*. London: Verso.
Wallman, S. (1996) *Kampala Women Getting By: Wellbeing in the Times of AIDS*. London: James Currey.
Wardle, H. (2000) *An Ethnography of Cosmpolitanism in Kingston, Jamaica*. Lampeter: Edwin Mellen Press.
Wedgwood, R. (2007) Education and poverty reduction in Tanzania. *International Journal of Educational Development* 27 (4), 383–396.
Wedin, A. (2005) Language ideologies and schooled education in rural Tanzania: The case of Karagwe. *International Journal of Bilingual Education and Bilingualism* 8 (6), 568–587.
Wedin, A. (2010) Classroom interaction: Potential or problem? The case of Karagwe. *International Journal of Educational Development* 30, 145–150.
Weiss, B. (1993) 'Buying her grave': Money, movement and AIDS in north-west Tanzania. *Africa* 63 (1), 19–35.
Weiss, B. (2002) Thug realism: Inhabiting fantasy in urban Tanzania. *Current Anthropology* 17 (1), 93–124.
Weiss, B. (2009) *Street Dreams and Hip Hop Barbershops: Global Fantasy in Urban Tanzania*. Bloomington, IN: Indiana University Press.
Werbner, P. (2008a) Understanding vernacular cosmopolitanism. *Anthropology News* 47 (5), 7–11.
Werbner, P. (ed.) (2008b) *Anthropology and the New Cosmopolitanism*. Oxford: Berg.
White, L. (1990) *The Comforts of Home: Prostitution in Colonial Nairobi*. Chicago, IL: University of Chicago Press.
Whiteley, W.H. (1968) Ideal and reality in national language policy: A case study from Tanzania. In J. Fishman, C. Ferguson and J. Das Gupta (eds) *Language Problems of Developing Nations* (pp. 327–344). New York: John Wiley and Sons.
Whiteley, W.H. (1969) *Swahili – The Rise of a National Language*. London: Methuen.
Wilk, R. (1998) Miss World Belize: Globalism, localism and the political economy of beauty. See www.indiana.edu/~wanthro/beaaauty.htm (accessed July 2013).
Williams, E. (2006) *Bridges and Barriers: Language in African Education and Development*. Manchester: St Jerome.
Williams, M. and Bekker, S. (2008) Language policy and speech practice in Cape Town: An exploratory public health sector study. *Southern African Linguistics and Applied Language Studies* 26 (1), 171–183.
Winter, J. (1979) Language shift among the Aasáx, a hunter-gatherer tribe in Tanzania. *Sprache und Geschichte in Afrika* 1, 175–204.
Wright, M. (1965) Swahili language policy, 1890–1940. *Swahili* 35 (1), 40–48.
Wojcicki, J.M. (2002) Commercial sex work or *ukuphanda*? Sex-for-money exchange in

Soweto and Hammanskraal area, South Africa. *Culture, Medicine, and Psychiatry* 26, 339–370.

Woolard, K. (1989) Language convergence and language death as social processes. In N. Dorian (ed.) *Investigating Obsolescence* (pp. 355–367). Cambridge: Cambridge University Press.

Woolard, K. and Schieffelin, B.B. (1994) Language ideology. *Annual Review of Anthropology* 23, 55–82.

Wortham, S. (2008) Linguistic anthropology of education. *Annual Review of Anthropology* 37, 37–51.

Yahya-Othman, S. (1990) When international languages clash: The possible detrimental effects on development of the conflict between English and Kiswahili in Tanzania. In C. Rubagumya (ed.) *Languages in Education in Africa*. Clevedon: Multilingual Matters.

Yoneda, N. (2010) 'Swahilization' of ethnic languages in Tanzania: The case of Matengo. *African Study Monographs* 31 (3), 139–148.

Zentella, A.C. (1997) *Growing Up Bilingual: Puerto Rican Children in New York*. Malden, MA: Blackwell.

Index